CW01499158

It's been an amazing year since Choc Lit published my first novel 'Things They Never Said' so I want to dedicate this second novel to all the readers who have taken the time to read it. For all of you who have got in touch or left a review, I am especially grateful.

It's also been a difficult year for me health-wise, so a big shout out to the NHS who have supported me, particularly Dr Puthuran and his team at The Walton Centre, Liverpool, without whom this second book may not have been written.

CHAPTER ONE

Anna checked Google Maps on her phone, trying to figure out where she was and, more importantly, where she needed to be. Knightsbridge was unfamiliar. To her horror, she realised she must have taken a wrong turn at the station and was walking in the opposite direction. If she didn't get on the right track soon, she'd be late for her interview.

Muttering under her breath, Anna retraced her steps. The backs of her new shoes were rubbing against her heels, the pain intensifying as she walked. Maybe she should just give up on the idea of this job — she didn't hold out much hope of getting it anyway.

The interview was for a photographer's assistant to Daniel Redfern, a high-profile photographer with a bad reputation. He was right at the top of his game, commissioned by all the top fashion magazines. He was also drop-dead gorgeous — tall, well-muscled but lithe, with dark-blond hair, strong cheekbones, a square chin and piercing blue eyes. Since his divorce from former top model Lucinda Russell, he was often seen in public with a variety of beauties on his arm. If that wasn't intimidating enough, he was reported to eat his assistants for breakfast, hence the current job vacancy.

Anna wondered if her life wasn't stressful enough without jumping out of the frying pan into the fire. But the thought of carrying on where she was — having to face her ex-boyfriend and his new girlfriend as they flaunted their relationship in front of her — was too much to bear. No matter how horrible Daniel Redfern might be, surely it couldn't be as bad as having her nose rubbed in *that* every day?

Filled with new resolve, Anna walked quickly, determined to ignore the pain stabbing at her heels. Just as she reached Knightsbridge Tube station and located the road she should have taken in the first place, the heavens opened. Not just a smattering of raindrops but a deluge, which would soon soak her. It had been sunny when she'd left home so, of course, she hadn't brought an umbrella with her. This day was turning out to be a complete disaster.

* * *

Daniel Redfern looked at his watch. 'She's late.'

His friend, Charlotte, handed him a cup of coffee. 'Here, drink this. It's only a few minutes. I'm sure she'll be here soon.'

'Not exactly a good first impression, is it?'

'No, but look at the weather. She might be sheltering somewhere.'

'I suppose so.' Daniel really wasn't in the mood for interviewing a new assistant, but his workload was hectic. He couldn't afford to be without one at the moment. The last one had left him in the lurch, not even serving a notice period. 'She'd better be good, though. The rest have all been pretty useless and I can't face going through this again.'

'Maybe if you weren't so difficult to work with, you wouldn't have to keep finding new assistants,' Charlotte said.

Daniel stared at her, open-mouthed. 'I'm not difficult. I just like things to be done properly.'

'You mean your way or the highway?'

He stared for a moment more, then smiled. 'I wouldn't take that from anyone else, you know.'

2

'I do know. That's why I can be honest with you. And it's why I'm here to help you find the perfect person.'

'I doubt that will happen, not judging by the shower we've interviewed already.'

'Have faith, my friend, have faith,' Charlotte replied.

Daniel's phone rang.

'Bet that's her cancelling,' he said as he picked up. Then, seeing the name on the screen, he groaned and answered it. 'Hi, Lucinda. What's up?'

'I'm sorry, darling.' She launched straight in. 'I know it's your weekend to have Ben, but Axel has sprung a last-minute surprise on us. He's taking us all to Disney — Paris, not Florida. Can you do next weekend instead?'

For a moment Daniel was speechless. How dare she jeopardise access to his son for some momentary pop star with a name like Axel?

'It's a bit short notice, Lucinda. I was planning on leaving in a few hours. Can't you go next weekend instead, rather than messing up my plans at the last minute?'

'I'm sorry, the tickets are non-refundable. I do sympathise, but that's Axel for you, always acting on impulse. He's just trying to do something nice for Ben. He really wants to get to know him better.'

'Buy his affections more like.'

'Oh, don't be like that!' Lucinda's voice turned sharp. 'You can see him next weekend and the weekend after if you like. What difference does it make?'

'It makes a difference to me.'

'It never used to. You never used to see him from one week to the next.' Her words cut into him as they always did, more so because she was right. But that was then. It was different now. 'Shall I tell Ben the trip's off, then? Because his father won't let him go?'

'No, of course not.' How could he possibly compete with a trip to Disney? Either way it was a lose-lose situation, for him at least. 'But you might have given me a bit more notice.'

'I only just found out myself.'

'Typical. Tell Axel that if he wants to take my son any-where, in future, he does it on your time, not mine. Don't start messing me around, Lucinda, or you'll be hearing from my solicitor.'

'Oh, Danny, don't be like that. As I said, he's only trying to do something nice.'

He cringed at the shortened version of his name that only *she* ever used. A term of endearment he didn't want to hear anymore.

'Well, seeing as I can't see my son, can I at least speak to him?'

'Sorry, darling, he's gone out with Axel to get some treats for the journey. I'll get him to video call you when we get there.'

'Make sure you do.' Daniel ended the call as the doorbell rang.

* * *

Anna finally found where her interview was — a white-fronted Georgian house, on a terrace of other white-fronted Georgian houses, each with railed steps up to brightly coloured front doors. Without an umbrella, her painstakingly straightened hair was framing her face in unsightly strings, and her new black suit, which she'd thought had fitted her so well, was limp and sodden. So not only was she fifteen minutes late but she looked like a drowned rat. She just hoped that she had made it at all showed her determination. In a hurry, Anna climbed the steps to Daniel Redfern's house and rang the bell, praying her make-up hadn't run and mascara wasn't now streaking her face.

'Oh my!' The woman who opened the door was tall and slim, with a dark-brown shiny bob. She wore a crisp white linen shirt, buckled at the waist, and wide-legged black trou-sers. The whole effect was incredibly chic.

'Hi, I'm, erm, I'm Anna Wright.' Anna reached to wipe away a raindrop that was rolling down her forehead.

'You're here for the interview?' the woman asked in a clear, clipped, upper-class voice.

'Yes,' Anna replied. 'I'm sorry, I'm a bit late. I got lost.'

'Of course, what am I thinking, leaving you dripping on the doorstep? Come on in.'

Anna walked through the door into the entrance hall, conscious of the obviously expensive parquet flooring beneath her wet feet.

'Here, let me get you a towel.' The woman disappeared behind a door further down the hallway. When she returned, proffering a white towel, thick and luxurious, Anna took it from her gratefully and began to dab her face, wondering if this day could possibly get any worse.

'Let me take your jacket. It's sopping wet,' the woman said. 'And then maybe you'd like to use the facilities?'

'Yes, please.' Anna shrugged herself out of her suit jacket and handed over the limp offering.

'It's just down here.' The woman led her to a downstairs cloakroom.

'Thank you.'

She closed the door behind her and searched in her handbag for a brush. She looked in the large ornate mirror. Her dark red hair was plastered to her head in a wet mess. She brushed it through, water dripping onto the floor. She looked a state, but she would just have to do her best, get the interview over with and leave. She'd probably blown any chance she might have had of getting the job anyway, so she had nothing to lose.

'Is that her? Finally.' A gruff voice came through the doorway.

'Anna Wright, yes. She got caught in the rain, poor thing.'

'She should have been on time, maybe then she would have avoided the rain.'

Anna quaked at his words. She presumed this was Daniel Redfern and he sounded as bad-tempered as his reputation suggested. She put her hairbrush back in her bag and opened the door.

He was standing in the hallway, looking even more handsome in the flesh than he did on social media, except for the deeply grooved frown creasing his forehead.

'Hi, I'm Anna Wright,' she said, holding out her hand for him to shake. He ignored it. Feeling like a fool, she returned it quickly to her side.

'You're late.'

'I'm sorry about that. I got lost and caught in the rain, but I'm here now.'

'You'd better come through, then.' He turned towards the doorway of another room.

Meekly she followed him into a dining room, which contained a huge white polished table with ten tall chairs surrounding it. The carpet was pure white and so thick her feet sank into it with every step. She should have offered to remove her wet shoes and could only hope she wasn't leaving muddy footsteps as she followed him.

'Sit down.' He pointed to a chair halfway down, while he sat himself at the head of the table. The woman who had let her in positioned herself to his right. Anna clasped her hands on her lap, hoping to quell the shaking. Her shirt felt damp against her skin and she prayed it hadn't gone see-through.

'This is Charlotte.' Daniel Redfern gesticulated towards the woman. 'She's helping me with the interviews today.'

'Pleased to meet you,' Anna said.

Charlotte smiled back. 'And you, Anna.'

Anna was glad there was at least one friendly face in the room.

Daniel Redfern glanced down at the papers in front of him and then looked up. Anna tried to settle her features into something resembling a calm expression, but as he scrutinised her face she couldn't help noticing how startlingly blue his eyes were. If only they'd held a hint of kindness, he would be absolutely devastating.

'I see you're currently working at The Whigmore Gallery?' he asked, forcing her to pull her thoughts away from how she would feel if he looked upon her with warmth. She needed to focus on getting this job, not whether she found her potential employer attractive.

'Yes, that's right.'

'Why do you want to leave?'

'Well, I've been there for the last four years and, while it's a great job, I feel the need to move on to fresh challenges.'

'Fresh challenges?' he asked, and she bristled at the sarcasm in his voice.

'I feel that I've learned all that I can in my current position and I want to do something that stretches me.'

'Right.' He sounded bored by her answer. 'I need someone who is reliable. Is that you?'

'I'm very reliable.' She stared him straight in the eyes. She wasn't going to be cowed by his abrupt manner. 'And whatever job I do, I give it my all.'

'Why does this particular job interest you?' he asked, giving nothing back.

She'd rehearsed the answer to this question and had settled on what an honour it would be to work with such a celebrated photographer. But now that answer didn't sound right. It wouldn't be an honour working with him, it would be a complete nightmare. She decided to be honest. She was beyond caring now.

'I've enjoyed working with the artists at the gallery, but my real interest is in photography. I feel I could learn a lot from working with you.'

His eyes widened in surprise and she congratulated herself that, for the first time today, she'd managed to elicit some kind of positive response.

'So you fancy yourself as a photographer, then?' he asked. 'Done a media course at university and think you know everything?'

She clenched her teeth before replying, furious — it was obvious he hadn't even bothered to read her application. How rude was that?

'No, as my CV quite plainly states, I left school at sixteen and have worked ever since.' She paused. 'My mother died when I was fifteen which interrupted my studies. I've done a few evening classes but most of what I do is self-taught.'

'Oh, I see.' At least he managed to look contrite. 'I'm sorry for your loss.'

'Thank you,' Anna said. 'You weren't to know.'

'All the same, that must have had a pretty big impact on your life.'

'Yes,' she said simply. 'Which is why I want to learn as much as I can to follow my dream and make my mother proud.'

'Of course.' He nodded. Silence hung in the air, until he seemed to pull himself together. 'There will be quite a lot of boring, dogsbody jobs to do, like making sure all my equipment is packed and ready for shoots, uploading photos onto the website and keeping my diary. How would you cope with that?'

'I'd be quite happy to do whatever the job takes. Mundane or not.'

'Good.'

'Do you have any questions, Anna?' Charlotte asked as silence descended once more.

Anna stood up. 'Yes. Can I have my jacket back, please?'

* * *

'So what do you think, then?' Charlotte asked after Anna had left.

Daniel didn't know what to think. He needed an assistant who was reliable, not one who got lost and had poor timekeeping, so even before the interview had begun, he'd written her off as unsuitable.

At first her answers had backed up his instinct. She'd looked as though she was visibly shaking, and her responses were predictable, as though she was saying what she thought he wanted to hear. Then part way through the interview she'd rallied and stood up to him. She'd shown herself to be assertive and that she knew what she wanted. But she had changed from mouse to tiger in an instant, with an unpredictability that he definitely didn't want in an assistant.

There was something about her though, something that he couldn't quite put his finger on. He was intrigued by her and felt that he wanted to get to know her better. She had nowhere near the sophistication of the women who appealed to him. She was pretty, with large green eyes, a heart-shaped face and a straight nose, in a kind of a girl-next-door look. There was very little artifice about her, but that was probably because the rain had washed away most of her make-up. And the way her damp shirt had clung to her, accentuating her curves — well, he would defy any man not to be stirred by that. But as his employee? No, he didn't think so.

'None of them were suitable.'

'Really?' Charlotte asked. 'I know she got off to a shaky start but I thought Anna was well qualified.'

'Maybe, but she was spikey. She'd probably spend the whole time arguing whenever I asked her to do anything.'

Charlotte said nothing for a moment, then replied, 'Well that might depend on how you asked her.'

Daniel shook his head. 'She was the best of a bad bunch. I'm either going to have to carry on, on my own, or re-advertise the job.'

'As you wish.' Charlotte got up from the sofa. 'You asked for my opinion but you obviously don't want it, so I'll leave you to it.'

'Oh, Char, don't get all huffy with me. I'm sorry, I am listening to you. I'm just so fed up with being messed around.'

'I know. And I understand you must be really upset about not seeing Ben this weekend. But, Daniel, you can't keep taking it out on everyone else. You'll get yourself a bad reputation.'

Slowly Daniel smiled. 'I think it's too late for that. Have you read the papers recently?'

'I never believe what I read in the papers, or on social media,' she replied. 'But seriously, have a re-think about Anna. She could be the one.'

He frowned. 'I seem to remember you saying that before, and look how badly that ended.'

CHAPTER TWO

The rain had stopped by the time Anna left Daniel Redfern's house and weak sunshine was trying to break its way through the grey clouds. She limped towards the Tube station, her shoes rubbing on the patches of skin on her heels, which had blistered and were now bleeding. She was bedraggled, in pain and furious. She didn't care if she didn't get the job — in fact, she'd decided that she'd turn it down if she did. She'd never be able to work for such a rude and obnoxious man. She couldn't believe he hadn't even bothered to read her CV.

The Tube was busy, but thankfully she managed to find a seat. When she reached her stop at Canada Water she began the short walk to the Angel pub, where she'd arranged to meet her friend Daisy. She would have preferred to go straight home and sink into a nice warm bath, but she knew that as soon as she arrived home, her evening chores would immediately engulf her and there would be no time for relaxation until much later. So, maybe a glass of wine and a moan with her best friend would revive her a little and put off the inevitable.

Inside the pub she stopped to adjust her vision to the gloomy interior. When she saw that Daisy hadn't arrived yet, she headed to the ladies', ran a brush through her now frizzing hair and reapplied her make-up. Feeling slightly more human, she went to the bar and ordered herself a large glass of white wine. Several groups were sitting at tables chatting loudly, obviously pleased that the weekend had started, and there were several regulars propping up the bar. She grabbed an empty table in a secluded corner and sat down gratefully.

A few minutes later, Daisy bustled in and headed towards her.

'Sorry I'm late,' she said, her face lit up with her ever-ready wide smile. As usual she was full of life, her walk as bouncy as her dark curly hair. Anna had always admired Daisy's rather bohemian style, her love of puffy-sleeved blouses and long skirts. As a personal assistant in a banking firm in the city, it wasn't a look she should have successfully carried off, but it matched her bubbly personality and somehow she seemed to get away with it.

'Don't worry, I've not been here long either,' Anna replied.

'I'll just get myself a drink and I'm all yours.'

Once Daisy sat back down she got straight to it. 'So come on then, how did the interview go?'

'Horrendous.' Anna cringed at the memory. 'I wish you'd never persuaded me to apply for it.'

'Oh, I'm sorry. What happened?'

'Put it this way, I got lost, was late, the heavens opened and I ended up looking like a drowned rat. And to top it all, Daniel Redfern is the most obnoxious man I've ever met. The whole afternoon felt like one of those dreams where you're try-ing to get somewhere but obstacles keep getting in your way, and then when you look down you realise you're wearing your pyjamas in public, or worse you're wearing nothing at all.'

'Ow.' Daisy pulled a face. 'So you didn't hit it off, then?'

Anna laughed at the thought of getting on well with Daniel Redfern. 'Just because he's successful and semi-fa-mous, doesn't give him the right to be so rude.' She took a slurp of her wine. 'When I told him about my interest in photography, he asked me if I'd done some media course at college and thought I knew everything. He hadn't even bothered to read my CV!'

'That's a shame,' Daisy said soothingly. 'On paper it sounded like the perfect job for you and, goodness knows, you need to get away from the one you're in. How you can bear to work with toxic Mark and his up-herself new girlfriend I really don't know.'

Anna sighed. 'It is becoming unbearable, but I can't leave until I've found something else. And I'm not going to jump into some crappy job to get away from them. I've worked hard in that gallery and I deserve a decent job, not to be pushed away because Mark can't keep it in his pants.'

'Too right.' Daisy nodded in agreement. 'But unfortunately the kind of job you're looking for doesn't come along very often. That's why this one looked so perfect.'

'I know.' Anna sighed again.

'What would you do if he offered it to you anyway?'

Anna laughed. 'Believe me, that's not likely to happen. The interview was a complete car crash.'

'But if he did? Maybe his bark's worse than his bite. Or maybe you could win him round. You'd probably learn a lot more about photography from a man like him than you could from any course.'

'I know. And that's the pity of it.' Anna had another sip of wine. 'But, no, I really don't think I could work with him. At least at the gallery they more or less leave me to get on with it.'

'Okay, fair enough.' Daisy paused. 'So apart from his obnoxious character, what was he like in the flesh? Was he as good-looking as he is in his pics?'

'No . . . he was much better in the flesh. The photos don't capture his eyes. They're so startlingly blue they take your breath away.'

'Really?' Daisy asked, a small smile playing on her lips.

'I'm speaking from an aesthetic point of view,' Anna replied, despite the fact that she felt herself growing slightly warmer at the memory of him. 'Nothing more.'

'Shame.' Daisy continued smiling.

Anna drained her glass. 'I'm sorry, hun, but I'm going to have to go. Dinner won't cook itself.'

'It would if those lazy boys pulled their fingers out,' Daisy said. 'Honestly Anna, you pander to them. They're old enough and ugly enough to look after themselves, even if it's only occasionally. It shouldn't all be down to you just because you're female.'

'I know, I know.' Anna had heard this rant from Daisy before, but it didn't change the fact that she felt obliged to look after them. 'When Mum died, it sort of became my role and now it's very difficult to undo.'

'You just need to put your foot down. Divide up the chores and get them to do their bit.'

'Tried that,' Anna said. 'All that happens is they do the jobs so badly it ends up taking me twice as long to sort it out after them.'

'Well, move out, then.'

'I wish I could afford to, Daise. But even if I could, there's Harry to consider. He's revising for his A-levels and I really don't want to rock the boat for him. I want him to do well so that he can get away to university. It would be nice for at least one of us to achieve that.'

'That could have been you,' Daisy said quietly.

'Should've, could've, would've,' Anna said. 'The circumstances were very different and there's nothing I can do about that. But, in September, when he's settled, things will change. I promise you.'

'I really hope so,' Daisy said. 'You need to be able to live your own life.'

'I know. So, are you walking with me?'

Daisy looked at her watch. 'No, you go on. I said I'd meet Tom and he should be here any minute.'

'Want me to wait until he gets here?'

Daisy shook her head. 'No, you get on.'

'Well, have a good time.'

As Anna made her way out of the now-full pub, the Friday-night crowd seemed ready to enjoy the weekend. What did the weekend have in store for her? she wondered. Washing, ironing, cooking and cleaning would be the limit of what she was doing, and then Monday morning would come round soon enough. Another week ahead of her facing Mark and his new girlfriend. Not exactly a lot to look forward to.

With a sigh of relief, Anna reached the terraced house she called home, eager to be rid of her painful shoes. Compared to the beautiful Georgian terrace of Daniel Redfern, the house she lived in was undeniably working class, but it had always been her home and, for that, she loved it. She put her key in the lock, opened the door and walked down the short hallway towards the living room. The blare from the television told her that someone was watching the football and, sure enough, she stepped inside to find her dad and her elder brother, Jack, sprawled on the two large sofas, each with a beer can in hand. Their eyes were fixed on the large TV as one of the strikers took a shot. As the ball went wide, both men groaned in mutual dismay. She looked around the room and compared it to the pristine mansion of Daniel Redfern. She did her best to keep the house clean and tidy, but the shabbiness of the room, which was long overdue redecoration, filled her with dismay.

When the noise died down, Anna said hello. Both men turned to face her, a look of shock on their faces as they hadn't realised she'd come into the house, let alone the room.

'Hello, love.' Her father, Andrew, was the first to recover. Jack didn't even bother to say hello and, after taking a glug from his can, fixed his eyes firmly back on the football match.

'Have you had a good day at work?' Andrew asked.

'I wasn't at work today, Dad. I told you I was going to an interview.'

'Oh, yeah, that's right. The posh photographer. How did it go?'

She sighed at the memory of it once again. 'Well, let's just say I don't think I'll be getting the job.'

Andrew snorted. 'Well, that's his loss. Shame. You could do with getting away from that idiot of an ex-boyfriend of yours.'

'I know. But I'm not going to be pushed out before I'm ready.'

'Quite right,' Andrew replied, then added, 'So what's for tea, love?'

Anna stared at him in disbelief. She'd had a disastrous day, her feet were killing her and here were her father and the eldest of her brothers, sitting in the comfortable living room, each with a can of lager in their hands, waiting for her to get home so she could cook them dinner. Something inside her snapped. Daisy was right, she'd pandered to them for far too long. She wasn't a wife or a mother, and just because she was the only female in the house didn't mean she should have to wait on them hand and foot.

'No idea,' she said, resisting the instinct to head to the kitchen and see what was in the fridge. 'To be honest, I'm not really hungry. I've had one hell of a day, so I think I might just have a soak in the bath. I'm sure there's plenty of stuff in the freezer if you want to sort yourselves out.' She rushed out of the living room before they had a chance to protest. She'd quite happily go hungry tonight if it made a point.

As she reached the top of the stairs, her younger brother, Harry, opened the door to his bedroom.

'Hiya, I thought I heard your voice. How did your interview go?'

Gratified that at least one member of her family had remembered, she told him all about it.

'Oh, that's a shame. It sounded like the perfect job for you.'

'In theory, yes, but things aren't always as they seem. I'm going to have a bath now. Dad and Jack are sorting out tea.'

Harry's eyes widened in surprise. 'Or not as the case may be,' he said. 'I can always do it if you like?'

Anna smiled at him. If anyone else pulled their weight in the house it was Harry. But his A-level exams would start in just over a month and he needed to revise.

'No, let them get off their backsides for once — you've got enough to do.'

He smiled back. 'Well, I was hoping to go through some past papers tonight.'

'Then that's what you should do. If they don't get anything sorted, make something for yourself. I've been too soft with them for too long.'

CHAPTER THREE

On Saturday afternoon, Anna escaped the house for a few hours, enticed by the April sunshine — and a desperate need to get away from the chores of washing and cleaning that had mounted up during the week. She loved to walk around the streets of Rotherhithe, taking pictures. As she walked she noticed that the trees were starting to bud, a sure sign that spring was on its way after the drabness of winter. Her passion was architecture, both old and new, and she liked recording buildings through the different seasons. Before she realised, several hours had passed and her legs were beginning to ache. With a sigh she decided to head for home.

As she walked she contemplated her life. She certainly wasn't where she'd expected to be at this age. She'd hoped to have achieved so much more by the age of thirty but, with her twenty-ninth birthday approaching in the next week, time was rapidly running out. And here she was, still living at home, looking after her dad and brothers, in a job she was desperate to get out of, with no boyfriend and very few friends. Not so long ago, she and Daisy would have been out on the town together, drinking in a bar or a club, with or without their boyfriends, or going out for meals or to the cinema as a foursome. But now that Daisy's relationship with Tom seemed to be getting more serious, and Mark had dumped her for the boss's daughter, Anna was like a spare wheel. Daisy had mentioned that she and Tom were contemplating moving in together, so Anna imagined she'd be seeing even less of her friend in the future. Binge-watching Netflix looked to become a Saturday night norm for her. She'd spent a large part of last night scouring through job ads, but nothing had appealed to her. Maybe she should be less picky, keep her photography as a hobby and find a job, any job, which was better paid and gave her some chance of a social life.

But it wasn't just her job that needed to change. Daisy had been right yesterday. She really needed to do something about her home life too. While she continued to pander to them, her dad and brothers weren't likely to get up and help her out. They were used to living on easy street. Why would they want to change that?

After she'd flounced out of the living room last night, she'd hoped it would be enough to galvanise one of them into doing some actual cooking, but instead her dad had gone to the chippy and brought back fish and chips. At least he'd bought a portion for both her and Harry, but it was still a takeaway and required little effort on his part. This morning she'd got up to find their plates left on the worktop in the kitchen, with congealed smears of ketchup, and an avalanche of empty beer cans on the coffee table in the living room. So, before she'd started her weekend clean, she'd spent a good hour tidying up their mess. Part of her had been tempted to leave it and see how bad the squalor would get before they actually did something about it, but the other part of her was unable to live like that. Her mum had been house-proud and for the house to be anything but neat and tidy, even if it was to make a point, would feel like she was betraying her mother's memory. Also she didn't want any rows or arguments — she wanted a tranquil environment for Harry to study. With his A-levels approaching, he needed peace and quiet to make the most of his education, to give him the chance she'd never had. She decided she would try to start putting her foot down gently, to try to get the boys to do more, and then when Harry had finished his exams she'd sit them all down and tell them how she felt and how she wanted things to change. For the meantime, though, she decided she would just have to carry on.

* * *

Daniel woke on Sunday morning relieved to find that he was alone in his bed and there was no evidence of anyone else having been there. He lay back on the pillows, his head thumping.

At a loose end because Ben was away, he'd gone out to a bar last night with Charlotte and a bunch of others. He had a vague recollection of chatting to one of Charlotte's model friends, Victoria, whom he'd had a fling with in the past. He'd only begun talking to her to alleviate the boredom of the evening. He used to enjoy going out to crowded clubs, where the drinks flowed freely and everyone gave the impression that they were living their best lives, but last night it had all seemed superficial. Perhaps he was getting too old to be socialising like that, he thought. These days he'd much rather spend his weekend nights snuggled up on a sofa with a woman he loved. Not that Victoria fitted into the snuggling category. She was incredibly glamorous and, from memory, very passionate, but he couldn't imagine her settling down on the sofa in joggers and a T-shirt with a bowl of popcorn and a box set. He was ridiculously relieved that he'd come home alone last night and could spend the rest of his weekend doing whatever he liked. Perhaps he should change not only his lifestyle but also the women he went for. Going out with glamorous women was good for his ego, as well as his society image, but did little for his soul. And that was what he found himself yearning for — someone he could have a greater connection with.

Daniel sighed as he pushed back the duvet and headed for the shower. At least next weekend he'd spend Saturday night with Ben. He was determined to make their time together as special as possible. Not that he was trying to compete with Lucinda and Axel, of course.

In the kitchen, Daniel made a strong coffee and went up to the attic that he used as a studio. Last week had been busy, finished off with that interminable day of interviews, and he had a stack of photographs that needed to be uploaded and edited before he could send them off. He switched on his computer and began the laborious and often slow process of uploading the images from his camera.

Several hours later, Daniel's stomach began to rumble and he decided to make himself some breakfast. He still had a long day's work ahead of him if he had any chance of starting the week without a backlog. He quite enjoyed the editing process, particularly the fine-tuning to make the images as perfect as possible, but he wished he had a reliable assistant who could start the process off, so that he could just come in and perfect them at the end. Last night, Charlotte had been pushing him to give the job to the last applicant of the day on Friday, and he had to admit he was coming round to the idea. Yes, he could foresee a clash of temperaments, but if he laid the ground rules down from the very beginning, maybe it could work? The fact that she was interested in photography would certainly be of benefit, especially when it came to editing the photos. She'd said she was self-taught, which indicated she had a willingness to learn. Without wanting to appear big-headed, he felt there was a lot he could teach her.

His thoughts slipped back to his uncle, who was sadly no longer with them. Uncle Lewis had been regarded as the outcast of the family, and Daniel's father had had a fit when Lewis had introduced Daniel to photography. His father had had much loftier aspirations for Daniel, pushing him into doing a business-studies degree with an emphasis on finance. Daniel, though, had hated the course. It was only when he'd found his love of photography that he'd had the courage to quit. His father had flown into a rage and their relationship had been strained ever since, even though Daniel had made a success of his chosen career. That day his father had vowed never to speak to Lewis again, and he'd kept his word, even when he'd found out that his brother had been diagnosed with terminal cancer. His attitude had pushed Lewis and Daniel closer together, and Lewis had become a father figure as well as a mentor. Daniel wouldn't be where he was today without Lewis, and he would always be grateful for the time and love his uncle had lavished on him. So perhaps that's what he should do, use his skills and knowledge to help another young hopeful get their foot on the ladder. He smiled for the first time that day. The thought was certainly appealing.

After eating his breakfast and heading back upstairs, he'd made up his mind. He would offer Anna Wright a trial period. If nothing else, it would free him up so that he could spend more time with Ben. If Lucinda allowed it, that was.

CHAPTER FOUR

Anna arrived at work early on Monday morning. Even though she wasn't due to start until nine o'clock, she normally liked to be the first to arrive. She loved the peace and quiet when no one else was around, and she often took a few moments to wander around the gallery, viewing the current artwork. Often she'd imagine what her photos would look like framed on the walls, if she was ever lucky enough to have an exhibition. And then she would sigh in frustration, because the chances of that happening were non-existent. She'd broached the subject with Mark previously but he'd told her in no uncertain terms that The Whigmore was an art gallery, not somewhere that would display someone's amateur snaps. And he'd been so derogatory of her photography that she hadn't dared show her work to anyone else, least of all any prospective agents. But deep down she hadn't been able to let go of the dream, that one day, with a lot more work on her part, she might become good enough to secure an agent and have her own exhibition.

She'd woken at six this morning in a very unsettled mood. Feelings from the weekend had lingered. She was increasingly frustrated at how her life was stagnating and how much she dreaded going into work each morning. Sitting on the Tube, she'd contemplated whether she should just go for any job to get away from the toxic situation she was in with Mark and Jemima.

She was just switching on the computer at the reception desk when the door pinged open. She looked up, surprised to see anyone so early. She usually had at least half an hour to settle herself into the day before she was interrupted. Her stomach sank when Mark walked through the door. He grinned when he saw her, his smile lighting up his hazel eyes. The smile that had never failed to make her stomach flip over in the past. And even though it was over, whenever she was alone with him, she was always tempted to reach out to him. But she couldn't do that. He was with someone else and she'd never be able to touch him like that again.

'Anna, you're in early!' He walked towards the reception desk. 'Did you have a good day off on Friday?'

'Yes, thanks,' she said tightly.

'Do anything interesting?' He was getting closer and she tried to deepen her breathing in the hope that her heart rate would slow down.

'Oh, went out with some friends.' She had met up with Daisy, so she was only half-lying, but the last thing she wanted was for him to find out that she'd gone for a job interview. He'd be even more smug if he found out she'd tried to get away and failed.

'That's good,' he said. He'd reached the counter now and casually leaned against it, so close to her that she could smell the musky scent of his aftershave. She took a step back. 'Nice to see you getting out and about,' he added. 'Not at the beck and call of your family as usual.'

The amount she did for the boys had always annoyed him. In his eyes he should have taken priority, not them, and no matter how much she'd tried to explain why she felt obliged to look after them, he hadn't wanted to understand. He hadn't got it when she'd gone on her photography expeditions either, or when she'd done anything that hadn't been directly connected to him. In the logical part of her brain she could see their relationship would never have worked out, even if he hadn't betrayed her, but all that logic didn't stop her from being physically attracted to him.

'We missed you on Friday,' he said. 'The place was in chaos without you. You'll have a lot of sorting out to do today.'

'I'm sure it's not that bad. Running this place isn't exactly rocket science.'

'That's because you make it look so easy.' He inched his hand across the desk as though he was going to touch her. She tried to move to the side — there wasn't much room behind the desk — to get away from him. What the hell was going on here? He hadn't been nice to her in weeks and this charm offensive was alien. She sensed he was playing a game and she didn't want any part of it.

He sighed. 'When I said we missed you on Friday, what I really meant was that I missed you.' His gaze was intent on her, sad puppy-dog eyes, which in the past would have her hurtling into his arms.

She swallowed, remaining as calm as possible. 'I was only gone for a day.'

'Yes, but it was a very long day.' His head was only inches away from hers.

She almost sprinted from behind the reception desk and marched over to the coffee machine, changing the subject. 'Do you want a coffee?'

'No,' he said. 'I want you.'

She turned around abruptly.

'I'm sorry?'

'I made a mistake, Anna. Jemima is a lovely girl, but I thought the grass was greener and it's not. I should have stuck with you.'

Not so long ago she'd have been delighted to hear those words, had even longed for him to say them. But now? Now she feared it was too late. She could see the holes in their relationship all too clearly.

'You want me back?' She almost whispered the words she was so shocked.

'I do.' He stepped towards her and put his hand on her arm. She looked up, almost drowning in the depths of his eyes. Almost.

'And it's over with Jemima?'

'To me, it is, yes. But she's, well, she's a little bit fragile. She doesn't look it, but underneath she's very insecure. I'd have to let her down gently. But in the meantime . . .'

'But in the meantime you want to two-time her with me. Just like you did to me?'

'No, no, it's not like that.' His grip tightened, but she shook him off and stepped away. This time he didn't move towards her. 'It's you I want to be with, not her. But she is the boss's daughter, so I'm going to have to tread very carefully.'

Anna felt a cold, hard lump settle in her chest as she realised one woman would never be enough for Mark and he didn't care who he hurt in the process. She wondered if he'd used the same line on Jemima? That Anna was flaky and he'd have to let her down gently. She seethed at the thought of it.

'I'm sorry if it's not working out with you and Jemima, but that's nothing to do with me. Our relationship is in the past and that's where it's going to stay.'

'But, Anna!'

'No buts, Mark. We have to work together, so I'd like to keep things civil, but that's all.' She moved back behind the reception desk and smiled as the door pinged open.

Mark glared at her and said in a low growl, 'You might just live to regret that.'

Jemima swept into the gallery, her long cream cashmere coat swishing around her calves, knotted tightly at her slim waist. Her dark hair cascaded down her back and, as ever, her beautiful face was exquisitely made up.

'Darling, hello.' She put her arm proprietarily around Mark. 'It's a lovely morning.'

'Feels like ages since I've seen you.' He leaned down and gave her a peck on the lips.

She giggled. 'Even if it is only a short while that you left our warm bed.'

Anna cringed at their canoodling. Honestly, she was better off out of it — she just didn't see why they had to flaunt it in front of her face. Jemima was like a cat marking her territory. If only she knew the conversation that had taken place moments ago. That would wipe the smile off her face. Although Anna doubted she would believe it.

Jemima turned her attention to Anna. 'Well, I hope you're ready for work, Anna, there's a lot to do following your day off. Gregory, our debut artist, has been in touch and he's got lots of questions for you, so I suggest you deal with all his queries as soon as possible. We want to make sure he feels like he's being heard.'

'Of course.' Anna anticipated there would also be a backlog of other emails too, emails that no one had bothered to open in her absence on Friday.

'Mark and I have lots of paperwork to do in our office, so if you could bring us both a coffee and then leave us undisturbed.'

'My pleasure,' Anna replied through gritted teeth, guessing there wouldn't be a piece of paper in sight.

* * *

After taking the coffees into the office and resisting the temptation to accidentally spill the mugs on them both, Anna returned to reception. As she had expected, no one had bothered to open any of the emails since Thursday and there were several from Gregory, growing increasingly annoyed that his previous emails hadn't been answered. Anna sighed and set to catching up with everything, pacifying Gregory in the process.

In reality, it wasn't even her job. She was employed as the receptionist, with Mark as manager and Jemima his assistant. When she and Mark had been together, she hadn't minded the extra work. It had given her a chance to develop her skills, even if she was fully aware it allowed Mark to get away with doing very little. But then she had been the one coming up with the ideas, and it made her feel important in his eyes. Having orders snapped at her by Jemima was a completely different matter. Jemima had been brought in as Daddy's little girl to learn the ropes. In theory she was supposed to be learning the job from the bottom up, experiencing all the jobs in the gallery so that, one day, she could take over. Anna had always suspected Jemima was only here to give her something to do, to stop her from lunching with her friends and spending Daddy's money. There certainly didn't seem to be much learning going on.

At twelve-thirty Jemima breezed through reception and said, 'I'm going out to lunch.'

'You will be back in an hour, won't you?' Anna asked, not entirely hopefully. She couldn't go for her own lunch until Jemima was back — and that was getting later and later these days. In fact, she'd started bringing sandwiches into work. Although she wasn't supposed to eat in the gallery, quite often it was the only way she got a chance to eat at all.

Mark left the gallery shortly after Jemima, throwing a glare towards Anna as he walked out, and once more she was alone. She sat back in her chair as she watched him go. She really wasn't sure she could carry on much longer like this.

Predictably it was closer to two hours by the time Jemima arrived back. This time she was arm in arm with Mark and the pair of them were grinning like Cheshire cats. She waltzed through reception towards Anna, waggling her left hand at her.

'Look what we've just bought.' She thrust her hand towards Anna. Even from a distance Anna couldn't have failed to notice the huge rock on Jemima's finger, or the way it glinted in the early afternoon sunshine.

'You're engaged.' Her voice came out in a croak. 'Congratulations.'

'Thank you,' Jemima said. 'I can't wait to tell Daddy.'

Anna glanced at Mark and he smiled smugly back at her, as though his words this morning had never been spoken.

'Let's go now, then.' Mark looked down fondly at his fiancée. 'You don't mind holding the fort this afternoon, do you, Anna?'

'I don't mind.' Anna reached for her bag and coat. 'But I haven't had my lunch yet so I'll take over when I get back.'

She kept her back straight and her eyes on the door as she tried to walk away in as dignified a manner as possible.

'Just half an hour, if you don't mind,' Mark said as Anna opened the door. 'You can take a longer lunch tomorrow.'

She walked out without turning back, not least because she didn't want either of them to see the tears that were welling in her eyes. It wasn't that she was upset about them getting engaged, or that she wanted Mark for herself. It was more the way he'd tried to manipulate her that very morning, and then how smug they were at their engagement. If she'd thought her work situation was bad this morning, it had just got a whole lot worse.

* * *

Sat in the nearest café with a cappuccino in front of her, Anna reached for her phone. She needed to get on the job sites, refresh the categories of what she was looking for and find something new. She'd settle for anything right now.

As she was scrolling through the adverts, the phone's ringtone startled her. When she saw the name of Daniel Redfern on the screen, she was even more surprised.

She answered it hesitantly. 'Hello?'

'Is that Anna Wright?'

'Yes.'

'Daniel Redfern here. I'm phoning about the interview you attended on Friday.'

'Oh, okay.' She hadn't expected to hear from him again. Most employers these days didn't bother to let you know if you were unsuccessful.

'I'm phoning to say that I'd like to offer you the job.'

'You would?' Today was beginning to feel surreal.

'Yes.'

'I'm, er, a bit surprised, that's all.'

'Well.' He paused. 'You were the best candidate for the job, all things considered.'

'All things considered?'

'Yes, well, do you want the job?'

'I . . .'

She didn't know what to say. She thought back to the encounter in the gallery earlier. Although she and Daniel hadn't hit it off, would working for him be worse than working in the same place as Mark and his new fiancée? At least her emotions wouldn't be involved.

'I'd love to accept,' she said.

'Great.' He sounded relieved. 'Well, obviously it would be on a trial basis. Say three months?'

'Yes, okay.'

'That would give us the opportunity to see if we suit each other.'

'Of course.' It would give her some breathing space, a chance to be paid while still getting away from Mark. And even if she didn't like him, she knew she could learn a lot from Daniel Redfern.

'So,' he said. 'How much notice do you have to give at your current job?'

'A month.'

'Ah. I don't suppose you could make it sooner, could you?'

'They do owe me holiday. I could use that in lieu of my notice, so, say, two weeks?'

'That would be great. I'll ask for a reference from your current employer and then hopefully we can make this official.'

'I'll look forward to it,' she said, before ending the call.

She sat for a while in a daze. She'd woken up this morning feeling as though her life was stuck and now her whole future was about to change. For the first time that day, Anna smiled. She might be jumping out of the frying pan into the fire, but she felt elated at the chance she was about to take.

She arrived back nearly an hour after she had left. Mark was pacing the reception area, looking angry and red in the face.

'I thought I told you, you could only take half an hour for lunch?'

'I'm entitled to a full hour and you have no right to stop me from taking it.'

'Well, now that you're back, I'm going to join my fiancée in celebrating our happy news.'

'Oh,' Anna said, pretending to look surprised. 'Has she gone ahead without you?'

'Please make sure you stay open until five. I don't want you slacking just because we're not here.'

'Wouldn't dream of it,' she said with a smile.

She waited until she was sure Mark had left and wouldn't be coming back before switching on her computer and writing her letter of resignation. After printing it off she folded it into an envelope and placed it on his desk where he would be sure to see it, first thing in the morning. Then she took a copy of *Amateur Photographer* out of her bag and read it from cover to cover, relishing that she was skiving off work, just like they were. At five o'clock on the dot, she grabbed her coat and bag and locked up the gallery, a smile on her face.

The next morning, she arrived back at the gallery at two minutes to nine o'clock. Mark was in front of her, trying to unlock the door with unfamiliar keys.

'You're late,' he said as she reached him.

She made a show of looking at her phone. 'No, I'm not. I've got two minutes to spare.'

'But you're usually so early.' The key turned in the lock and he pushed the door open. Anna moved inside to turn off the alarm.

When it was quiet once more, Anna said, 'Well, maybe things are going to be different from now on.'

He frowned at her. 'What does that mean?'

'You'll find out soon enough,' she said. 'No Jemima this morning?'

'No, she's, er, a little under the weather today. She might be in later.'

'I see, a bit too much celebrating last night, then?'

'Well, you only get engaged once,' he replied, smiling smugly at her.

She turned her back on him and switched on her computer, imagining his expression when he opened the letter that was waiting for him on his desk.

She was scrolling through her emails when he stormed back into reception from his office, waving her letter at her.

'What's this all about?'

She turned to him and smiled sweetly. 'I'd have thought that was quite obvious. It's my letter of resignation.'

'But you can't go.' He paused. 'Why do you want to go? Is it because I'm engaged? Is the thought of me marrying someone else too much for you?'

'No, it's not because you're engaged.' It was a part-truth. 'It's because I've got a new job. A better one.'

'What job? What could be better than this? The Whigmore is one of the most prestigious art galleries in the West End.'

'Where I'm employed as a receptionist, on a receptionist's wage, even though I'm the one who contributes most to the running of it. Whereas you and Jemima are paid so much more than me for doing . . .' She paused. 'Tell me, what is it you actually do?' She knew she was sailing close to the wind, but she'd spent so long biting back her words and her feelings and she wasn't prepared to do it anymore.

He spluttered. 'How dare you?'

'What are you going to do? Sack me?' She smiled.

'I've a good mind to, yes.'

'Fine.' She reached for her coat and her bag.

'No, no, don't go.' He barred her exit. 'At least, if you go now, you won't get a reference and you'll need that for your new job, won't you?'

'Yes, I will. But I'm sure you'll give me a good reference. Well, at least an accurate one, which amounts to the same thing.'

'And what makes you so sure of that?' He seemed confident he had the upper hand.

'Because you wouldn't want Jemima to find out about our conversation yesterday morning.'

'What conversation?'

She laughed. 'Oh, Mark, you must remember — the one where you said that you'd rather be with me than her, but you had to let her down gently because she's so fragile.'

He paused for a moment. 'And why would she believe you?'

'Because I'm pretty sure they're the same lines you used on her when you were seeing me. And when I quote you word for word, I think she'll recognise them and know I'm telling the truth.'

When his face paled, she knew she'd hit the bullseye. Mark was far too lazy to be original. She almost laughed out loud, but stopped herself just in time.

'Fine, I'll give you a reference, but only if you work your full four weeks' notice.'

'I've given you four weeks.'

'No, you've only given me two.'

'The last two weeks I'm taking as the holiday you owe me, so you don't need to pay me for that.'

'But two weeks isn't long enough to find a replacement.'

She forced herself not to smile. 'Then maybe Jemima can help out? She was given the job to learn the ropes and she's been here long enough. It should be easy enough for her to fill in for a lowly receptionist until you find a replacement.'

Mark moved towards the reception desk and looked own at her. Softly he said, 'Anna, you know you're more than just a receptionist. You're very much more than that.'

'Everyone is replaceable,' she answered coolly, delighted for once that his puppy-dog eyes and cajoling compliments didn't move her one little bit.

'Morning, everyone.' Jemima breezed into reception and then stopped in her tracks. 'Oh, I'm sorry, am I interrupting something?'

'Not at all,' Mark said, pulling himself together. 'Anna here has just handed in her notice. I was trying to persuade her to stay but she's obviously impervious to my charms.'

'Oh, you're not going, are you?' Jemima asked, barely able to keep the glee out of her voice. 'Where to?'

It was then Anna realised Mark hadn't even bothered to ask her where she was going.

'I've got a job as an assistant to a photographer.'

Mark scoffed. 'You and your photography. You were always more interested in that than real art.'

'Who's the photographer? Anyone we might know?' Jemima asked.

'You might, yes.' Anna paused. 'I'm going to work for Daniel Redfern.'

'*The* Daniel Redfern?' Jemima asked, her eyes wide.

'The very same,' Anna replied, smiling. She looked at Mark — his face was puce, but he quickly rallied himself.

'Well, you won't last two minutes with him,' he said 'He changes his assistants more often than most people change their socks.'

'We'll have to see,' Anna said as Mark turned on his heel and slammed his office door behind him.

For a moment both women stared after him, then Jemima glared at Anna before following Mark into the office.

CHAPTER FIVE

The first day of her new job dawned bright and sunny. Anna dressed carefully, not wanting to appear either too smart or too casual. She'd been fretting all weekend about what to wear and had eventually settled on a shirt, black jeans and boots. It wasn't exactly a corporate position, so a suit probably wasn't appropriate, but she didn't want to look as though she hadn't made an effort.

She'd woken early with butterflies in her stomach. She couldn't sleep and, when she'd got up, she'd been too nervous to eat. Instead, she'd made herself a sandwich for later and shoved it in her bag, unsure what her lunch arrangements would be.

The last two weeks working at the gallery had been almost unbearable. Both Mark and Jemima had gone out of their way to make life difficult for her. Considering that Mark still supposedly had feelings for her, he hadn't even acknowledged her birthday, halfway through her notice period. But then why should that surprise her? Mark usually only did things to serve himself. Her dad and Harry had made a fuss of her and she'd gone out on a girl's night with Daisy on the Saturday, so she'd enjoyed it without any contribution from him. During the last few weeks, the thought of her new job had kept her going, but now that the day had arrived, she wasn't quite so confident. In fact, walking into the unknown terrified her.

She left for the Tube station in plenty of time. The journey passed without hazard and she was on Daniel's doorstep half an hour early. She wondered whether she should bide her time and find a coffee shop somewhere. But half-afraid she would get lost and end up being late again, she rang Daniel's doorbell with a trembling finger.

He took a while to answer the door and when he did he was dressed casually in jeans and a T-shirt, with a towel wrapped around his neck, as though he'd just got out of the shower.

'I'm sorry, I'm early.' Anna wondered if he was going to be as cross with her for being early too.

'Well, it's better than being late, I suppose,' he said somewhat gruffly. 'Go through to the kitchen and I'll be in with you when I've finished getting ready.'

Inside the gleaming white kitchen, with stainless-steel appliances and black granite worktops, Anna put her bag down and perched on a stool beside a huge island in the centre of the room. Five minutes later Daniel arrived, looking more composed.

'Sorry again about being early. One day I'll get it right,' she said.

'Let's hope so.' He wasn't smiling at her attempt to joke.

There was a silence until he said, 'Sorry. I'm not a morning person — not at least until I've had my first cup of coffee.'

Anna jumped off her stool immediately. 'Then let me make you one.'

'No, it's okay, I'll do it,' he replied quickly and then, as if he'd spoken too hastily, added, 'At least on your first day. I can show you where everything is and then you can do it in future. I need plenty of coffee in the mornings.'

She nodded. 'Noted. Happy to be chief coffee maker.'

When the coffees were made he said, 'Come on then, let's take these upstairs.'

'Upstairs?' she asked, panicked.

'Yes, of course,' he replied. 'My studio is in the attic.'

'Oh, right, yes, of course.' She felt foolish at her overactive imagination.

* * *

Daniel led Anna back through the house and up the sumptuous stairway. The whole house looked like something out of an interior-design magazine and everything was white — the walls, the woodwork, the curtains and the plush carpets. Anna tried to imagine her lot living here and almost burst out laughing. The place would be grubby as soon as they walked through the door. The house was enormous for just one person. What was so amazing about it was how high the ceilings were, each containing intricate ceiling roses with hanging chandeliers. This was definitely how the other half lived. As they made their way up the second flight of stairs to the attic, Anna was tempted to pinch herself to make sure that her new workplace was actually real.

At the top of the stairs, Daniel opened the door into a large, open-plan area. The loft was the length of the house, with large roof windows that let in an abundance of light. Anna gasped at the sheer size and splendour of the studio. Again, it was all white, with blonde-coloured flooring. At one end was a huge desk with a large-screen iMac. At the other, an area where portrait photos could be taken. This was interspersed with comfortable sofas, racks for clothing and built-in wall cupboards, which Anna presumed would contain Daniel's equipment.

'Wow!' It was all she could say as she moved inside the doorway.

'Like it?' Daniel asked, his face beaming with obvious pride.

'It's magnificent.' She gazed around the room.

'Good, because when we're not on shoots, this is where you'll be spending most of your time.'

'Suits me,' Anna said. She just hoped they would be able to get on —this looked like it could very well turn out to be her dream job.

'Right, well, first things first.' He walked over to the desk and picked up a large A4 desk diary. 'This is my bible — it contains all my appointments, telephone numbers and addresses, times and directions.'

'Right,' Anna said.

'What's the matter?'

'Nothing. I just assumed that it would all be computerised.'

'No.' He shook his head. 'It all goes in here. You can't go wrong with pen and paper.'

'What if the book got lost? You've got no backup.'

'It can't get lost,' he replied grumpily. 'That diary doesn't move from the desk.'

'But what about if you need the information when you're on a shoot or on the way to one?'

'Then I have this.' He pulled a much smaller notebook from the pocket of his jeans. 'I transfer any relevant information into this before I leave the studio.'

'Right,' she said slowly.

'What's the matter with that?' He frowned at her and she could tell that if she mentioned sharing an online diary on their phones he might just explode. She decided to go along with his system for the moment. Maybe, bit by bit, she could bring him into the current century.

'Nothing,' she said lightly. 'It just seems a bit laborious, that's all.'

'Well, it's a system that's worked for me all my life, so I don't intend to change it now.'

'Whatever works for you,' she replied, trying to be diplomatic. 'But if it's all right with you, I might just put all this information into a calendar on my phone, which is backed up to the cloud. That way we can be doubly sure that we don't lose anything.'

'If that's the way you want to work, it's up to you.' He didn't sound pleased about it. 'As long as you don't forget to put everything into the desk diary first.'

'I won't,' she said. 'I'm not about to upset your system.'

'Good.' He turned his back to her. 'Why don't we go through the diary together? You need to get up to speed with what's coming up so we can plan accordingly. Let's sit down on the sofa. We might as well be comfortable.'

Comfortable was not how she felt sitting next to him on the small sofa. She could feel the heat of him, suddenly aware of his hard and muscular form, and the room became stifling as warmth spread through her entire body. She tried to concentrate on the diary, to not think about his proximity, but she was struggling to focus on what he was telling her.

As he talked, she realised how busy he was. It was hard not to be starstruck at the amount of top models and celebrities he was about to photograph, but she was too hyper-aware of his body next to hers. She told herself she was being ridiculous. She had vowed, after Mark, she would never fall for her boss again, and here she was getting all hot and bothered after only a few moments in his company.

'So you need to learn exactly what equipment you will need for each shoot,' he said. 'Why don't you grab a fresh notebook from the drawer over there and you can make some notes?'

She smiled as she got up to retrieve a notebook and a pen — she was still smiling when she sat back down again.

'What's so funny?' he asked as she opened up the book to a fresh page.

Realising she was at risk of offending him, she said, 'Nothing's funny, just happy to be here.'

'Good.' He nodded. 'Let's get on with it, shall we?'

'Of course.'

* * *

Daniel found it very disturbing sitting so close to Anna, but he was doing his best not to show it. She was wearing a floral perfume, something he didn't recognise. The women he mixed with often wore much heavier, more obvious scents, but hers was light and fresh, just like her. He shook his head. He must stop thinking about her like this. She wasn't his type and she was his employee — or at least she would be if she passed her probation period. And he wasn't entirely convinced about that. He wasn't sure he could work with someone he felt was silently mocking him for how he organised his work. He knew it was old-fashioned, but it was a system his uncle had used, and if it was good enough for Uncle Lewis, it was good enough for him.

He continued to go through the appointments for the week, bombarding her with information. She was scribbling down his comments so quickly he was sure her hands must be aching.

Taking pity on her, he closed the diary. 'You might think I'm a technological dinosaur, but when it comes to editing software, you'll find I use up-to-the-minute kit.'

'Really?' Her eyes widened in surprise, making her look even more endearing. And all of a sudden he found he couldn't be cross with her.

'Yes, come on, I'll show you.'

He got up, walked over to the desk and switched on his iMac, showing her some of the photographs he had taken last week and how he liked to edit them.

* * *

Although she had been dreading today, working with Daniel was turning out to be a lot easier than she'd expected. Spending the entire day immersed in the world of photography was like a dream come true. So much better than having to cram the thing she loved most into the slivers of space between her everyday life. Although Daniel had been terse with her at times, she'd seen flashes of softness in him too. But she also realised he was a complete perfectionist and she'd have to work incredibly hard to meet his expectations. Especially if she wasn't going to go the way of his previous assistants. And that, she realised, was what she wanted to do. To impress him. She was going to do everything in her power to achieve that.

As she watched him explaining the software to her, she imagined how she could improve her own photographs, if she was ever allowed the chance, forcing herself to push away the feelings he aroused when they were leaning over the keyboard together. So close that they were almost touching. She wasn't going to have a repeat of Mark.

She'd been attracted to Mark from the moment she'd first met him at her interview for the receptionist's job at the gallery. He was smooth and sophisticated, and although she'd known nothing about art galleries, he'd made her feel important and worth something. She'd rarely felt like that before. At school she'd struggled with academics, much to her teachers' consternation. The only thing she'd ever been any good at was art. From her art classes she'd developed a love of photography and from then she'd been hooked. Those classes had been the highlight of her school week, pitted against the frustration of not being able to understand most of her other subjects. She'd dreamed of doing an art foundation course, and even a degree, but then her mum had died and her whole life had changed.

Her mother's death from a brain haemorrhage had been completely unexpected and all the more traumatic because of it. There hadn't even been any signs that anything was wrong. One moment she was standing in the kitchen, laughing and joking, the next, she cried out in pain, holding her hand to her head, and then slumped to the floor. Anna flew to her, trying to get her to speak while their father rang for an ambulance. Her mum was already gone by the time the ambulance arrived, leaving the whole family lost and in shock. Afterwards, her father went through the motions of running his plumbing business, but losing his wife knocked the stuffing out of him and he lived on autopilot. When he came home after work he would slump in a chair, watching mindless television programmes, without even seeming to take any of them in. At first Anna tried to tempt him to eat by cooking her mother's recipes, but, rather than encouraging him back into the world, the memories of the food her mother made for him caused him to push his plate away. Anna then tried to find new recipes that were nothing to do with their mother, imploring him to eat. As if taking pity on her, and not wanting to cause her any more worry, he forced the food down, and slowly, very slowly, he began to heal and return once more to the head of their family. But without his wife by his side, he was never the same again — very much a shell of the man he'd been before.

In an effort to keep things together, and also to keep busy so that she didn't have to deal with her own grief, Anna took on the running of the house — shopping, cooking, cleaning and doing all the laundry — as well as looking after her brothers. Jack was nine and felt the loss of his mother clearly, whereas Harry was only four and didn't really understand. She tried to comfort them as best as she could, but she was ill-equipped to be a mother. Sometimes she'd get really angry with her mum, not only for leaving them so suddenly, but also because she'd done everything for all of them, and now she was gone it was all down to Anna.

She was so busy in the year after her mum's death that she didn't have time to put any effort into her GSCEs and, although she never expected to get good grades, she barely scraped through the exams. Luckily she managed to pass maths and English, and excelled in her art, having thrown herself into it as a means of escape. But she certainly didn't have the grades she needed for the further education she dreamed of. Instead, she enrolled at a secretarial college to learn something practical that would get her a job at the end of it. On leaving college she managed to get a boring office job in a stationery company, but each day going to work had filled her with dread. She moved from job to job, trying to find something she enjoyed more, but nothing seemed to hit the mark. And then she saw the advert for a receptionist at a West End art gallery and knew she had to go for it.

She splurged some of the housekeeping money on a new suit and was a bag of nerves as she approached the gallery. But Mark soon put her at ease. After being offered the job, over the next few months, he brought her out of herself, making her believe that she did have skills and talents, and that she could be really good at her job if she put her mind to it.

He became a lifeline to her then, and so it was little wonder that she fell in love with him. And to her amazement he seemed to reciprocate her feelings — for the first six months of their relationship she felt happy again. But he never took to her family or they to him, and more and more Anna began to feel as though she was playing piggy in the middle between them all. He resented it when she put her family first, and they thought he was too smarmy and not to be trusted. Despite Mark's protestations about how much time she gave to her family, and that he should have her whole attention, Anna refused to give in. Their arguments were followed by painful periods of Mark completely ignoring her, as though in punishment for caring about people other than him. And then one day, when Anna walked into the office, she found him in the arms of Jemima, their boss' daughter. And her world once again imploded.

'So what I try to do when I'm editing is to first look at the focus of the picture, and what I want to direct the viewer's eye to.'

Anna was brought out of her reverie at the sound of Daniel's words. She quickly pushed all thoughts of Mark from her mind. He was in the past. This was her present and she was going to do her best to make it her future too.

CHAPTER SIX

Daniel took a cold bottle of beer through to the living room and sank down into the plush white sofa. Today had been hard work. Spending all day showing Anna the ropes had forced him to concentrate on the things he did that he usually took for granted but, apart from one point where it looked as though she'd drifted off, he felt she was keen to learn. She certainly seemed to pick things up quickly enough, though only time would tell. On Friday he was doing a photo shoot for *Vogue* in a central London hotel — that would be the real test of whether they could work together. By the time he went back into the kitchen to make himself something to eat, he was feeling optimistic that this might work out after all.

After finishing the omelette he'd made and stacking the dishwasher, Daniel switched on his laptop to find some places to take Ben at the weekend. Beeston Castle was a current favourite — Ben was obsessed with knights and battles — and Daniel was delighted to find a medieval re-enactment was taking place at the weekend. He couldn't keep the smile off his face as he booked the tickets. He knew it could never compete with Disneyland. Ben couldn't stop talking about the rides and the wonderful characters he'd 'met', and while Daniel was pleased Ben had enjoyed himself, he just wished he didn't feel he was in competition with Lucinda and Axel. He also hated that he only got to spend time with Ben every other weekend. Daniel sighed as he shut down his laptop. The saying that you only really appreciated something when you didn't have it anymore definitely rang true. He often wondered if he could have done more to prevent it from happening, but thinking that way was a sure route to madness.

The truth was, Ben's arrival in his and Lucinda's life had changed everything. Daniel had met Lucinda when he'd gone to a weekend party on a country estate with Charlotte. Several other guests were invited, including Lucinda, who was part of that Cheshire set. At the time he was busy building up his photography career and didn't have the time for a long-term relationship, and certainly not one at a distance, but on first meeting Lucinda he fell head over heels in love. The rest was out of his control. She had beautiful long dark hair, which rippled down her back in a glossy sheen. Her oval dark-brown eyes had stared at him intently, making him feel as if he was literally melting. She had exquisite bone structure too. His first instinct was that he wanted to kiss her, followed very closely by the desire to photograph her. And he did plenty of both. She was naturally photogenic and knew just how to pose in front of a camera to get the best results. Later she admitted that she'd always had a desire to become a model and had practised these poses in front of her bedroom mirror from when she was a little girl. She was delighted when his photographs launched her into a modelling career, and readily moved to London. For a while they were the golden couple, his blond good looks contrasting with her darker ones, and both of them successful and becoming rich in their own right. They ate out at the best restaurants, danced in the most expensive clubs and jetted off on luxury holidays whenever their schedules would allow.

Now, Daniel remembered those early days with a pang of regret. They were some of the best years of his life and he'd thought they'd never end, but of course they had.

Two years into their relationship, they'd married, at Peckforton Castle in Cheshire, surrounded by all their friends, family and countless hangers-on, followed by a honeymoon in Antigua. When they'd returned home they'd continued their life and careers as normal. Until one day, Lucinda announced that she wanted to stop modelling and become a mother. Daniel wasn't keen. He didn't want to give up the lifestyle he had for the responsibility of caring for a child, but when he saw how much it meant to Lucinda, he caved in to her wishes. He could never deny her anything and he was actually delighted when a few months later she announced she was pregnant. But that's when everything changed. She suffered horrifically with morning sickness and mood swings, which lasted well into the pregnancy. Although he was sympathetic to what she was going through, and did everything he could to make it better for her, he didn't really know what to do, and everything he tried always seemed to be wrong. He kept telling himself this was just a stage and things would change when Lucinda had the baby, and they did. For the worse. Caring for a newborn was completely out of both their comfort zones. They were exhausted, constantly snapping at each other, and Lucinda's mood swings, if anything, were worse than before. Then she stopped caring for both herself and Ben.

Bewildered and inexperienced, Daniel tried to look after both of them. It was Charlotte who suggested Lucinda go to see a doctor, where she received a diagnosis and medication for postnatal depression. Gradually Lucinda started to improve and Daniel returned some of his attention back to his business, which suffered during her illness. He had to work hard to build it back up again, to fund the lifestyle they were used to and Lucinda didn't want to live without. Over the next months she finally bonded with Ben. But, as if trying to overcompensate for those early days, she went completely the opposite way. She wouldn't let Ben out of her sight and wouldn't let anyone else in, including Daniel. He retreated to something he understood — photography — and worked as much as he could to overcome the feelings of being shut out.

Thinking back to those times, that was what Daniel regretted most of all. He should have persevered to be part of his wife's and his child's lives. Work had become a habit he'd found difficult to break, and Lucinda had been on her own most of the time with Ben. Daniel had been in such a state of denial that he'd been genuinely shocked when Lucinda announced she was leaving him. She'd hated being alone in London and had wanted to go back to Cheshire where she would be surrounded by family and friends. He'd understood why she would want to do that, but had known he couldn't move with her. His career was here. He'd nearly lost it once and he wasn't prepared to lose it again. And so he'd let her go. She hadn't seemed bothered by that. In fact, she'd seemed relieved to be out of their marriage, and that had made him feel doubly rejected. But he'd never anticipated how much living so far away from Ben would affect him. His life was here, but his son was in Cheshire, and he couldn't figure out how he could possibly combine the two.

CHAPTER SEVEN

Anna watched in fascination as Daniel photographed the models. He seemed to know instinctively which poses would suit their faces and their bodies, and he charmed them with gentle words to get the right reactions, ones that Anna knew would look good in the glossy magazine they'd end up in. She concentrated hard on making sure she had all the right equipment to hand — she'd memorised where everything was so that she could find things quickly. On the whole the day was running smoothly, but that didn't stop him barking instructions at her when she didn't get it quite right. She envied the models for the way he spoke to them, with a soft caress in his voice, and wished he would speak to her like that.

They worked hard all morning, barely even stopping for a coffee. Her body ached from moving equipment and backdrops, and she realised how little physical activity she'd done in her old job. But she was enjoying the experience, and just by watching Daniel — the kind of lighting he used, which camera angles and lenses worked best — she felt as though she'd already learned so much, things that would benefit her own work. With the exception of the photographer in question, this was the perfect job for her.

By the time they finished the shoot at three o'clock, she was exhausted but elated, and a rather gruff, 'You did well for a first big shoot,' from Daniel had her spirits soaring.

'Let's get packed up and this lot back home as soon as possible,' he said. 'I'm going up to Cheshire this evening, so I'd like to get on the road as soon as possible.'

'Of course.' She immediately started to pack up the equipment. 'Doing anything nice up there?'

He stopped what he was doing for a minute and stared at her, frowning. She wondered if she'd overstepped the mark. Throughout the week, he hadn't said anything about his personal life.

'I have a house there,' he said. 'My son lives in Cheshire with his mother and it's my weekend with him.'

'Oh, I see.' She was stunned. She hadn't realised he was a father. She didn't really know anything about him, other than he was often photographed coming out of a restaurant or a nightclub with some beauty on his arm. 'That will be nice for you.'

'Yes,' he said. 'It's just a pity I only get to see him every other weekend.'

'I can see that must be difficult,' Anna said softly.

'It is.' He turned away and continued putting the equipment back in the right containers. They worked in silence until everything was in the Range Rover and they were on the road towards Kensington. After encroaching on his personal life, Anna was hesitant to start up another conversation, so sat in rather uncomfortable silence beside him. She decided that, over the weekend, she'd have a look to see what was on the internet about his personal life. It might help prevent her from putting her foot in it in future. It was a relief when they arrived and she could start unpacking everything, glad of something to do.

When they were finished he said, 'I tend to go to Cheshire every other weekend. I don't normally plan shoots for a Friday if I'm going away but this one was delayed. It's likely that every other Friday will be a short day, but there will be other days when you will need to work longer. Is that okay with you?'

'Yes, that's fine,' she said. 'Whatever suits you.'

'Well, I'll let you go, then. Have a good weekend.'

'And you,' she said quietly before leaving.

Anna walked towards the Tube station, wondering what to do with her unexpected time off. If she went home, she would only get bogged down in the numerous jobs that needed to be done around the house. It was a sunny afternoon, too good to be wasted on chores, so she wandered around Kensington instead, taking snaps of whatever took her fancy, before settling at a table outside a café, contemplating the weekend ahead. She was actually looking forward to next week, wondering what she would learn from Daniel. On Monday they would be editing the photos they'd taken today and she couldn't wait to see the results. Suddenly life seemed to be getting a whole lot better.

CHAPTER EIGHT

The next week was incredibly busy, either working with groups of models for magazines or with individuals at Daniel's studio. Anna was completely in awe of some of the beautiful women she'd met, knowing that she could never look that good, even with loads of styling and make-up. Instead, she kept herself in the background, making sure she did as good a job for Daniel as she possibly could. He was a hard taskmaster and she was often the brunt of his terse commands, but she hoped in time, as she got better at her job, that he would soften towards her. Because she was learning so much working with him and was loving every minute of it.

'You're home late.' Her father frowned at her as she arrived home on Wednesday evening. It was nearly seven o'clock and they'd been working on a difficult shoot. One of the models hadn't turned up and another had been in a mood because she'd had an argument with her boyfriend. All the photos taken of her had turned out to be sulky rather than sultry and had had to be redone. Of course, that had meant Daniel had spent the whole day snapping at Anna, and the grumpier he'd become, the more nervous she'd felt, making mistakes that had worsened his mood. When they returned from the shoot, he'd insisted on them looking at what he had taken together, and he hadn't been happy with the results. The last thing she needed now was a lecture by her father.

She had to admit the hours she worked for Daniel were rather erratic. What time they finished often depended on how well a shoot was going and how much editing the photographs needed. Daniel was certainly in demand, which often made for long days, something her family weren't pleased about.

'I should have a word with that boss of yours,' her dad said. 'He's working you far too hard.' It was a constant gripe of his when she wasn't around to do what he felt was her role in their lives, a role that she was increasingly beginning to resent. When she wasn't working she wanted to be out following her own photographic instincts, not looking after her dad and brothers.

'It's the nature of the job, Dad,' she replied tiredly. 'I'm learning so much and I'm finally doing a job I'm interested in.'

'Yes, but we need you here. I never know what time you'll be getting home these days.'

Finally, Anna had had enough. 'What? Does it put you out because I don't have tea on the table waiting for you when you get back from the pub?' Both her father and Jack often went to the pub for a couple of pints after they finished work, and when they came home they were hungry for their tea. 'It wouldn't hurt you to get your own meal for a change.'

'How can we when we don't know what you've got planned?'

'Well, from now on you can assume that I haven't got anything planned and you can do your own.'

'Don't be like that, Anna — you know we rely on you.'

She relaxed slightly at his softer tone, but wasn't fooled by it. This was the tactic he used when she snapped, to sweet-talk her round. But not this time.

'Well, then, maybe we should sit down at the weekend and plan the meals together. And each night take it in turns to cook.'

'What would we want to do that for?' He sounded genuinely puzzled.

'Because I'm sick of being the only one who does anything around the house, so maybe we should have a rota for the cleaning too.'

'And when would we have time for that? You know how hard me and Jack work, often seven days a week. Why should we have to come home and start doing the housework?'

'Don't you think I work hard too?' She was incensed by his words.

'Taking pictures is hard work now, is it?'

'What would you know, Dad? You've never taken any interest in my career.' Suddenly the frustrations that had built up over the years came tumbling out, and, although she knew her words would hurt him, she couldn't stop herself. 'You know I wanted to go to art college, that I wanted to be creative. But I never got a chance, did I? And you don't care about that because you think all I'm good enough for is to be a skivvy for you lot.'

She could see the way his jaw was clenched, tightened in anger, and as she ran out of words she realised she'd said more than she should have. She also saw that Jack and Harry had come into the room at the sound of an altercation. Harry looked stricken at her words — Jack just plain angry.

'You didn't get to go to college because you didn't get the grades. That's not my fault,' Andrew replied.

'No, and neither was it mine.'

'So what are you saying, girl?' His tone was low, as though he was fighting to keep control. 'Are you blaming your mother for dying?'

His words knocked the stuffing out of her — she deflated like a balloon. Feeling tears prickle in her eyes, she blinked them back. She wouldn't let him see her cry.

'No, of course not,' she whispered.

'Because that's what it sounds like to me.'

'I didn't mean it like that, Dad. Mum died thirteen years ago and we've all had to deal with that. What I meant was, Mum dying changed everything for me.'

He almost snarled. 'And it didn't for the rest of us?'

'No, but now I'm finally doing something I've always wanted to do and I want to concentrate on it. All I'm asking for is a little bit of help in running the house.'

'I'll help, Anna, you know I will,' Harry said. Anna looked on him fondly. She knew he felt guilty — he was being given a chance she'd never had, but she wanted him to make the most of that opportunity.

'I think everyone should,' she said, glaring at Jack.

'You've changed since you got that job,' Jack said. 'Think you're so high and mighty now you're mixing with celebrities. Too good for us, are you?'

'No, but I'm fed up of being your skivvy and I was fed up long before I got this job. What's wrong with you all helping out around the house? Just because Mum did everything for you doesn't mean I should have to. Cooking and cleaning aren't just women's work, you know. You're such a chauvinist.'

'Anna, that's enough.' Her dad took Jack's side, as she'd known he would.

Jack laughed, completely unperturbed by her words. 'Bet you're doing the boss like you did in your last job. And look how well that ended.'

'And that's enough from you, Jack.' Andrew finally rounded on his eldest son. 'All this arguing is getting us nowhere. And I for one am hungry.' He stared at Anna meaningfully. 'So, what's for tea?'

Anna stared at him dumbfounded. All she'd said hadn't meant a thing. Nothing was ever going to change. He just didn't care.

'I don't know. I'm sure you'll find plenty in the freezer. I've lost my appetite.'

She barged past Jack and ran up the stairs to her bedroom. Only when she was safely inside, with the door firmly shut, did she allow the tears to spill over. And, when they did, they came in torrents, soaking the pillow that muffled her anguish.

CHAPTER NINE

'Damn, damn, damn.' Anna sat up in bed and realised she was late. *Of all the days!* She and Daniel were doing a shoot in Leicester Square, a promotion of the iconic bronze film-star statues outside the cinema. Only yesterday Daniel had impressed on her the importance of getting there early, before too many members of the public were around, getting in the way of the shots. They'd arranged to meet at seven o'clock, but it was nearly that time now. She hurled herself across the landing and into the shower, avoiding getting her hair wet so she didn't have to dry it. Instead she scraped it back into a ponytail and threw on yesterday's clothes, the nearest ones she could find.

At the station luck was with her and she managed to run onto a train just before it left the station. Predictably there were no seats left, so she stood at the end of the aisle, hanging on to a metal pole as the train rumbled towards central London. As she caught her breath she reached in her bag for her phone. There were two missed calls from Daniel and a voicemail. Her blood ran cold as she listened to it — he was instructing her to meet him at the location rather than his house, because if he didn't leave now there would be no shoot at all. She'd be lucky if she still had a job by the end of today.

* * *

Daniel lugged the equipment into his car, cursing Anna as he did so. In times gone by this would have been perfectly natural to him, but recently he had got used to her being by his side. It was unfamiliar not to have her here today. He'd been predisposed not to like her when he'd first taken her on, but he had to admit that, over the last few weeks, she'd proved him wrong. She was hard-working and perceptive. She had a feel for photography, which had surprised him, and which helped a great deal — she seemed to instinctively know what he needed. Until today she had always been punctual. Sod's law that when he really needed her to be in on time, she was late. She couldn't have picked a worse moment. And to top it all, it was a damp grey day, which would make getting the good shots even harder, especially if the models were grumpy. He'd just have to hope the weather brightened by the time he got there, and that there weren't too many people around. And he'd have to hope that Anna got there soon, because he would need her to help set up as quickly as possible. He cursed her again. Why did she have to choose today of all days to be late?

When he arrived and parked up, he was glad to see the weather meant Leicester Square was relatively quiet, but there was still no sign of Anna. Some of the models had arrived, shivering despite the thick coats they were wearing. He'd start with some of the easy shots first, with the models cosying up to the statues of Paddington Bear and Mr Bean that were posed sitting on benches. Suddenly Anna arrived, breathing heavily as she'd obviously been running. She was wearing yesterday's clothes, had her hair scraped back into a haphazard ponytail and was wearing no make-up. No guesses what she'd been up to.

'I'm so sorry, Daniel,' she said between gasps. 'I overslept and—'

He held up his hand. 'I don't want to hear it. You've obviously had a boozy night out and certainly not got home, judging by the look of you, but I can't have your social life interfering with work. Work has to come first and if you're not going to be committed to that, I suggest you find yourself another job.'

'No, I am committed. It's just that my alarm didn't—'

'I told you I don't want to hear your excuses. There isn't time. The light isn't great and the locals are starting to get curious. We need to get this shoot in the bag as soon as possible. The images have to be delivered first thing Monday morning and we're going to have a hell of a job editing them if the weather doesn't improve.'

'Of course.' She lowered her head. 'What do you need?'

'I'm going to do some shots on the benches, but I need you to set up some steps next to Mary Poppins and then Gene Kelly, so that the models can be at the same height. Can you manage that?'

'Of course, I'll do it straight away. Is there anything you need for your shots first?'

'No. I'll sort that out for myself.'

He felt a pang of guilt as she nodded and slunk away, but he couldn't have her social life interrupting his work. Her social life. Envy pierced him as he thought about what she might have been doing last night and who she might have been doing it with. She was young and attractive, if in a girl-next-door kind of way, and she could be with whomever she wanted to.

He watched as she carried the mounted steps across the square towards the Mary Poppins statue. She was probably cursing him like mad, he thought now, judging by the way her forehead was creased in a frown and how her jaw was held tightly, as though to stop herself from saying what she really thought of him. He didn't blame her really. Okay, so maybe he had a right to tell her off today, but most of the time he was exceptionally short with her for a completely different reason. As much as he didn't want to admit it, as unprofessional as it was, the honest truth was that his feelings for her were growing by the day. Being grumpy with her was one way he could stop himself from telling her how he really felt.

* * *

An hour later and it had begun to rain, putting an end to the hope of getting any more decent shots.

'Come on, we might as well call it a day. Go back to the studio and see if we've got anything salvageable.'

Anna felt a pang of guilt at his words. If she hadn't over-slept, they might have been able to get some better shots earlier. She hated to think what would happen if they had to reshoot. Would he want to take the cost out of her wages? She hoped not, she certainly couldn't afford it.

They packed up in silence. It wasn't until he was driving back to the studio that she attempted to apologise again.

'Daniel, I really am sorry about this morning.'

'I don't need to know,' he said. Then he added more softly, 'Look, it's not as important if we're in the studio, but if we're out on a shoot or up against a deadline then I need to know I can rely on you.'

'You can. This was just a blip. Last night I—'

She was about to explain her family situation but he inter-rupted her.

'Let's just move on, shall we?'

'Sure,' she replied and lapsed into silence. But she couldn't say she was happy. He'd automatically assumed she'd been late because she'd been out drinking — her red puffy eyes had probably made him think that. Would he even believe her if she told him it was because she'd spent most of last night crying? Even though she felt they treated her badly, after what they'd all been through her family was important to her. She just wished they could show her a little bit of respect in return.

She supposed it was natural for Daniel to automatically assume she'd had a heavy night out. It's what most people her age did, not running a household and looking after grown men who couldn't seem to do anything for themselves. If she told him a bit more about her family life, it might help them get on better and stop him making assumptions about her. But now was certainly not the right time, as he'd made it quite clear he wasn't interested in any of her explanations.

* * *

'It's no good.' Daniel sighed after spending an hour poring over the photos he'd uploaded from the camera. 'None of these are suitable. We're going to have to reshoot.'

His words filled Anna with dread. Was he going to blame her for this?

'Let me have a look,' she said, desperate to try to salvage the situation.

'What, think you know better than me?'

He gave her a sideways glance. She was amazed to see there was almost a twitch of a smile on his lips. *Where had that come from?*

'No, of course not, just a different perspective, that's all.'

'Fine, fill your boots. I'm going to make a coffee. You want one?'

'Please.' She nodded and settled down into his chair, scrolling through images. She was filled with despondency when she realised he was right. The light was poor on all of them. She selected three that might be salvageable and tried to filter the light to make them more presentable.

'How about these three?' she asked when he returned with the coffees.

He paused for a moment, considering, as she flicked through them.

'Um, they're okay, I suppose. But I don't think they'd withstand being blown up into large posters. Are they the only ones you found?'

'Just about.'

'Then we are going to have to reshoot. The promoter needs more than three and they've got to be much better than this. I'll give them a ring and explain about the weather. In the meantime, do the best you can with those — we'll send them through and see what they say. Let's hope we can reschedule for tomorrow and get some better weather. Can you look up the forecast for me?'

Anna picked up her phone and was happy to see that the forecast for tomorrow was much better than today.

Daniel nodded. 'Good, if they give us the go ahead, we'll need to get on to the agency and book some more models for first thing tomorrow. Let's just hope everyone can accommodate us.'

Anna nodded silently, not daring to ask the question of who was going to pay for the reshoot, although at least he seemed to be blaming the weather more than her late arrival.

When Daniel came off the phone, he seemed relieved that a reshoot due to the weather conditions had been accepted and Anna quickly set about rebooking the models for tomorrow morning.

'So that's that, then,' Daniel said once it was all in place. 'Seven a.m. at the same place tomorrow and don't be late!'

'I won't, I promise.' Anna felt contrite. She would set her old alarm clock as well as her phone to make sure that she woke up in time. The last thing she wanted after today was to be late again.

'Of course, having to shoot tomorrow is going to make the deadline really tight.'

Anna thought she could make amends. 'I'm happy to work the weekend to meet the Monday morning deadline.'

'I'm afraid you're going to have to,' Daniel said. 'But I need to leave here at lunchtime tomorrow. Ben's in an athletics competition after school and I promised I'd be there to watch him.'

'That's okay, I can edit the photographs here and send them to you.'

Daniel shook his head. 'No, I need to do them myself, but I don't want to eat into my time with Ben. It would be better if you came with me to Cheshire. You can do the preliminary editing and we can work on the final images together when Ben's asleep.'

'You want me to come to Cheshire?' she asked, astounded at his comment. 'But I—'

'Sorry. I'm sure that's going to upset your social life, but we've already cocked up on this once and I need to make sure what we send over on Monday is as good as it can be. I'm not comfortable working at a distance on this one.'

'Yes, of course. I wasn't thinking about my social life, it's just . . .'

'Just what?'

'Nothing,' she said. 'Of course I'll come to Cheshire. I'll make these the best pictures they can be.'

She did feel partly responsible that they had to reshoot, so she really had no choice but to go along with what he wanted. Though, after last night, she wondered what her family would think of her going away with her boss for the weekend. Her dad would hit the roof and Jack would be full of snide comments. Well, she'd just have to deal with that when she got home.

'Thank you, Anna. I do appreciate it.'

'That's okay. But, as it is short notice, do you think I could have some time off today to get myself sorted?'

'Of course,' Daniel said. 'You can take the rest of the day off. I'm sure you'll want to make it up to your boyfriend, not being around for the weekend.'

Anna didn't bother to tell him that it wasn't her boyfriend who would need consoling, but her dad and brothers.

CHAPTER TEN

On her way home, Anna called into Tesco to buy food for the weekend. She knew her dad wouldn't be happy about her going away, but she needed to do this and he would just have to put up with it. She thought that if she stocked up the fridge, cooked some meals for the freezer and did all the washing before she went, then maybe they wouldn't be too put out. And if they were, it might show them how much she did for them, and that she wasn't going to put up with doing it all on her own any longer.

By the time her father and Jack returned home, the house was clean, the washing had all been dried and ironed, and she was just about to dish up a beef casserole with mashed potatoes. Harry had said he was going to the library to study, so she plated some food up for him for when he got home.

The response from Jack was surly, but her dad came over and gave her a hug. 'Thanks, love, I hate it when we argue and it's good to know you want to make amends for last night.'

Anna was so stunned she couldn't speak. And now was not the time to tell him the real reason she'd cooked dinner. That would be better said once he'd eaten.

After he'd had his fill, her father leaned back in his chair and patted his stomach. 'That was lovely, Anna, thank you.'

'Glad you enjoyed it.'

Andrew looked to Jack. 'Jack, say thank you to your sister for dinner.'

'Thanks,' Jack said gruffly. Anna and Jack had always squabbled, but recently he'd changed, becoming more chauvinistic, and he wasn't a person she liked anymore. She tried to do as little as possible for him, purely because he expected her to do it and never offered any thanks for her efforts.

'That's better.' Her father ignored how ungraciously Jack had said the words. 'We're family and we need to stick together. No point in us falling out with each other.'

'I'm glad you said that, Dad, because you might not like what I've got to tell you.'

'What's that then?'

She took a deep breath and then splurged straight into it. 'I've got to work this weekend.'

'I don't believe this! That man's taking advantage of you.'

'He's not. But the fact is, we've got an urgent job on and the deadline is Monday morning. There's not much he can do about it. And I'm sure he'll give me time off in the week.'

'He'd better.'

'There's something else, though. He's got to be in Cheshire this weekend, so I'll need to go with him.'

'What!' Andrew exclaimed.

But Jack laughed. 'I knew it! I knew you were doing the boss. I have to hand it to you, Anna, you're a quick worker.'

'Jack! Take that back!' her father said. 'That's a terrible thing to say.'

Jack smirked but didn't apologise.

'Mind you, I can't say I'm happy about you going to Cheshire with him.' Her father ignored Jack's silence.

'Dad, I'm a grown-up and I can handle myself. Besides, it's all completely above board.' While Anna was furious with Jack for his snide comment, now was not the time to confront him. It would only exacerbate an already volatile situation. 'I've stocked up the freezer so you won't go hungry. All you'll need to do is take something out in the morning to defrost, then heat it through in the microwave.'

'You want us to eat microwaved crap!' Jack said.

Anna gritted her teeth. 'No, it's home-cooked food that has been frozen — nothing to turn your nose up at. And if you don't like it you can always get a takeaway.' She turned to her father. 'I've done the shopping so there's plenty of food in the fridge too, and all your washing is in clean piles outside your rooms. I doubt you'll even notice I'm away.'

'I'm sure we will,' he said. 'And thanks for doing that, love. I do appreciate what you do, even though I don't always tell you. We all should.'

'Thanks, Dad. But I meant what I said last night. The best way you could show your appreciation is by you all helping out a bit more.'

Jack scoffed, but her father said, 'Yes, maybe you're right. You deserve to have a life too.'

Anna was elated. Maybe her point of view had been understood after all. 'Well, I've got an early start in the morning and need to pack, so I'll go to my room now.'

Her father got up and gave her a hug and a peck on the cheek. 'You take care now. And don't let that man take advantage of you.'

'I won't.'

'And if there's anything you don't like, you get on a train straight away and come home.'

'I will, Dad,' Anna said, although she didn't for one minute think she'd need to.

* * *

Thankfully the shoot went much better the next day and, as Daniel headed towards the motorway in his white Range Rover, Anna had a quick look at the camera roll.

'Oh, these are much better,' she said. 'There's a number we could use just by a quick look at them.'

'That's a relief,' Daniel said. 'We can make a start on them tonight if that's okay with you? Ben will be exhausted after his competition and he's a good sleeper, so he'll be out like a light.'

'Right, okay then.' She wondered where she'd be staying.

'You don't sound too sure. I can always make a start myself and you can carry on tomorrow morning while I look after Ben. He's got a party in Chester in the afternoon so I won't be around then, but if we can break the back of it by tomorrow afternoon, we can both have a bit of time off.'

'No, I don't mind working tonight,' Anna said hesitantly. 'I was just wondering where I'd be staying. Do I need to book a hotel?'

Daniel roared with laughter. 'Don't be daft. I've got a five-bedroomed house and you can take your pick of the spare bedrooms.'

'Oh!' she said in surprise. He'd told her before he had a house in Cheshire but she didn't think it would be that big, especially when he only visited every other weekend.

'When Lucinda moved back here with Ben, I ended up staying in hotels. It didn't feel as though I could spend proper time with him like that, so I bought a house and made it a home from home. He's got all his own stuff there so it makes it a little easier.'

'That's very thoughtful of you,' Anna said. She wondered how much of a different side she would see to Daniel this weekend. From the way he talked about Ben, there was no doubt he loved his son very much.

'Well, my split from his mother wasn't amicable at first, but we realised how much our animosity was affecting Ben and had to sort ourselves out. It's not always easy. Lucinda has a tendency to move the goalposts, especially when she wants to fit in with her new boyfriend, but I do my best to not let it affect Ben. He's my priority.'

'I can see that,' Anna said. She hadn't expected this softer side to her boss, but found that she liked it.

'And what about you?' Daniel asked when Anna had been silent for a moment. 'I hope going away this weekend at such short notice didn't mess up any plans with your boyfriend.'

'I don't have a boyfriend,' she said quietly.

'Really?' He sounded surprised. 'But I thought, the other night . . .'

'No, you assumed. The reason I was late wasn't to do with my social life.'

'Oh, I see, I'm sorry. I shouldn't have jumped to conclusions.'

'That's okay, I can see why you might think that.'

She didn't elaborate and they fell into an uncomfortable silence. She felt that if she told him the truth, it would ease their working relationship, but she was worried he might think less of her if she did. Her family's opinions were certainly old-fashioned — maybe he wouldn't understand them. She'd rather make sure her job was secure before she opened up to him.

* * *

Daniel glanced across at Anna. She was staring straight ahead and had a closed expression on her face. He realised he knew absolutely nothing about the woman who was sitting next to him, who he'd be sharing his home with for the weekend. Normally he liked to keep business relationships and friendships completely separate, but there was something about Anna that made him want to cross that line. He could see already that she made a brilliant assistant. That she loved photography was an added bonus. But he was beginning to think that she'd make a very good friend, if he let her in. And if she let him in too, of course. It looked like the latter was going to be the hard part. He decided to ask her about something he suspected she'd be a lot more willing to talk about.

'So, when did you become interested in photography?'

'My art teacher at school. She was a keen photographer and shared her interest with me. Art was the only subject I was ever any good at, the only thing that kept me interested in school if I'm honest, and she could see I was willing to learn as much as I could.'

Her voice had softened and he knew he'd chosen the right subject to engage her.

'I'm surprised you didn't want to go on to art college.'

'I couldn't.' The closed tone was back and he could see her jaw tighten as she spoke. He returned his eyes to the road, wondering what he'd said to make her so obviously annoyed.

'If you remember,' she continued, 'I told you at my interview that my mother died when I was fifteen.'

'Oh, yes, of course.' He kicked himself. How could he have forgotten something as important as that? Because, at the time, he reminded himself, he hadn't been interested in listening to her, as he didn't think she was right for the job.

'You didn't really like me at the interview, did you?' she asked.

He sighed. He could hardly deny it. 'It was the end of a very long day, where I'd been interviewing people who were definitely not right for the job. And . . .' He paused, remembering his disappointment about not seeing Ben. 'I was supposed to be coming up here that day, but my ex-wife had just phoned to tell me that she was taking Ben away for the weekend. I wasn't in the best of moods.'

'Yes, I can see that,' she said. 'So what made you decide I was the right person for the job after all?'

'I didn't really. But Charlotte did. She wouldn't let it drop until I offered you the job.'

'I see.'

He realised he'd said the wrong thing again and cursed himself for being so honest. 'But she was right. She saw something in you that I was too blinkered to see and I'm pleased she did. You've only been working with me for a few weeks, but you've picked things up really well.'

'So I'm doing all right on my probation, am I?' There was a hint of laughter in her voice.

'You wouldn't be here right now if you weren't.'

'Good, I'm glad about that, because I'm enjoying working for you.' She paused. 'When you're not bawling me out that is.'

He looked across, worried, but when he saw that she was smiling, he felt a pang of relief. 'Charlotte says I'm too hard, but I'm a perfectionist and I suppose I expect that in the people I work with.'

'Well, you certainly keep me on my toes.'

They lapsed into silence until she spoke again. 'So how old is Ben?'

'He's nine,' Daniel said proudly.

'And this competition he's in. Athletics, you say?'

'Yes, there's only three of them from his school who've been picked for the county championships. He loves his sport.'

For the rest of the journey they chatted amicably, mainly about Ben, and before he knew it Daniel was turning off the motorway and heading for home.

* * *

Anna had thought the journey would be tiresome, having to sit so long next to someone who was a virtual stranger, but it had passed more quickly than she'd expected. She found she enjoyed talking to Daniel. When he wasn't working he was much more relaxed. He was certainly besotted with Ben, who sounded like a lovely boy, but Anna wondered if Daniel was seeing him through the lens of a devoted father. And one who was trying to make up for the fact that he was no longer a full-time dad. She only hoped Ben turned out to be as nice as Daniel said he was. She wondered what he would think of her coming to stay. Even though this was purely a working relationship, would he resent her for being there on a weekend, when it should be just him and his dad? But if he did, there was nothing she could do about it. She was here to work because Daniel had asked her, so Daniel would have to deal with any repercussions.

Daniel turned the car into the picturesque village just outside of Chester and she almost gasped in wonder as they headed down the tiny main street. It was completely chocolate-box, with a smattering of brick cottages, a few shops, a church and even a village green.

'Oh, this place is beautiful,' she said as Daniel slowed to let another car pass.

'I grew up in a similar village in Sussex,' he said. 'Back then I thought it incredibly dull and boring, and I couldn't wait to escape to the city, but now I can see the appeal of villages like these.'

'I've always lived in London,' Anna said. 'I didn't know places like this actually existed. I thought they were just made up on a film set.'

She wondered if she would get any time to take some photographs — she could picture the shots in her mind. Photos of a countryside village would contrast perfectly to the ones she'd taken of the urban landscape.

They continued on through the village and out the other side, travelling along a winding country lane, until eventually Daniel indicated and turned into a small driveway that was blocked by a set of wrought-iron gates. He reached for a remote in the centre console, pressed it and slowly the gates began to swing open. Further down the driveway, which was flanked by lawns, was a huge white house. Anna could hardly believe this was Daniel's second home. Most people, herself included, would give their eye teeth to have this as their first home.

Daniel stopped the car in front of the house and looked at his watch.

'We're a bit pushed for time. I need to pick Ben up and go straight to the athletics track. We'll drop our stuff off and I can quickly show you round if you want to stay here. Or . . .' He paused. 'You could always come with us.'

'Erm, I . . .' She didn't much fancy being in a strange house on her own, waiting for them to come back. 'Would Ben mind if I tagged along?'

'God, no.' Daniel laughed. 'One more person to cheer him on. He'll love it.'

'Then I'd love to come,' she said.

Anna stayed in the car while Daniel grabbed their bags from the boot and put them in the hallway, then got back in the car.

'Let's go then,' he said, and she could tell that he was dying to be with his son. She decided that, over the weekend, she would stay out of the way as much as possible so that she didn't encroach on their time together.

She had a smattering of nerves as she waited in the car for Daniel to collect Ben from school, but she needn't have worried. Ben jumped into the back of the car, thrust his hands between the front seats, leaned forward and said, 'Hello, Anna. I'm Ben.'

Although surprised, she took his outstretched hand in hers and shook it. 'Hello, Ben, it's nice to meet you.'

Daniel put Ben's belongings in the boot. 'Dad said you work with him?' Ben asked.

'That's right. We've got a bit of work to do this weekend, but I'll try not to let it interfere too much with your weekend with your dad.'

'That's okay.' He smiled. 'I've got loads of homework to do. Dad's rubbish at homework, so maybe you could help me if you've got time?'

She grinned at how easily he had accepted her. 'Well, I don't know if I'll be any better than your dad, but I'm certainly willing to try.'

'What's this?' Daniel got into the car and shut the door. 'Ben, don't tell me you're already trying to pass your homework on to Anna? You know you need to do it yourself.'

'It's worth a try,' Ben said, grinning, and Anna realised she could very easily get to like this little boy.

'Dad, Mum said she'd meet us there, and Axel too when he finishes band practice.'

'That will be nice,' Daniel said, and Anna could tell he was trying to keep the hostility out of his voice. She knew

Lucinda used to be a model and, from her photos, was incredibly glamorous. Anna hadn't even had time to check her make-up since she'd slapped it on early this morning and goodness knows what her hair looked like. What would the lovely Lucinda make of her in all her scruff, she thought — but then banished it to the back of her mind. What did it matter what Lucinda thought of her? Anna was a work colleague and probably wouldn't even meet the woman again. She'd have to push her feelings of inferiority away if she was going to be part of this world, as it looked like she might be.

The car park to the athletics ground was already filling up by the time they reached it and Anna realised this was no run-of-the-mill village competition.

'Wow,' she said before she could stop herself. 'I didn't realise how big this event was.'

'It's an annual thing,' Daniel said. 'There'll be lots of scouts here for the county teams. It's a big deal.'

'I really want to get picked for the county running team,' Ben said. 'But I've only got a chance if I win all my heats. It's a bit scary.'

'Well, you sound to me as though you love running and that's all that matters,' Anna said, feeling guilty that her words might have added to his nerves. 'Go out there and enjoy yourself, and if it's meant to be the rest will follow.'

Ben nodded seriously as he took in her words. 'Thanks, Anna. Yes, I'll do that.'

'And whatever happens,' Daniel added. 'Me and your mum are proud of you. It's a big achievement to make it here in the first place.'

As they got out of the car and walked to where the rest of Ben's schoolmates had congregated, Anna hung back. Ben rushed over to a woman, who was obviously Lucinda, and gave her a big hug. She bent down to hug him back, her long, glossy dark hair falling over him in a curtain. As she stood up, she casually brushed it behind her ear to reveal her face — high cheekbones, enormous eyes and perfect smiling lips.

Anna looked from Lucinda to Daniel as he gave his ex a brief kiss on the cheek. She could see what a glamorous couple they had made. It was a shame it hadn't worked out for them. But at least they were both supportive of Ben.

As Ben's teacher herded the children off, Daniel turned round and motioned for Anna to join them.

'Lucinda, this is Anna — she's my new assistant. We've overrun on a project, so she's going to stay for the weekend to help me meet the deadline.'

Lucinda held out her hand and said coldly, 'Pleased to meet you.' Anna shook her hand but noticed that Lucinda withdrew it as quickly as she could. Lucinda turned to Daniel. 'I hope this doesn't mean you're going to spend all weekend working. If you'd let me know, we could have swapped.'

'You know I don't like doing that. It only upsets Ben and I wouldn't have missed this for the world.'

'All the same, it's no good to him if you spend all weekend huddled up in your darkroom.' Lucinda threw what Anna considered to be a hostile glance in her direction.

'We don't use darkrooms anymore,' Daniel said, obviously annoyed. 'And, besides, that's why Anna's here, so she can do most of the work while I spend time with Ben, then when he's asleep we can finalise the submission.'

'How very cosy.' Lucinda looked at Anna as though she had just crawled out from under a stone.

'Does anyone fancy a coffee? There's a van over there,' Anna asked, wanting to make her escape.

'No, thanks,' Daniel and Lucinda replied in unison.

* * *

Anna hoped that the queue for the drinks would be very long, so that she could delay her return. The less time she had to spend with Lucinda the better. Fortunately, by the time she got back, Axel had arrived and Lucinda was making a show of draping herself around him while Daniel stood at a distance.

'I'm sorry about before,' Daniel said quietly when she approached him. 'Lucinda can be a bit . . . territorial.'

'It's okay,' Anna said, trying to sound upbeat. 'It's understandable, really. I am going to be spending the weekend with her son.'

Anna lapsed into silence as she feigned an interest in the races that had now started to take place. The atmosphere was electric, but it was difficult to get involved as she didn't know any of the participants. Until she spotted Ben's race, and then she cheered as loudly as the rest of the parents, feeling inexplicably proud as he raced first over the finish line. She was so elated she almost turned to hug Daniel, but stopped herself just in time. The grin on his face was enough to show how proud he was of his son.

Ben was in another two races and then had to stay to the end to take part in the finals, where he came second. By the time they left, Ben was literally bouncing with adrenaline and Anna wondered whether they'd get a chance to start work tonight — she didn't think he would ever go to sleep. Thankfully she'd managed to avoid Lucinda for the rest of the afternoon and felt a wave of relief as she buckled up her seatbelt and Daniel drove them home.

'My teacher said the scout for the county team was interested in me joining the club. He's going to speak to Mum later in the week. Is that okay with you, Dad?' There was no doubting the joy and pride in Ben's voice, which was matched in equal measure by Daniel's.

'Of course, you did really well today. Mum and I are very proud of you.'

'Thanks, Dad,' Ben said. 'What's for tea?'

Daniel groaned. 'That's all that boy thinks about. Sport and food.' But he said it jokingly. 'Well, it's getting late, so it will have to be something that's really quick or . . .'

'Or we could get a Chinese?' Ben asked hopefully.

'Chinese it is, then, if that's all right with you, Anna?'

'Of course it is. I'll eat anything.'

'That's good.' He paused. 'Is everything okay? You're frowning.'

'I was just wondering how you organise everything. If you haven't been here for two weeks, won't you need to go and do a food shop?'

'I have a lady who comes in every fortnight to keep the house tidy, and I do an online delivery and arrange for it to arrive when she's at the house. Debbie, bless her, puts it all away for me. I don't know what I'd do without her, but it means I don't have to spend all weekend doing chores when I want to spend time with Ben.'

'That's very organised,' Anna replied, impressed. Yes, he was still relying on a woman to do things for him, but Anna would bet she was well paid and he certainly seemed to appreciate her. The fact that he did the shopping himself, albeit online, was more than any of her family ever did. She was certainly getting a different impression of Daniel Redfern this weekend to the one she'd been expecting.

* * *

They sat around the table in the large open-plan kitchen, which gleamed with white cupboards and black granite surfaces, just like his kitchen in Knightsbridge. As she often did when she was at work, she compared it to their tiny shoe cupboard of a kitchen at home, which badly needed redecorating.

While Daniel was sorting out the food, Ben had shown her to a spare room that overlooked the garden. It was as large as their living room at home and had its own ensuite. Everywhere in this house screamed money, and she only hoped that when she got home she wasn't spoiled by the experience. But if the house was luxurious, the conversation over dinner was very down to earth, with Daniel catching up with what had been going on in his son's life since he'd last spoken to him, and what was going to happen over the next few weeks.

Daniel certainly did his best to make up for lost time when he was with his son, and that really impressed her.

Later that evening, once Ben was asleep — contrary to Anna's earlier predictions, he had been more than ready for his bed — Daniel poured two glasses of wine. 'I know it's getting late and it's been a very long day, but do you think we could make a start on the editing?'

'Of course, that's what I'm here for after all.'

'Good. We don't have to spend too long on it, but if we make a start at least you'll know what you need to do in the morning.'

Anna reached for her laptop. 'Let's get to it, then.'

While Daniel had been dishing up the Chinese, she'd started to upload the pictures they'd taken that morning. Although she'd been tired when they'd first started work, the next few hours sped by as they both concentrated on the thing they loved doing.

CHAPTER ELEVEN

When Anna woke, the sun was streaming through the large bay window. They'd worked late into the night, both losing track of time. By the time she'd finally come to bed, she'd been exhausted, falling instantly into a dreamless sleep. Stretching in the comfortable bed, she couldn't remember a time when she'd slept so well — she had half a mind to turn over and drift back off again. Then she remembered where she was and why, and hurriedly grabbed her phone from the bedside table. *Shit!* It was already nine thirty. In a panic, she threw back the covers and raced into the shower, hoping she wouldn't receive the sharp edge of Daniel's tongue for getting up so late.

When she reached the kitchen it was to the delicious smell of coffee and bacon. It was a surprise to find Daniel standing in front of the hob, turning the rashers over in the pan.

'I'm sorry I'm so late up.' Anna blurted out her apology as she entered the kitchen. Daniel turned and, to her surprise, smiled at her.

'Not to worry, we had a late night last night. You deserve a lie-in.'

'Oh, thank you,' she replied, slightly at a loss. Daniel smiling at her was an unfamiliar sight and she wasn't sure how to react.

'Help yourself to coffee. Will bacon and eggs do you?' he asked.

'That would be lovely, thanks.' It was also an unusual experience to be waited on by a man, but she wasn't going to turn her nose up at the experience.

'Ben's already eaten, up with the lark as usual. I'm going to take him to football shortly and then this afternoon he's got a party in Chester, so you'll have the house to yourself.'

'Oh, okay, that should give me plenty of time to do the editing and then maybe we could finalise everything tonight?'

'That would be good, give us both the day off tomorrow. If we can get them sent over early, we can have a day out? Go to a country park and maybe lunch in a pub somewhere?'

'Sounds good.' Anna smiled. Although she was here to work, this was turning out to be more of a holiday than her usual weekend.

'And if you manage to get everything done this morning, maybe you'd like to come into Chester with us and you can have a look around while Ben is at his party?'

'I'd like that,' she replied. 'Only if I get finished in time.'

Daniel served up breakfast and she realised how hungry she was. If she'd had any time today, she'd been planning on walking into the village and taking some pictures, but Chester sounded like a good place to take pictures anyway. It was a different type of city to add to her portfolio.

As she ate she noticed that Daniel was staring at her and smiling.

'What?' she asked, uncomfortable at his scrutiny.

'Nothing. I was just enjoying watching you eat. Lucinda always picked at her food and it used to really annoy me when I'd gone to the trouble of cooking for her.'

'Do you cook often?'

'All the time. I have to, living on my own. But really, I was the one who used to cook the most when we were married. Lucinda did try, but it was costing a fortune in replacement pans.'

Anna laughed. 'It's not like that in our house. The men barely know how to work the microwave.'

'You live with a lot of men?'

She put her fork down with a clatter, realising that she'd let her guard drop. 'I live at home with my dad and two brothers.'

'Wow, and they don't help out?'

'Not if they can avoid it.' Anna sighed. After the last twenty-four hours, and the fact that Daniel had been so open and honest with her, she felt that maybe she should open up to him after all. 'My mum was a traditional housewife, who did everything for us all. We were her life's work and when she died, everything fell apart. Dad was distraught and the boys were only little, so it was up to me to keep everything together.'

'That must have been really difficult for you.'

She nodded. 'I still miss my mum every day. And I know she would have wanted to keep the family together, but she also wanted me to have my own life. It's just difficult getting the others to understand.' She felt herself close to tears as she explained, but the last thing she wanted was for him to see her cry, so she pulled herself together. With a smile she added, 'But I'm working on it.'

* * *

As he cheered Ben on from the sidelines of the football pitch, Daniel thought about what Anna had told him over breakfast. He'd been stunned by her revelation, and not a little ashamed of himself. He'd just assumed that as a single twenty-something she'd be out on the town every night, living her best life, not holding together a household consisting of three men, who it seemed couldn't even boil an egg. Both his parents had worked, his father in finance and his mother as a barrister, and both he and his brother had been taught to cook and fend for themselves. It must have been such a burden for Anna to take on that kind of responsibility when she was just a teenager herself. And he hadn't exactly been kind to her, he thought with a pang of guilt. His thoughts slipped back to his uncle and how he'd mentored him. Anna hadn't been given opportunities in life, but maybe he could help to redress the balance. Maybe he could even go further than that and extend it to other youngsters keen to learn. Preferably ones who came from disadvantaged backgrounds, who would never normally have such an opportunity. But first things first, he'd start with Anna. She'd made a good job at being his assistant so far, but now he wanted to find out what her own photography skills were like.

When he got back from football, he made them all sandwiches. He settled Ben in front of the television and took the food and fresh coffee into the study where Anna was working. She looked up blearily as he came through the door.

'Oh, Daniel, hi, are you back already? I'd completely lost track of time.'

'That happens to me too when I'm editing. How are you getting on?'

She leaned back in her chair. 'Good, I think. In fact I'm just about finished. Do you want to have a look?'

He put down the tray he was carrying and walked round to her side of the desk. As she flicked through the photos he couldn't help but grin. She'd done a brilliant job, and so much quicker than he'd expected. 'Well done, Anna, I'm impressed, and I'd say with just a few more tweaks we can send them over and have the rest of the weekend off.'

'Really?' she asked. 'Are they okay?'

He was touched by her lack of confidence. 'More than okay. You've done a great job and I'm really pleased you came with me. Time with Ben is precious and I either would have had to work here this weekend or swap my weekend with him, which I hate doing.'

'I've enjoyed it,' Anna said. 'It's nice to see how the other half lives.'

He laughed with her. 'Well, the other half are going into Chester if you'd like to join us?'

'I'd love to. I've never been to Chester before. In fact, I haven't really been much outside London.'

Her mention of London made him realise he'd taken her away from her family for the weekend. As she'd finished the work she'd come here to do, maybe he should give her the opportunity of going home early?

'Unless, of course, you'd like to go home?' he asked hesitantly. He really hoped her answer would be no, but he felt he had to offer. 'I could drop you off at the station if that's what you'd prefer?'

'God, no!' she answered straight away, delighting him. 'I've managed to escape chores for the weekend — I'm not going back until I absolutely have to.'

'Good, I'm glad,' he said. 'Now, this coffee's going cold. Let's eat and, while we do, there's something I want to talk to you about.'

CHAPTER TWELVE

Anna had been glowing with pleasure at his words of praise, but her throat had gone dry when he'd offered her the chance to go home. When she'd said she'd rather stay, he'd seemed pleased. But had he secretly wanted her to go, so that he could spend the rest of the weekend alone with Ben?

'Okay, but just to make things clear I'm happy to go home, if you'd prefer it? I don't want to impose on your time with Ben.'

'Not at all. He's really taken to you. He told me on the way home from football.'

'I like him too. He's a great boy. By the way, how did the football go?'

'We won. Three-one and Ben scored a goal. He was chuffed to bits.'

'I'm glad. He's a great athlete. I was never very good at sports myself. I much preferred the art room.'

'Me too actually — he must get it from Lucinda's side of the family. Anyway, I'm glad you mentioned art, because that's what I wanted to talk to you about.'

'Oh, yes?' Her throat went dry again — she reached out for a sandwich and took a bite, although she didn't think she'd be able to swallow.

'Yes, it's about your photography. What are your subjects?'

She managed to get the food down, surprised at his question. He'd never shown the slightest interest in her photography before, but this weekend was a revelation. They were certainly getting to know each other better.

'Urban landscapes mainly,' she replied. 'I can't do people because of data protection, but I like comparing old and new buildings, especially around the East End where there's such a contrast.'

'Sounds interesting,' he said. 'I think you'll find there's quite a bit of contrast around Chester too. There are some beautiful old buildings and some very ugly modern ones. Would you like to take a camera with you?'

She gasped. 'I'd love to. I usually just use my phone. It's got a decent enough camera on it, but it will be a treat to use a proper one. Only if you don't mind.'

'Not at all.' He smiled. 'And later tonight, perhaps you'd show me what you've taken. I'd be interested to see what kind of photographer you are.'

'Really? You'd do that?'

'I'd love to,' he said. 'I've learned a lot over the years, particularly because I had some good mentors. I'd like to mentor you, if that's okay?'

Anna nearly fell off her chair. She couldn't believe her luck. This was the opportunity she'd been waiting for all her life. 'That would be more than all right,' she eventually managed to say.

* * *

It was a beautiful late May afternoon when Daniel dropped Anna off in the centre of Chester.

'I'll pick you up here at four. Is that okay?'

'Perfect,' she said as she looked around her. Daniel had pulled into a layby next to the cathedral, its stone structure surrounded by magnificent gardens. Instantly she was itching to get Daniel's camera out.

'Now, you won't get lost will you?'

'Of course I won't.' She looked up to see a playful smile on his lips. 'I've always got Google Maps, and a tongue in my head,' she added, returning his smile. 'I usually get there in the end.'

'See you later, then.' He switched the engine back on and she waved to them both as they drove off.

After taking some pictures of the beautiful cathedral and the town hall opposite, Anna walked into the tourist centre and picked up a map. She spent the next two hours happily wandering and photographing, walking along the city walls, which had been erected as part of a fort to protect the city when the Romans first occupied it, around 75 AD. She read that the walls were the most complete Roman city walls in Britain and were almost two miles long. As she walked, she thought the views were amazing, both for her own eyes and for her camera, and she knew she could fall in love with this city. The East End fascinated her with its own history and regeneration, but here she felt something much more peaceful, as though the city was proud of its ancient architecture. Daniel had been right though — standing between the beautiful buildings were modern monstrosities, mainly restaurants glaring in their gaudiness, but she took pictures of them too, because they provided the perfect contrast to the sense of history.

By the time she made her way back to the cathedral, her legs were aching but she was elated at having had such a pleasant afternoon. It was a joy to be away from the constraints of her life at home. It almost felt like a holiday and it made her even more determined to sort things out when she got back.

* * *

'Let's see what you took today, then,' Daniel said when Ben was tucked up in bed and they'd finished editing the photos from the shoot. While he'd been preparing a delicious steak meal for them both earlier, she'd spent a pleasant hour with

Ben helping him build Lego from an enormous box. He was a lovely boy, bright and entertaining, and she enjoyed spending time alone with him. She was amazed at how well he had adapted to her being around and she was looking forward to going out with them both tomorrow. She couldn't believe how much her life had changed in such a short time.

She uploaded the photos from the camera onto the laptop and passed them over to Daniel, biting her lip with nerves as she wondered what he would think of them. She prayed he wouldn't have the same reaction as Mark, and tell her that they were no good. She waited, her nerves increasing by the second as he stared intently at the screen, clicking from one photograph to the next.

Eventually he looked up. 'They are really good.'

'Sorry? What did you say?' Were her ears deceiving her?

'They are really good,' he repeated. 'Look, let me show you.'

She moved up on the sofa so that he could sit beside her and felt her heart quicken at the heat from his leg so close to hers. She mentally shook her head to disperse that thought. He was only sitting so close to her so that he could give her the benefit of his experience. And he was her boss. What he was about to say was far more important than how she felt sitting next to him.

'You see here, how you've captured the light?'

She nodded as he pointed to the screen. It was a picture she'd taken of a bridge spanning the River Dee. The sun had dipped just behind the trees as she had taken it, making the bridge almost ethereal. 'It's perfect. And this one.'

He flicked to the next photo and she listened in earnest as he pointed out what was good and what could be improved with each photo, and how she could have adjusted the camera angle or lighting to create a different effect. He made it all sound so simple and she wished she had a notepad so that she could write down everything he said.

'You make a good teacher,' she said. 'I wish I'd known someone like you when I'd first started out. Most of what I've learned has been self-taught.'

He smiled at that comment. 'It's not just about teaching, though. You have to have instinct too, which you certainly seem to have. The next quiet day we have in the studio, can you bring in some of your other work? I'd like to see what else you've done.'

'Really?'

'I'm not saying this lightly, Anna. I think you have incredible talent. That's not to say that there isn't work to be done here. A lot of work in fact, but if you're willing to put the effort in, I can see you creating photographs worthy of exhibition.'

'Really?' she asked, again unsure if her ears were deceiving her. The fact that Daniel Redfern thought her photographs were, or could be, good enough to exhibit was completely mind-blowing. Then reality kicked in.

'I haven't got the money for an exhibition.'

'All you need is a venue.'

'And an agent.'

'You don't really need an agent. Not if you have the right people on your side,' Daniel said, a thoughtful expression on his face. He fell silent and she was unsure how to respond. Eventually he said, 'There's work to be done on the photos first though.'

'Okay, and you really think they might be good enough?'

'Let's not run before we can walk. As I said, you have instinct and talent, but you still need to back that up with hard work.'

She nodded, still not really taking it all in. 'Well, hard work isn't something I've ever been afraid of.'

He cut her off. 'And as for money, I can stump up the cost of the venue and you can pay me back with your sales, if you want to.'

'You think I'd manage to sell anything?'

He smiled. 'I'd put my career on it.'

* * *

Anna was in a bubble of happiness as Daniel's Range Rover sped its way down the motorway to London. They'd spent a glorious day on a tree-top walk around Delamere Forest. She'd thoroughly enjoyed being immersed in nature, and it was the perfect way to use up Ben's boundless energy, as well as an entirely new experience for Anna. After that, they'd eaten well in a country pub — huge portions of roast dinner with large fluffy Yorkshire puddings. It had been the first time she'd eaten Sunday lunch without having to cook it herself for a long time. She'd sat back in her chair, savouring a cup of coffee, thinking life couldn't get much better, and thanked both Daniel and Ben for their company. She'd thoroughly enjoyed her 'working' weekend.

But the bubble of joy burst the moment she got home. The house itself seemed suddenly cramped compared to Daniel's house, though that wasn't the only thing. There was no one in when she opened the front door, but the smell of stale beer assaulted her nostrils. She went into the living room, which looked like a bomb had hit it. A bomb that contained empty beer cans, crisp packets and empty takeaway cartons, littering practically every surface in the room and over most of the floor. Anna gasped in shock and moved down the hallway towards the kitchen. That was even worse — the sink was piled high with dirty crockery and rubbish covered the worktops. Anna was utterly dismayed. She'd only been gone for two days, and to think she'd spent Thursday afternoon cleaning the house and cooking for them to make life easy while she was away. They didn't deserve her.

Her first instinct was to start clearing up the mess, because she knew she couldn't live like this, but something stopped her. Why should she clear this up? This was their doing, not hers, and if she let them get away with it, like she had for so many years, this would be her lot for evermore. This weekend had shown her all too clearly that life didn't have to be this way. She wished she had the finances to move out and let them fend for themselves, but that was just wishful thinking.

She might not have the money to leave, but she was damned if she was going to put up with this kind of behaviour anymore.

With a determination that surprised herself, she turned away from the mess and walked upstairs. As she got to the top, Harry came out of his bedroom, his face stricken at the sight of her.

'I'm sorry, Anna, I tried to clear up today, but Jack told me not to. And you know what he's like when he's on one.'

Anna certainly did know. When Jack went into one of his rages, it was best to keep out of his way. She nodded in sympathy and Harry continued. 'He said it was your punishment for going away for the weekend.'

'My punishment?' She gaped at him, astounded. 'So, I'm to be punished for trying to have a life, am I?'

'I tried to tell him it wasn't fair on you, but he wasn't having any of it. And Dad just lets him get away with it, because he doesn't want the confrontation.'

'It's okay, I know what they're both like.'

'I've spent most of the weekend in my bedroom, but it was pretty hard to study because of the noise they made, watching the football during the day and inviting their mates round last night. That's why everything is in an even worse state, I had to put my ear plugs in and even then I still couldn't concentrate enough to revise properly.'

Anna felt a pang of sympathy for her youngest brother. He was the only one who ever tried to help, and that selfish lot couldn't even go out to the pub to give him the peace and quiet he needed to study. With a jolt she remembered what tomorrow's date was.

'Oh, Harry, I'm so sorry. You've got your first exam tomorrow as well. Why didn't you just tell them, or at least tell Dad, so that they could've given you some peace and quiet?'

He shrugged. 'You know what Jack's like when he's been drinking. I thought it would cause more trouble than it's worth. Yesterday I went to the library and spent most of the day there. If nothing else, it was a change of scene.'

She really hoped that, despite them, he did well in his exams so that he could get away from this place.

'How are you feeling about tomorrow?'

'Okay. To be honest I'll be glad to start ticking them off the list.'

'I'll bet.'

She'd never had the experience herself, but this was the result of two years' hard work and he must be looking forward to the end of it, so he could move on to the next stage.

'Just think, in a month it will all be over and you'll have the summer to do as you like, with no revision.'

'Sounds like heaven.' He closed his eyes.

'I'll do whatever I can to help you through it,' she said, although how she was going to fit it all in, she didn't know. 'But I think the next few days are going to be difficult. I'm not going to give in to Jack, so we might be in for a bumpy ride.'

'That's okay. I'm with you on this. I don't see why they can't pull their weight.'

'It's a pity there isn't somewhere else you could go and stay for a bit so that you can study in peace.'

Harry smiled. 'Don't worry about me. I'm not going to let them put me off. I'm going to get my grades so that I can move away.'

'That's the spirit. Although, I'll miss you.'

'I'll miss you too. I missed you this weekend. But did you have a good time?'

She grinned back at him. 'Oh, I had a brilliant time.' She told him all about Daniel, Ben, his house and the glorious countryside. And then she told him that Daniel had offered to become her mentor.

'Oh, that's fantastic, Anna. It's just the thing you need to get what you want out of life. You really should go for it and don't let the rest of them get in the way.'

'I won't,' she said. And this time she meant it.

CHAPTER THIRTEEN

'You look different,' Daisy stared at Anna, a puzzled expression on her face. 'I can't put my finger on why, though — you haven't changed anything.'

Anna grinned back at her. They were at the Angel on Monday night and she'd been struggling all day to keep the smile off her face. Working with Daniel today had been the best and she was positively fizzing.

Daisy gasped. 'Oh my God! That's what it is! You're happy.'

'Oh, I am.'

'I can't remember the last time you were happy,' Daisy said. 'That's why you look so different.'

Anna laughed. 'I'll get us some wine, shall I?'

'You'd best get a bottle. I think this is going to take some time.'

When Anna returned from the bar and poured them both generous glasses of wine, Daisy said, 'Right, now, I want to know everything. Have you met someone?'

'No!' Anna shook her head. 'Not like that anyway. Oh, Daise, you won't believe what a difference my new job has made.' They hadn't had a chance to meet up since Anna had started working for Daniel. They'd spoken briefly on the phone a few times, but Anna had been guarded at first — she couldn't figure Daniel out — but now she wanted to tell Daisy everything.

'The job that you didn't want to take, because your new boss was rude and difficult?'

Anna smiled again. 'He likes things a certain way, that's true, but his bark is worse than his bite when you get to know him.'

'And you've got to know him?' The insinuation was clear in Daisy's voice.

Anna scolded her friend. 'As a person, yes. Not in any other way.'

Although, when he'd leaned over her, to look at her photographs this afternoon, she couldn't help remembering that her heart had started to beat more quickly.

As soon as the photographs had been delivered to the promoter, Daniel had turned to his famous diary. 'We haven't got much on for the next few days. How about we look at your work?'

'Are you sure?'

He nodded. 'I told you on Saturday I wanted to see them.'

Hesitantly Anna switched on her laptop, opening up the folder that housed her latest work. She bit the inside of her cheek nervously, still unused to showing her photographs to others. Daniel didn't say anything as he flicked through the images, his face so expressionless that Anna didn't know what to think. Her stomach clenched with anxiety until he reached the last one and turned to her.

'They're exceptional,' he said simply.

'They are?'

'Yes, they are. I love the way you've captured the old and the new architecture. You have a good instinct with light and angles — these images aren't what the average person would see. They make you look at the buildings in a different way. These alone would be enough for an exhibition. You don't need the ones you took in Chester. In fact, I think a different location would muddy the waters.'

'You think they're good enough for an exhibition?' she asked incredulously.

He nodded. 'With a bit of work, yes. The only thing I don't understand is why has no one spotted your talent before?'

She bowed her head, her face flushing with heat. 'Because the only person I've ever showed them to before was my ex, Mark, the manager of The Whigmore. He made me believe they weren't good enough, and so I've never been brave enough to do anything with them.'

'Well, he was wrong. They are good enough, or they will be, and so are you. He's done you a disservice in stopping you from believing in yourself.'

Anna stared at him open-mouthed. She had never once doubted that Mark was telling her the truth about her talent. But judging by the way he had treated her recently, she should have realised he may have acted to serve himself. Now she felt foolish for taking his opinions at face value.

Daniel broke her silence. 'The first thing we need to do is decide which photographs we want to use, then we can get to work on making them the best they can be. Are you up for that?'

'Oh, definitely.' And suddenly the past and Mark didn't matter. It was the future which counted, and she had a feeling that the future looked bright.

She and Daniel had worked all afternoon, selecting the best photographs. He was right — there were more than enough for an exhibition. Daniel suggested how she could edit some of them, and some that she should retake at a different angle, and she couldn't wait to get started. The new photographs would have to wait until the weekend, but she had every intention of getting out first thing on Saturday morning, regardless of what was going on with her family.

'That's amazing, Anna,' Daisy said now. 'It's what you've always dreamed of.'

'I know.' Anna took a large gulp of her wine. 'I can barely believe it's actually going to happen. I keep having to pinch myself.'

'And it's all down to one man,' Daisy said. 'I thought you were going to work for Daniel Redfern, not the other way around.'

'Oh, I'm still working for him. We've got a shoot on Wednesday and I'll be the one lugging all the equipment around. Nothing's going to change in that department. And I don't want it to, either. I'm learning so much just by watching how he works.'

'I see.'

Anna turned to her friend and looked at her sharply. 'What's that supposed to mean? I know that tone of voice.'

'Nothing . . . it's just that you sound as though you're a little bit in love with him.'

Anna almost choked on her wine. 'Don't be ridiculous. I've done that before, remember? And look how badly it ended. I'd never be stupid enough to do it again.'

'Okay, I believe you,' Daisy said guardedly. 'It's just that you sound really enamoured with him.'

'Because I admire him as a professional. You know how long I've wanted to take my photography seriously and this is my chance. I'm blown away that he wants to mentor me and I'm not going to risk that by getting emotionally involved.'

'No, I can see why you wouldn't want to do that,' Daisy said. 'But why is he taking such an interest in you? What's in it for him?'

'He was telling me at the weekend about his uncle who helped him when he was starting out, and he wants to do that for me, to give something back.'

'That's good of him.'

'It's certainly good for me.'

Daisy frowned. 'What do you mean, he told you at the weekend? What were you doing with him then?'

'Oh, we needed to work because a shoot had gone wrong last week and the deadline was first thing this morning. He had to be in Cheshire, where his son lives, so he took me with him so that we could work on the images together.'

It was Daisy's turn to splutter on her drink. 'You went away for the weekend with him?'

'Yes, for work. It was all totally above board. I stayed in the spare bedroom if that's what you're thinking. Well, one of them.' Anna carried on regardless of her friend's expression. 'You should see the house he's got up there, and that's just his weekend home.'

'Anna, please be careful.'

'I will and I am.' Anna put her glass down. 'Oh, Daisy, of all people I thought that you at least would be happy for me.'

'I am.' Daisy reached over and gave her a hug. When she pulled away she added, 'I don't want you to get hurt, that's all, and if you're pinning all your hopes on just one person — well, that's a risk isn't it?'

'I can see where you're coming from,' Anna said. 'But it's the thought of an exhibition that's making me so giddy, nothing else.' Although, as she tried to convince her friend, Anna couldn't help remembering the look of admiration in Daniel's eyes as he assessed her photographs, and the way it had made her feel — as though her whole body was glowing. She shoved the thought away and changed the subject, before it became even more uncomfortable.

'Anyway, I bet you can guess who wasn't happy at me being away for the weekend.'

'That doesn't take Einstein to work out. I'm surprised they even let you go.'

'I didn't give them a choice. Although Jack . . .' She broke off, remembering all she had done for them and the state they'd made of the house while she was away.

'Although Jack what?'

As she told her, Daisy's expression was one of pure horror. 'That brother of yours is a complete misogynist. How dare he say it was your punishment for going away. I hope you didn't clear it up!'

'Nope.' Anna smiled. 'And I have no intention of doing it either. It can stay like that until they do it for themselves, and I mean it this time.'

Daisy smiled back. 'Good for you. And, seeing as how I'm sure you don't want to go home just yet, how do you fancy going for a pizza?'

'I'd love to,' Anna said.

* * *

'You look like the cat that got the cream,' Charlotte said as she and Daniel were seated in the Olive Grove, a Mediterranean restaurant in Chelsea that was a favourite of theirs.

'Do I?' Daniel couldn't help smiling. He'd really enjoyed working with Anna today. When he'd seen the photographs she'd taken in Chester at the weekend, he'd thought she had talent, but he'd been completely blown away when she'd shown him the rest of her work, although he still seethed with anger when he thought about how her ex-boyfriend had convinced her not to have any faith in herself. If he ever bumped into him, he knew what he would like to do to him. If Anna hadn't applied for a job as his assistant she may never have realised just how talented she was. It made him even more convinced that he wanted to mentor people who wouldn't normally have a chance.

'You know you do,' Charlotte said. 'So what's it all about?'

'Well, you could say I've had a bit of an epiphany and I've got you to thank for it,' he said cryptically. 'That's one of the reasons I asked you to dinner tonight.'

'You've got me intrigued now.' She took a sip of champagne.

'You were the one who encouraged me to give Anna the job.'

Charlotte put her glass down onto the table with such a jolt that some of the champagne splashed over the top. 'You haven't!'

Shocked at her response, the smile slipped from his face. 'No! Of course I haven't! She's my employee.'

'Oh, that's a relief.' Charlotte visibly relaxed. 'For a moment there I thought—'

'You've got a filthy mind,' he interrupted her.

'It's all working out, then?'

'And then some.' He smiled again. 'Not only is she a good assistant, and I have to admit I was wrong about her being difficult to work with, she's the complete opposite, but she also has considerable talent as a photographer.'

'Really? You've seen what she does?'

'Oh, yes, it's amazing. She's completely self-taught, but a good photographer needs to have instinct and she's got plenty of that.'

'And why does the fact that she's a good photographer make you so happy?' Charlotte looked puzzled.

'Because . . .' Daniel paused before continuing. 'She's given me my spark back.'

'For your own photography?'

'No, well, yes, maybe, but I was thinking more for other people.'

Charlotte frowned. 'I don't follow.'

'I've been getting bored with the amount of photoshoots I've been doing recently.'

'You've got such a good reputation. Everyone wants your photos to grace their magazines.'

'I know, but seeing what Anna is doing has made me realise how lacking in creativity my work is these days.'

The waiter took their order and left them to continue their conversation. 'Without influence and without contacts, it's not easy to be successful in the art world. I was lucky I had my uncle to mentor me and I've realised that I want to give some of that back.'

'So you're going to mentor Anna?'

'To start with, yes. But I'm thinking about setting up a photography school for underprivileged kids.' He paused, but before she could answer he continued. 'In Manchester.'

She gasped. 'You're moving!'

'No, at least not at the moment. I still need to be in London, because I'll need my commissions here, but I want to spend more time in Cheshire . . . I miss Ben. He's growing so fast and I don't want to miss out.'

She reached out and put her hand over his. 'I know you don't.'

'So this way I get the best of both worlds.'

'It will mean more travelling.'

'I don't mind that.'

'And what about Anna? Will you expect her to travel with you?'

'Sometimes, maybe. But everyone's working so much more remotely since Covid, I don't see why she can't keep things ticking over here while I'm away.'

Charlotte gasped for the second time. 'I don't believe it. Daniel Redfern, control freak extraordinaire, is actually loosening the reins.'

He grinned at her. 'Complete personality transplant.'

'You're telling me.'

The waiter came with their food. As they started to eat, Daniel said, 'Besides which, with my help, I think Anna will be busy in her own right.'

'In what way?'

'I want to set up an exhibition for her.'

'Ah, I see.' Charlotte smiled back at him. 'That's the real reason you invited me here tonight. You want me to use my contacts to get her some exhibition space?'

'Oh, you got me there.'

'I might be able to do that. I'd have to see her work first, though, to get some idea of the kind of space we'd need.'

'Come round tomorrow morning?'

'Says the man in a hurry?'

'What's the point of hanging around? I reckon she'll be ready in about six weeks' time — we need to do some editing and some reshooting, but that should be enough. So we could aim for early July?'

'You'll be hard pushed to get a venue so soon,' Charlotte said, but then smiled at him. 'But I'll come round in the morning to have a look. It will have to be first thing, though, I've got an appointment at ten.'

'That's fine.' Daniel raised his glass to her.

* * *

'Hiya, I've brought coffee and croissants,' Anna called out happily as she nudged open the door to the studio. 'Oh!' She stopped short at the sight of Daniel and Charlotte huddled by the Mac that was used for editing. When they both turned to face her, Anna tried to regain her composure and said, 'Sorry, if I'd known, I'd have brought an extra coffee.'

'Not to worry.' Charlotte smiled at her. 'I've got to dash soon anyway. We've just been looking at your work.'

'Have you?' Anna felt affronted that Daniel had sought to share her photographs with someone else without even consulting her.

'Yes, they really are rather good.'

'Thanks.' Anna put the coffee and croissants down, no longer hungry.

Daniel looked at her, frowning. 'Charlotte has lots of contacts in the art world and she's agreed to find a venue for your exhibition. She wanted to get a feel for your style so that she could find a space to complement them.'

'Oh, I see.' She was slightly mollified at his explanation, but still wished he'd spoken to her first.

'We were thinking in about six weeks' time,' Charlotte said. 'So we need to start looking for a venue as soon as possible. They usually get booked up months, if not years in advance.'

'Yes, I know.' She was dumbfounded. This had all happened so quickly and, because it had been taken out of her control, made it feel a little surreal and actually very scary. She turned to Daniel. 'Do you think I'll be ready so soon?'

'Of course you will,' Daniel replied, smiling confidently at her.

She suddenly felt lightheaded and clutched a table to steady herself. She'd waited so long for this moment, but it was nothing like she'd expected it to be.

'Are you okay?' Daniel looked concerned.

'Yes, I'm fine.'

Charlotte looked at her watch. 'Well, I must get going.' She picked up an oversized Armani handbag and stood up. After giving Daniel a peck on the cheek, she turned once more to Anna. 'Your work is really good, you know. I'm sure you'll be a hit at your exhibition.'

'Thank you.'

And with that she swept out of the studio, leaving a waft of Coco Chanel in her wake.

Anna watched her leave, still unable to move.

'Ah, you sure you're okay?' Daniel asked again, frowning.

'I'm fine.' She forced a smile. 'It's just a bit of a shock, that's all.'

'What's a shock? The exhibition?'

'Yes.'

'But we spoke about this yesterday.'

'I know, but I didn't think it would all happen so quickly.'

He smiled at her. 'I'm sorry, I've steamrollered you, haven't I?'

'A little bit.'

'One of my traits, I'm afraid,' he said. 'When I get an idea I like to run with it straight away. And, besides, you've waited for this for a long time. There's no point hanging around now.'

'But will I be ready?' she asked again.

'Of course you will. We'll do it together.'

She liked the sound of that, of someone holding her hand through this. Of Daniel holding her hand through this. She pushed that last thought away. He was her employer and mentor. Nothing more.

'So, come on then, let's get to work. Let's sort out what we need for the shoot tomorrow and, if we have any time left over, we can run through some of my ideas for your exhibition.'

Anna smiled and shook her head. Daniel was incredibly dynamic when he put his mind to something. Even if it was rather scary, it was good that he was being dynamic about her. No one had ever championed her like this before and, although it was a strange feeling, she was going to try to live in the moment and enjoy it.

CHAPTER FOURTEEN

Anna felt as though she was floating in a bubble of happiness as she got off the train and headed home that evening. Even the thought of facing her family couldn't dim her mood. If the worst came to the worst, she'd just retreat to her bedroom and ignore them as she worked on a list of photographs for the exhibition. But as she walked into the kitchen she was surprised to see her father standing in front of the sink, doing the washing-up.

'Hello, love,' he said pleasantly as she stopped in surprise.

'Hello, Dad. What's all this?'

'Well, it wasn't going to do it itself, was it? And to be honest it was starting to smell.'

She nodded as she noticed that all the kitchen windows were open. She picked up a tea towel. 'I'll dry then, make more room for the rest.'

'You don't have to do that. It's not your mess.'

'I know that. And neither should it be my punishment for going away. But as you're showing willing, I will too.'

He frowned at her, holding a plate just above the water, his wrists dripping with soap suds. 'What do you mean, punishment for going away?'

'That's what Jack said to Harry. That the mess was my punishment for going away, so I needed to clear it up.'

'He said what!' Andrew looked furious. 'Are you sure?'

She nodded. 'Ask Harry.'

'No, I don't need to.' He shook his head. 'I'm just shocked that he actually said that. Although I don't know why I'm so surprised. He's got out of hand recently and I've let him get away with it. I'm sorry. Not having you here this weekend, and the atmosphere since you came home, has made me realise how much we've taken you for granted.'

Anna was elated at his change in attitude. 'It's not that I mind doing things — most of the time I want the house to be nice, as Mum would have wanted it. I just wish we could pull together a bit more. It shouldn't just be down to me.'

'No, you're right,' he said, returning to the washing-up. 'I do appreciate how much you've held this family together since Maggie died. I couldn't cope, but you just got on with it. It should have been me being the strong one. Your mum would be so proud of you, love.'

Anna gulped, tears stinging her eyes. She turned away from him so that he wouldn't see, and managed to say in a croaky voice, 'Thanks, Dad.' She reached out to give him a hug. 'Everyone deals with grief differently. Mine was to keep busy, so perhaps that's what worked for me. There's no right or wrong way.'

'No, but it's time to stop burying my head in the sand. I'll start tomorrow by speaking to Jack. No point trying to do it tonight — he's out with his mates and by the time he gets back he'll have had a skinful. And I'm going to call a family meeting. Tomorrow night, and we're going to work out how we're going to pull together. All of us.'

Anna grinned at him. Finally, he was listening. 'That sounds like a good plan, Dad. What do you want for tea?'

* * *

Later, when they'd finished eating but were still sitting around the kitchen table, Anna said, 'I'm glad you mentioned the others helping out a bit more, because I'm going to have less time in the next few months.'

'Why's that? Is it your slave driver of a boss?'

'He's not a slave driver, Dad, and it's not my work for him that's going to take up my time.'

'What is it then?'

'He's seen some of the photographs I've taken and he's working with me so that I can have an exhibition.'

'Really?' Her father looked surprised. 'Don't exhibitions cost money? How are you going to afford that?'

'Daniel thinks I'll more than cover the costs from what I sell.'

'And you trust him, do you?'

'I do. He knows what he's talking about.'

'That's good then, isn't it? So you'll be a professional photographer?'

Anna laughed self-consciously. 'I don't know about that, but it'll definitely be the first rung on the ladder.'

He nodded thoughtfully.

'Please, Dad, say you're happy for me.'

He looked shocked. 'Of course I am. And I've always been proud of you, even though I don't always say it.'

'But my photography?'

'Ah, well, that's the thing you see.' He sighed. 'I'm a plumber, I see things from a practical point of view. I've never really understood the art world. I find it difficult.'

'Maybe you'd understand more if you came to my exhibition, when I have it?'

'Would you want me there?' He looked surprised.

'Of course I would, Dad!'

He smiled. 'I'd be delighted to come and see how far my one and only daughter has come.'

'Then you can be my guest of honour,' she replied, grinning.

'And in the meantime, I'll make sure everyone helps out more in the house. We may need some help at first, though, just so you can show us how it's done.'

'Of course. Jack won't be pleased.'

'Jack won't have any say in it. I'll make sure he pulls his weight.'

* * *

The three of them were sitting round the kitchen table when Anna arrived home from work the next night. Judging by the scowl on Jack's face, he wasn't happy about it.

'I hope this won't take long,' he said loudly as Anna walked into the kitchen. 'I've arranged to go out.'

'It will take as long as it takes,' her father said gruffly. 'And no one is going anywhere until we're all in agreement.'

'Agreement about what?' Jack asked.

Anna had told Harry yesterday about her conversation with their father, so he knew what was coming. Jack, it seemed, was the only one who'd been kept in the dark.

'Right,' her dad said. 'I've decided that things need to change around here. It's not fair on Anna doing everything around the house like she has for so long. She's got her own life to lead. So, from now on, we all need to pitch in.'

Jack scoffed. 'What? You want us to do women's work?'

'We all live here, so it shouldn't just be down to the only woman who lives here.'

'You've changed your tune!'

'Yes, I have,' Andrew said firmly. 'Anna works just as hard as the rest of us outside the home, so it's not fair to expect her to do everything.'

'Oh, what? Has the poor little baby been bleating to you? Too good to get her hands dirty now, is she?'

'No, she's not. She'll be doing her share — we all will. And if you don't like it, you know what you can do.'

Anna and Harry stared on, aghast. They'd never seen their father like this before. He'd never been one for confrontation, which was why he'd let Jack get away with so much for so long.

'What do you mean I know what I can do?' Jack looked shocked.

'I mean, I'm the head of the household here. I'm the one who pays the bills, so if you don't like my rules, you can find somewhere else to live.'

Jack laughed. 'You think I can afford to live somewhere else on the poxy wages you pay me?'

'I pay you what you're worth, Jack. So if I'm not paying you enough, that's on you.'

'What do you mean?'

'I mean your work is sloppy. I've lost count of the times I've had to check your work and redo it. I haven't said anything before and that's on me. You could be a good plumber if you put your mind to it, but you're lazy and slapdash and only interested in going to the pub. I've tried to teach you but you're not interested. So from now on, you'd better pull your weight at work and at home, or you might find yourself looking for another job as well as accommodation.'

Jack stood up abruptly, knocking his chair back in the process. 'I'm not staying here to listen to this. I'm off.'

'Pick that chair up before you go!' Andrew shouted at him, also standing up.

Jack bent down roughly, pulled the chair up and slammed it back down again. Anna found herself holding her breath at the altercation and almost gasped when he turned to her, venom in his eyes. 'I know this is all your doing, Daddy's little girl. But don't think you'll get away with this.'

He turned on his heel and strode out of the kitchen. As he reached the door Andrew said, 'Make sure you're on time for work in the morning. And don't be stinking of alcohol either. If you're not fit for work, I won't let you on site and you won't be getting paid.'

His words were met with silence and the crashing of the front door as Jack stormed out.

'That went well,' Harry said a few moments later.

Andrew sighed. 'My fault. It was probably too much in one go. But that's been coming for a long time, only I haven't been brave enough to confront him. Jack's going to have to make some changes and, if he doesn't, he'll be out on his ear.'

'That's a bit harsh, isn't it?' Anna asked, surprised by her father's turnaround.

'No,' he said, shaking his head. 'I meant what I said about his work. I can't keep covering for him. It's my business and my reputation on the line, and if he wants to make his living as a plumber he can't afford to keep making the mistakes he's been making.'

Anna and Harry stared at each other in silence. For so long now, it had seemed as though Andrew and Jack weren't just father and son but best friends, so it was a shock to realise how different things really were.

'Well, I don't know if you've got any ideas for tea,' their father continued, breaking the silence. 'But if you'd like to show me how to cook whatever it is, I'm willing to learn. Harry, you can watch too. You're going to need to learn some cooking skills for when you're at uni.'

Anna decided to start with something easy and began to put together the ingredients for a cottage pie. Her father and Harry watched as she showed them how to chop the onions and brown everything off in the saucepan.

'You'll have to write this down,' her dad said. 'I'll never remember it. I've never cooked in my life.'

'I'm sure you'll soon get the hang of it,' Anna said reassuringly.

'It all seems pretty straightforward to me,' Harry said.

'That's because you're the brains of the family,' Andrew said. Then he looked at Anna, stricken. 'No offence, love.'

She laughed. 'None taken. That's exactly right.' She turned to Harry. 'Harry, can you put your exam timetable up on the fridge, so we'll know when not to disturb you?'

'Will do.'

'I forgot to ask. How did the first one go on Monday?'

Harry grinned. 'Pretty good actually. It was a relief to get one out of the way. My next one is Friday. They're all pretty much spread out over the next month, so I should have enough time to revise between each one.'

'Great. I'm sure you're going to smash them,' Anna told him.

'You deserve to,' her father said, patting Harry on his back. 'After all the hard work you've put in.'

Harry grinned at the rare compliment and Anna felt a warm glow spread within her. Everything was finally coming together. The only fly in the ointment now was Jack.

CHAPTER FIFTEEN

For the next few days, it looked as though Jack was going to toe the line. He'd come home the night of the argument reasonably early — though he'd crashed and banged his way upstairs to make his presence known. But he'd been up early for work the next day and contributed to the washing-up that evening, though he refused to learn to cook. To everyone else it looked as though he'd taken their father's words to heart, but Anna couldn't help noticing the hostile looks he threw at her whenever he got the chance. This wasn't over yet. She did her best to avoid being alone with him.

Her father was the one who had surprised her most. He seemed to take to cooking instantly and had gone to the supermarket with her early on Saturday, after they'd discussed the menu for the week. This had left her plenty of time for photography during the rest of the day. During their shopping trip, he'd talked about taking a cookery course and had started coming home from work early each night, rather than going to the pub, eager to start cooking the evening meal.

Work was busy too. Daniel had been booked by *Fashionista Magazine* to do an extensive shoot at London Fashion Week, both in front of the catwalk and behind the scenes, and they were busy organising the various photoshoots that would take place before and during the four days of the event. He'd also been asked to contribute to a book that was being written by a retired fashion designer, on fashion through the ages, and was searching through his archives for fashion photographs from the noughties. And when they weren't concentrating on that, Daniel was helping her get together the photographs for her exhibition.

With work being so busy she was beginning to worry that she wouldn't be ready for her own exhibition, which was rapidly approaching on 1 July. Charlotte had found a venue, although she was keeping where it was going to be under wraps, building up to a big reveal nearer the time. When Anna pressed her to tell her where she had booked, all she would answer was that it was unique and perfect to showcase Anna's debut. This not only frustrated Anna but also made her very nervous. She decided that all she could do was concentrate on the actual photographs and hope that the rest would fall into place.

* * *

Daniel was puzzling over the photographs he'd collected and printed so far for his section of the book on fashion. Preferring to see things in actual format, he'd laid them all out on the large table he used when he was selecting photographs.

'What's the problem?' Anna came to stand next to him.

'I'm just struggling to make a decision on what to include,' he said, taking in how close Anna was to him and the way her floral perfume was tantalising him. Although they were growing closer each day that they worked together, and Daniel couldn't wish for a better assistant, he was growing increasingly aware of how attractive he found her. That wasn't something he was comfortable with at all. In fact, these days he was finding it very difficult not to reach out and touch her — he was experiencing such lurid dreams about her that he found it hard to act normally when she was standing in such close proximity.

He moved around to the other side of the table, anything to take away the temptation of wanting to reach out, take her in his arms and kiss those soft lips. He shook the thoughts away. 'This period was all about cropped tops and cargo pants or bootleg trousers, which looks great on these models but it's certainly not as extravagant as, say, the seventies or the eighties.' He showed her some of the photographs the author had collated so far. 'I might struggle to make my section stand out.'

'Hmm, I see what you mean.' She leaned across him as she selected some of the photos, too close to him for comfort. 'I think this period was more about attitude, though. Look at the women in these pictures. They're almost saying "I'm going to be me and I don't care what you think of me." You've certainly captured it here.'

'Do you think?'

'Definitely. They're so expressive, you'll easily stand out.'

He began to shuffle the photographs back into one pile, feeling his face growing pink at both her praise and her proximity to him. 'Oh let's forget this for today,' he said. 'I'll have another think about it when I'm feeling a little less jaded. Now, why don't you show me the photos for the exhibition you've been working on?' He breathed a sigh of relief as she moved away to switch her laptop on. He'd have to find a way to keep his distance from her in the future.

* * *

As Anna walked home, she contemplated Daniel's embarrassment earlier, when she'd praised his photographs. Why did he suddenly seem so shy around her? His behaviour was very different to the Daniel she had first started working for. She was still puzzling this when she opened the front door and made her way into the kitchen. The house was quiet, so maybe no one was home. She liked it when no one else was here. It was much more relaxing. Maybe she'd even run herself a bath and have a good long soak in the peace and quiet.

She stopped short when she saw Jack sitting alone at the kitchen table, a can of lager in his hand and several empty cans on the table.

'Hello, big sister,' he said with a snarl. She turned to go upstairs, anything to avoid being alone with him. 'Oh, don't run away,' he continued. 'Come on and sit down. It's ages since we've had a proper catch up.'

'I'm not sure we have much to say to each other.' She turned her back to him and tried not to show her fear.

'Well, I've definitely got a lot to say to you. Come and sit down.'

'I'd rather stand. Where is everyone?'

He shrugged. 'Dad's gone off somewhere on some kind of secret mission and who knows where Harry is. Probably at the library again.'

'He's in the middle of his exams and at least it's peaceful there.'

'I might have known you'd stick up for him. He always was your favourite, wasn't he? Good, quiet, hard-working Harry.'

'I don't know what you mean,' she said.

'Oh, come off it, Sis. I know you always found me the difficult one, whereas little Harry couldn't put a foot wrong, could he?'

'You were just very different personalities and had different needs,' she said, suddenly realising that jealousy was the root of Jack's anger towards her.

'Yes.' Jack got up from his chair and moved towards her. Too late, she realised the kitchen door had closed behind her, barring her escape. She tried to slowly reach behind her to open the door, but Jack was too quick. Before she had a chance, his hands were on her shoulders, he'd shoved her to the side and she was pinned against the kitchen wall, his beery breath in her face. 'I needed you to get me out of trouble with the teachers and Harry needed you to pat him on the back.'

'It was a very difficult time for all of us. People deal with things differently. That doesn't mean I loved you any less than I did him.' Anna hoped pacifying him would help her get away. Jack had never been violent towards her in the past, although she'd always felt the threat of it, but now she realised there might be a first time.

'Bet you do now, though, don't you?' Jack gave her a not-so-gentle shove.

'I still love you, Jack, you're my brother. It's just sometimes I don't like you very much.'

He sneered. 'Oh, the feeling's mutual. Although I'd go a bit further than that, because I hate you, and do you know why I hate you?'

Again she tried not to sound threatened by him. 'I don't, Jack, but I'm sure you're going to tell me.' She could feel her legs trembling and doubted they would be able to hold her up if it wasn't for his hands on her shoulders.

'I certainly am. Do you know how difficult you've made life for me recently?'

'What? Because I've asked you to help out a bit more around the house? Hardly a reason for you to hate me.'

'No. Because you've turned Dad against me. Life used to be sweet, but now he's on at me all the time. And working with him means I can't get away from him. In fact, he's worse when we're at work, always on my case.'

'What's going on?' They'd both been so intent on each other they hadn't heard Harry come into the house and open the kitchen door.

Jack didn't take his eyes off Anna. 'None of your business.'

'When you've got our sister pinned against the wall, I'd say it was very much my business. Get off her, Jack.'

'Make me.'

Harry sprang across the kitchen and tried to pull Jack off her, but Jack spun round, landing a fist firmly in Harry's face.

Anna gasped in shock as she watched Harry go sprawling away from them, landing on the floor.

'What the hell is going on here?' An angry voice came from behind them. Anna turned to see her father in the doorway, his fists clenched at his sides.

'I'm teaching these two a lesson, that's all,' Jack said.

'A lesson for what?' Andrew asked.

'For ruining my life,' Jack answered.

'The only person who's done that is yourself,' Andrew replied. 'And I won't have violence in my house, so you can get out.'

'What?' Jack sounded shocked.

'I said get out. I've had just about as much as I can take from you recently. I don't want you living under my roof. You've got fifteen minutes to pack and leave or I'll be calling the police.'

'What for?'

'Assault for one,' Andrew said. 'Now get out.'

Jack glared at him. 'Fine. I don't want to live here anyway.'

'And you can find yourself another job while you're at it. You don't work for me anymore.'

'Fine! If that's the way you want it.' Jack didn't even bother to go upstairs to pack, but stomped down the hallway, slamming the front door behind him.

Anna looked at her father. 'Dad, did you—'

'Anna, I know you mean well, but you really can't defend him,' he said 'He hit Harry and it looks like he had a go at you too.'

'He did, but—'

Harry pulled himself up from the floor, blood seeping from his nose. Anna quickly ran a tea towel under the tap, wrung it out, and began to gently dab Harry's face.

'And that's not the only thing he's done,' her father continued. 'I found out today that he's stealing from the business.'

'What?' Anna asked, pausing in her administrations.

'It's true. He's been overcharging customers, putting the right amount through the books and pocketing the rest. I only found out because someone mentioned their job was more than they were expecting. You know how useless I am with paperwork, but I've been going through the accounts. I should never have left it to him without checking it myself, but I trusted him.'

'Oh, Dad! I'm so sorry.' Anna left Harry's side and put her arms around her father.

'I would never have believed it from one of my own.' He leaned his head against hers. 'But he's a bad apple and now he needs to face life on his own. See how much he likes that.'

'Maybe he'll see the error of his ways,' Harry said.

'Maybe he will,' Andrew said. 'But I'm not sure I'll ever be able to trust him again. And neither should you. We need to get some ice on that face or you'll have a right shiner tomorrow.'

CHAPTER SIXTEEN

The following week was incredibly busy as they worked on the shots they had been commissioned to take prior to the show opening on Friday. Anna was grateful as it took her mind off what had happened with Jack. She'd known he could be chauvinistic, particularly where she was concerned, but she hadn't been prepared for the depth of his hatred, or the level of violence he'd shown towards both her and Harry. And she certainly hadn't been prepared for him stealing from the family business. She and Jack had definitely grown apart as he got older, and she wondered how much her easy relationship with Harry was a factor. But that wasn't because she loved Harry more than she did Jack, it was just that Harry was much easier to get on with. If she'd known Jack had been fostering jealousy all these years, maybe she could have done something to stop it from reaching boiling point.

Like her, Jack hadn't been academic and had shown no interest in school. If it hadn't been for their dad giving him an apprenticeship, she didn't know where he would have ended up. And yet even that hadn't been enough for him. Despite everything he'd done, though, she couldn't stop worrying about him. Their dad refused to even mention his name, but Anna wondered how Jack was managing without either a home or a job, and it distressed her that she couldn't do anything to help him.

On Thursday, after a particularly gruelling day of pandering to the temperamental personalities of both fashion designers and models, Daniel asked Anna if she'd like to join him at home for dinner. They were packing away the last of the equipment and she was bone-weary, dreading the long journey home.

'Just a takeaway and a bottle of wine,' Daniel said.

'That would be lovely,' she replied. 'Save me having to face the Tube in rush hour.'

They finished packing the equipment they needed for the next day's shoots and, after a short journey to his house, she was sitting by the kitchen island on one of the comfortable bar stools.

'This is great.' Daniel smiled at her as he poured a glass of wine. 'I really can't face another evening on my own, but I haven't got the energy for going out.'

He seemed to be going out less these days, and he certainly wasn't showing up on social media on the arm of a beautiful model. She wondered what was happening to him.

She took a sip of the wine, relishing the cool acidity as it slipped down her throat. 'I love it when I get an evening to myself at home, but it doesn't happen very often.'

'How is it at home these days?'

'It's getting better actually,' she replied. It was certainly a lot quieter and more easy-going without Jack. 'Dad's taken a fancy to cooking, so at least that's one chore that isn't my sole responsibility. But Harry is in the middle of his exams so he's really stressed.'

'And what about your other brother? Jack, is it?'

'Jack's moved out,' she said carefully, not wanting to reveal that he'd been thrown out, or the reason why. 'So it's just the three of us now. We're getting along okay. Better than we have in a long time to be honest. It's still a busy house, though.'

'Have you ever thought about getting a place on your own?'

'I've thought about it, but I've always felt the need to look after them. Besides, I couldn't afford somewhere on my own.'

He smiled. 'Maybe that will change after your exhibition.'

'I doubt that! One little exhibition isn't going to make me a fortune.'

'No, but it will set you on your way. The photos are great. Charlotte is determined to make it a success.'

Anna took another sip of her wine as she thought carefully about a subject that had been worrying her recently. 'Daniel, I know we agreed I'd pay for any costs of the exhibition out of my sales, but I'm conscious how much time both you and Charlotte are putting into this. I'm worried that the exhibition won't be enough to cover all those costs.'

Daniel roared with laughter. 'We're not expecting you to pay anything for our time. I offered to mentor you, and so your success will be payment enough for me. And it's the same for Charlotte.'

'Okay, maybe I can understand where you're coming from, but what's in it for Charlotte?'

'Charlotte has lots of contacts and has always dabbled in organising parties and events, but she's never taken anything seriously. Daddy's allowance means she's always had a safety net. But I've seen a change in her since I suggested this exhibition. She's got the bit between her teeth and she's decided she wants to give it a proper shot. If your exhibition is a success and her name is linked with it, she's hoping other work will come her way.'

Anna nodded. That did make sense, but it also put pressure on the exhibition going well.

'And what if it's not a success?' she asked. The reality of having her own exhibition was very different to what she had dreamed it would be. Going public with her photography was beginning to feel as though she was exposing herself. It made her feel vulnerable — that wasn't a comfortable place to be.

'Of course it will be a success. Your work is good, Anna. It's your self-confidence that's lacking.'

She nodded. Maybe he was right, but that didn't stop her feeling any less nervous. 'You know I'm extremely grateful for you helping me get my foot on the ladder, don't you?'

He nodded. 'I do, but that's not entirely altruistic either. Life was getting a bit jaded before you came along.'

'And now it's not?'

'Definitely not. Although, after a day like today, it does make me wonder. Truth be told I'm getting a bit fed up with the fashion world. Yes, the models look great, but having to deal with their egos and often their tantrums can be very draining. And I've decided that I want to do something worthwhile.'

'Which is?'

'I want to set up a photography school.'

'Oh!' She wasn't expecting that.

'You've made me realise there's a lot of talent out there that will go unnoticed if it's not given a guiding hand. I want to give people who are less privileged than myself the opportunity to follow their dreams.'

She paused, then put her glass down on the breakfast bar.

'So am I your guinea pig then?' She wasn't sure if she was pleased or offended.

'No,' he said. 'You're my inspiration.' The way he smiled at her made her heart start to beat a little faster. Was he flirting with her? No, he couldn't be. Confused, she looked away and tried to think of something else to say.

'So, when are you going to set up this school?' She turned back to look at him. He was still staring at her, but instead of that making her feel uncomfortable she had a sudden urge to kiss him. She pushed the thought away. She mustn't go there.

'It's just a thought at the moment. I haven't really had a chance to look into it properly. I'll need to wind up some of my business here, look into the legalities of it all, then find some premises, so that will take up more visits to Cheshire.'

'You're going to set it up in Cheshire?'

'Yes, well, Manchester anyway. Didn't I say?'

'No, I just assumed it would be in London. Is this about Ben?'

'Yes, I want to spend more time with him. Obviously I can't leave the business here, but if I set something else up nearer home then I can be nearer to him, at least some of the time.'

Anna stared at him, trying desperately to figure out what that meant for her and her job. The arrival of their food interrupted their conversation. As they ate, she didn't have the courage to ask, afraid of what his answer might be.

* * *

Working at London Fashion Week was thrilling. Anna had never experienced an event like this before. The atmosphere was electric, with everyone determined to make a success of their part of it, and with huge out-cries when things didn't go right — when things or people weren't in the places they were supposed to be. Anna would have loved to be a fly on the wall and watch the drama unfold, but she was far too busy for that, as both she and Daniel were in the epicentre of the action. Her legs and arms ached with the effort of making sure that every piece of equipment was in the right place at the right time, and her brain hurt with anticipating all of Daniel's needs to get the right shot in the smallest amount of time. But working behind the scenes had also shown her that the glamorous side the paying public saw was very different to the backstage reality. And Daniel was definitely right — the tantrums she'd witnessed over the weekend could rival any pre-school nursery. Although it was June, the weather was unseasonably cold, and so apart from the moans about who had been given the better designs or position on the catwalk, the main gripe among the models was that they were chilly. And while the whole experience had been exciting, Anna was exhausted, and was looking forward to a gentler pace of life when it was all over. At six o'clock on the last night, she felt something akin to relief when all the models lined up to begin the final parade down the catwalk.

Daniel was set to take his closing shots, Anna next to him, ready to assist him if there was anything he needed, when a deafening explosion ripped through the air. Suddenly she was flying — then everything went black.

CHAPTER SEVENTEEN

'Anna! Anna!'

She could hear a voice but it sounded like it was far away, as though it was underwater. Further behind that she could also hear muffled screams. And it was raining too — she could feel water dripping onto her face. She tried to open her eyes but it was too dark to see. Exhausted, she shut them again. The air smelt acrid and tasted of smoke. Her chest tightened and she began to cough.

'Anna!' There was the voice again, familiar but still sounding distant. She tried harder to open her eyes, this time managing to keep them open. Bending over her was a familiar shape, and a hand came out to clutch at her shoulder.

'Anna!'

She groaned, unable to form any proper words.

'Oh, thank God! I thought I'd lost you.'

She heard a scrabbling sound and suddenly her body felt lighter.

'You're covered in rubble. Let me get it off you.'

'Daniel?' She croaked his name, overwhelmed by the sound of his voice, relieved that she was not alone.

She started to pull herself up but his words stopped her. 'Lie still until a paramedic has checked you over.'

'No, I need to get off the floor.' She needed to get away from the dust that was filling her lungs. Gradually she pulled herself up until she was in a crouching position, then leaned on Daniel's arm as she managed to stand up.

'What happened?'

'Some kind of explosion, I think,' he replied. She tried to make out what was going on around her, but it was too dark to be clear.

'Why is it raining?'

'It's the sprinkler system.'

Through the ringing in her ears she could hear low moaning and intermittent screams.

'Let's try to get you out of here. You need to be checked by a medic.'

'No, I'm fine,' she said. Her head felt muzzy and her body battered and bruised, but she sensed there were people worse off than her and she had an overwhelming need to help them. 'It's so dark.' She felt at a loss. 'How can we help if we can't see?'

'Have you still got your phone?' he asked.

She reached into the back pocket of her jeans. Miraculously her phone was still there. She pulled it out and flicked on the torch, shocked at the sight of the devastation around her. 'Oh, Daniel!'

Daniel too had switched on his phone and seemed to be at a loss for words.

'We've got to help,' she said, suddenly galvanised into action. Taking a tentative step forward, she moved towards a body that was almost completely covered in rubble.

'Hello, can you hear me?'

The body made a slight groan.

'What's your name?'

When she didn't receive a response she asked again. Eventually a faint voice said, 'Eva.'

'Okay, Eva, we're going to get you some help. But a lot of stuff has fallen on top of you, so the first thing we're going to do is to try to get it off. At least make you a bit more comfortable.'

"Kay.'

It looked as though half the ceiling had fallen on the woman. Anna was afraid of what they would find under the debris, but both she and Daniel worked diligently at trying to release the weight of it from Eva's body.

Realising how quiet Eva had become, Anna said, 'Eva, are you still awake?' When there was no response, Anna said again, 'Eva? Eva?'

The woman groaned.

'Eva, you need to stay awake.'

After a while Eva mumbled, 'Tired.'

'Yes, I know. But you need to stay awake.'

"Kay,' Eva said.

'What were you doing here?'

'Model,' she mumbled.

Daniel continued to work at removing the debris, but as Anna looked across she saw that his hands were slick with a dark liquid. She could only assume it was Eva's blood. From the expression on his face she knew it was not looking good.

'Go and see if you can get some help,' she whispered to him. 'I'll stay here and keep her talking.'

Daniel moved hesitantly away as Anna tried to clear the rest of the debris from Eva's body. When her leg was clear she could see the blood pumping from a gash just above her knee. Silently thanking the recent first aid course she'd attended that no one else at The Whigmore was bothered about, Anna quickly pulled off the belt from her jeans and tried to slide it under Eva's leg. Eva moaned in pain.

'It's all right,' Anna explained. 'You've cut your leg, but I'm going to stop the bleeding if I can.'

"Kay,' Eva mumbled, and Anna tried to keep her talking while she tightened the belt in a tourniquet above the wound. After what seemed like an incredibly long time, Daniel returned with a paramedic by his side. Anna explained what she'd done and the paramedic nodded and said, 'Good job. I can take it from here.'

'Her name's Eva,' she said before turning away to where else she might be needed.

Daniel and Anna worked long into the evening, trying to help as many people as they could. For some they were too late and, although she wasn't religious, Anna offered up a silent prayer for them. As she held the hand of one young woman, who paramedics were desperately trying to save, she realised how lucky she was to be one of the walking wounded. If she'd been standing in only a slightly different space, her fate might have been very different. Most of those who had been badly injured, it seemed, had been lining up at the start of the catwalk at the time of the explosion, taking the full force of whatever it was.

Eventually, when it looked as though the paramedics had control of the situation, Daniel and Anna made their way outside into the dusk of the June evening. For a moment they looked wordlessly at each other, both in shock at the events of the last few hours. After a moment Daniel said, 'Your cheek, you're bleeding.' She reached up to where she now realised there was a dull throbbing. Her fingers came away wet.

He reached into his back pocket and pulled out a hanky, gently wiping the blood from her face.

A sudden flash caught Anna's attention and she realised they had just been photographed. Daniel put his arm around her.

'Come on, let's get away from here. I think we both need to be somewhere we feel safe, followed by a hot shower and a stiff drink.'

'I like the sound of that,' Anna said. And, shaken though she was by everything she had just witnessed, she too wanted to be as far away from the carnage as possible. And most of all she wanted to be with Daniel. Today she'd experienced the gentler side of him, which she'd seen when he was around

Ben. He had a compassion towards other people that she admired, and he made her feel safe.

'Excuse me, Miss, we need to get you checked out before you can go anywhere.' A paramedic moved towards them.

'I'm fine,' she said.

'That's a nasty cut you've got there. At the very least, let me clean it up and put a Steri-Strip on it.'

'Haven't you got more seriously wounded people you need to see to?'

'The worst are on their way to hospital now. I wouldn't be doing my job if I let someone with an injury walk away untreated.'

Realising he wasn't going to take no for an answer, Anna allowed herself to be led away into one of the many ambulances that were parked in front of the entrance to the building.

* * *

Anna sat in Daniel's dressing gown, after having showered away the grime of the explosion. Too shaken to travel home, Daniel had offered her his spare room for the night.

'Have you phoned your father? You need to let him know that you're okay.'

'No, I'll do it now.' She should have done that before now, she realised. The news of the explosion was all over the television and, knowing she was working at London Fashion Week, he was bound to be worried about her.

'Anna, thank God you're safe! Were you in it?'

'Yes, Dad. Sorry, I haven't had a chance to phone before. It's all been a bit of a blur.'

'That's all right. As long as you're okay. Were you injured?'

'Just a few cuts and bruises. Nothing to worry about.'

'Oh, that's a relief! Where are you?'

'Daniel has offered to put me up in his spare room to save me having to travel across town.'

'That's good of him.'

'Yes. I didn't feel like getting on a train on my own tonight.'

'I'm not surprised. Well, you take care and ring me tomorrow.'

'I will, Dad.'

Although she'd doubted him in the past, the concern in his voice told her how much he loved her.

She went back into the kitchen where Daniel handed her a glass of wine.

'Here, I think we could both do with one.'

'Thanks.' She took a sip, savouring the cold and crisp taste.

'Do you want anything to eat?'

She shook her head. 'No, I've got no appetite.'

'Me neither. I think we're both in shock . . . I'll never forget tonight.'

'Nor me.' She remembered how she held the hand of a woman as she slipped away while the medics were trying to save her. Then she thought of Eva and wondered if she was okay.

On the wall of the far side of the kitchen, the television burbled away with repeated news of the night's events. At first it had been assumed it was a terrorist attack but, as no one had claimed responsibility, it was looking more likely that it was a tragic accident. Investigators were already trying to piece together what caused the explosion at the start of the runway.

So far ten people had died and many more were injured. How easily it could have been them. They sat in silence watching the scenes unfold on the television. Scenes that, only a short time earlier, they'd been at the centre of.

'What about the photos?' She suddenly remembered what they'd been doing before the blast. 'Have they been lost?'

'No, the camera around my neck was damaged but the STD card is still intact, and all the earlier photos were already uploaded to the cloud.'

'Well, at least that's something.'

'Yes. All the equipment is ruined, but it's covered on my insurance. Not important.' He paused. 'Anna?'

'Yes?' She turned to face him, concerned at the worried expression on his face.

'This might sound crass, but we're going to need to get the photos uploaded as soon as possible. They might be needed as part of the investigation, but as they have been commissioned by *Fashionista*, they're the ones who are going to have to send them to the police. Then it will be up to them what they do with them, and we owe it to the models to send the best versions across as we can. Do you feel up to helping me or have you had enough?'

'Of course I'll help you.' She didn't need to think twice.

'We both deserve some sleep but we'll need to start editing first thing in the morning.'

She drained her glass. 'Whatever you think best.'

'In that case, I'll show you to your room and give you a call in the morning. The sooner we can get them over, the better. I think we should take the rest of the week off. There's nothing in the diary for the next few days, so I thought I might head up to Cheshire. I know I'm not due to see Ben, but under the circumstances Lucinda might let me have some extra time with him.'

'Of course you must. You'll want to give him lots of hugs after what you've been through and I'm sure he'll want to do the same. It's just . . .' She paused, not really knowing how to broach the question she wanted to ask him.

'What?'

'Well, I think I'd like to keep busy. I know this is your home and everything but, while you're away, would it be possible for me to do some work in the studio? I'd like to finalise the photographs for the exhibition and it will help me take my mind off what happened.'

'Of course you can. I think we have to do whatever works for each of us to get through this. I'll let you have a key and the security code, and you can come and go as you please.'

'Thank you.'

She got up to make her way to bed. For a moment they were standing so close to each other and he was looking at her as though he was about to kiss her. It felt as though time was standing still and she leaned towards him, longing to feel his lips on hers.

But Daniel took a step backwards and she flushed at the thought of what she'd wanted to do.

'I'd better get some sleep.' She turned away from him so he wouldn't see her blushing face.

'Good idea,' he replied.

* * *

Daniel couldn't sleep. Every time he closed his eyes, images of the previous evening flashed in front of him. The initial bang, followed by the dark silence and the strange floating sensation, then the buzzing in his ears and feeling like he was choking on black dust, before the sprinkler system turned the dust to mud. Then had come the terrible realisation that Anna, who had been standing by his side before the explosion, wasn't there anymore.

In a panic he'd shouted her name, but she hadn't replied, so he'd begun to gently explore the debris around him until he'd found her lying half-submerged under fallen rubble.

The relief when she'd answered him was overwhelming. How they had both survived relatively unharmed was a miracle. But if tonight had proved anything to him, it was how fragile life was. There one minute, gone the next. Over the last few weeks his feelings for Anna had grown dramatically. But he was her boss, so he'd always tried to push thoughts of her to the back of his mind. Like the way she crinkled up her nose when she was concentrating, and tucked her gorgeous auburn hair behind her ear when she was editing a photo. Or the way her skinny jeans fitted her long legs and neat little bottom to perfection.

Daniel groaned and tried to ignore his arousal. But tonight, after fearing he'd lost her, after seeing how compassionate she was, how her immediate response had been to try to help those who had been less fortunate than themselves, he'd begun to realise — boss or no boss — he was falling in love with her. And he didn't know how much longer he'd be able to keep that under wraps. Tonight, in the kitchen, he had been so close to her, breathing in her apple-shampoo-scented hair, that he had almost kissed her. Almost. At one point he'd felt as though she would welcome his kiss, but then his courage had failed him. The moment was lost and he'd moved away.

He groaned again as he thought how much he had wanted to kiss her. And how pointless his feelings were. One night over a glass of wine, Anna had gone into more detail about her previous relationship with her boss at The Whigmore. And while Daniel's blood boiled at the way she had been treated, what had really stuck in his mind was how emphatic she'd been about never mixing work with a relationship again.

Eventually Daniel slept but woke several hours later with a start, dreaming of the explosion and the horrors of the night before. Realising he wouldn't be able to get back to sleep for a while, he pulled on a bathrobe and padded downstairs.

The light was on in the kitchen and he wondered if he'd forgotten to switch it off before going up to bed. Then he saw Anna's figure huddled at the breakfast bar, her hands wrapped around a mug. She looked up when he walked in.

'Couldn't sleep,' she said as an explanation.

'No, me neither.'

'Kettle's just boiled.'

He walked over to switch the kettle back on and began to make a cup of tea. There didn't appear to be any words to express what they were both thinking and feeling, but he desperately wanted to talk to her, to tell her about the sense of loss he'd felt when he couldn't find her after the initial explosion, but he didn't know where to begin.

'I suppose as we're both up we could make a start on the photos.' She interrupted his thoughts.

'Yes, I suppose so.' He didn't want to think about the photos, didn't want to see the glamour of the night before, when in his head all he could see was the horror afterwards. But he knew they had to be done, that they were especially important after what had happened, and that time was of the essence.

They made their way upstairs and started to sort through them. He imagined that the police would want them in the order they had been taken so that they could identify the positions they had all been in, directly before the explosion. Anna gasped as they came across a shot of Eva, tall and glamorous, her soulful eyes looking into the lens as though she was seeing the person beyond.

As they waited for the images to upload Daniel was hyper-aware of his closeness to her, doing everything in his power to resist the urge to reach out and touch her. The sooner they could get these photographs over to the magazine, the better. A few days in Cheshire with Ben would give him the time and space he needed to get his feelings back under control. Maybe this was just a reaction to the night before and, after a few days, his feelings would settle down and they would be able to carry on working together as normal.

* * *

Anna was struggling to concentrate too. Her mind was just a whirlwind of emotions, and she couldn't stop comparing what was in front of her to the destruction of what had happened afterwards. They didn't even know whether the pictures they were looking at were of people who had survived.

'I think we should send these photos through to the magazine as they are. As soon as possible. Let them decide what they want to do with them. They might even decide not to run the article under the circumstances.'

'Yes, of course, you're right. My head's all over the place. As soon as they're uploaded, I'll ping them over to the magazine. Let's get something to eat while we wait, and I'll give the magazine a ring.'

When they reached the kitchen, Daniel flicked on the screen and the room was filled with scenes of devastation from the night before and the sombre voiceover. They watched in stunned silence as the faces of the dead appeared on screen, some of whom were the faces they had been looking at upstairs.

'I'm going to phone the editor. I imagine he'll be in the office already, despite the hour.'

Anna listened as he was put straight through. It was difficult to make out what was being said as Daniel merely answered, 'Yes,' then, 'No,' then, 'I'll send them over and let me know which ones you want me to edit later.'

When he switched the phone off he turned to her and said quietly, 'They want to run an article focussing on all the models who were killed or seriously injured in the blast. They want to run a sensitive tribute to them, with the correct permissions of course.'

Anna nodded. 'Better than some rag who is only going to sensationalise it all.'

'That's what I thought,' he agreed. As he turned to leave the room, he was stopped in his tracks as another image flashed up onto the television screen. It was the two of them outside the venue, Daniel looking tenderly at her as her hand touched the wound on her face. Anna's stomach lurched and her mouth went dry. Daniel Redfern looked like a man who was in love. She turned her gaze away from the screen and back to him. He was looking at her in exactly the same way as he had been last night.

Silently they moved towards each other. Just as they were only inches apart, and seconds away from the kiss she was aching for, his phone rang. Looking startled, he answered it, but after a few curt responses, switched it off.

'Gutter press,' he said in answer to her unspoken question. 'They won't get anything from me.'

She nodded. 'Me neither.'

'I'd better get those photos sent over and then I'll give you a lift home.'

When he left the room she felt bereft. His words had left her in no doubt that she'd been dismissed. Once more the moment had been lost — she wondered if they would ever be able to get back to that point again.

CHAPTER EIGHTEEN

It was strange working in the studio without Daniel. Anna kept expecting him to walk through the door at any moment, but of course he didn't. She couldn't help wondering what he was doing — whether he was getting to spend more time with Ben, as he'd said he had wanted to. She imagined him doing the school runs and going to the park or out for pizza in the evenings. She also wondered if he was working on his plans for a photography school. She still hadn't had a chance to ask him how his future plans might affect her. She supposed she'd just have to wait and see, though she didn't like that her future depended so much on someone else's decisions. But after Monday, she realised that no one could really know what lay around the corner.

She had returned home on Tuesday to an almost hero's welcome. Both her dad and Harry were so pleased to see her, and even Daisy had stopped by after work. Everyone wanted to know what had happened. As she had to go through it all again, the memory of it terrified her. Every night she relived it in her dreams, often waking with a start, sweat bathing her body. On Wednesday she'd visited the hospital in an attempt to see how Eva was doing. The nurses had told her that she was stable but, at the moment, she was only receiving family visitors. Anna wrote her a note, telling her she wished her well in her recovery, and went back home.

On Thursday, with everyone out at work, Anna had decided to come into the studio. Her exhibition was in two weeks' time and there was plenty to be done. Besides, she reasoned, keeping busy would occupy her mind. Despite her best efforts, though, she couldn't stop thinking about Daniel and how he had nearly kissed her, twice. She wondered what would have happened on Tuesday if they hadn't been interrupted. Perhaps it was best that they had, and that Daniel was now in Cheshire. The last thing she needed in her life was any more complications.

She was deep in concentration, studying a photo she'd taken recently of the River Thames, from the outside of the Angel pub, wondering why it wasn't quite right, when her phone rang. She picked it up without thinking, half-hoping it would be Daniel.

'Hi, Anna, it's Mark. How are you?'

For a moment she was startled by the sound of his voice, but eventually she managed to reply, 'I'm fine, thanks. How are you?'

'Good. I've been reading about you in the news and I wanted to make sure you're okay.'

'Yes, I'm fine, just a few cuts and bruises.'

'It must have been terrifying.'

'Yes, it was.' It was strange to be speaking to him like this after the way they'd parted. Strange and a little disconcerting.

'Lucky you had Redfern by your side, then.'

'Sorry?'

'I must say you two seem to be getting along. It hasn't taken you long to work your magic on him, has it?'

'What do you mean?'

'That photo of the two of you. You certainly looked close.'

She recognised the sneer in his voice — a cold shudder ran down her spine. The photo had been splashed across the papers with the caption, "Daniel Redfern and his pretty assistant, survivors of the explosion."

'We'd just been through a very traumatic experience and he was concerned that I was injured. That's all that photo was,' she said, trying to defend herself. To defend them both.

'If you say so, but you of all people know that a picture paints a thousand words.'

'And two and two doesn't make five. Is there anything else you want to say, Mark? Only I'm very busy—'

'I'm sure you are. Not long until your exhibition now, is it? And I hear Redfern is sponsoring that too. Very cosy.'

Briefly she wondered how he knew about the exhibition. Charlotte hadn't even told her yet where it was being held, which was beyond frustrating, but perhaps he'd heard through the grapevine. The gallery world was very small after all, and full of gossips.

'Yes, I'm looking forward to it.' She ignored the snipe. 'You know it's something I've always wanted to do, but up until now it hasn't been possible.'

'So the move has been to your advantage, then?'

'Oh, I would say so, Mark. Best thing I could have done to be honest. Thanks for your call and your concern, but I really am very busy.' And with that she cut him off. She dropped the phone onto the desk, as though it had just scalded her, and realised she was shaking.

Mark wasn't the kind of man who liked to be second best and she recognised the tone in his voice. It spelled trouble. With her hands still shaking, she made herself a cup of coffee. Mark was just jealous that she was doing well for herself without him, she reasoned. And, besides, what could he possibly do to hurt her now?

* * *

It was a relief when she walked into the studio on Friday morning to find Daniel sitting at the desk.

'Hello!' she said in surprise. 'You didn't say you were coming back.'

133

'I got back late last night. Lucinda let Ben stay at mine all week, but he's going on a school trip today so he went back to hers last night so she could make sure he had everything he needed. She was surprisingly accommodating, considering it was such short notice.'

'Well, she couldn't not be after what you've just been through.'

'Perhaps not, but I needed to get back anyway. We've got a lot to do here.'

'We have?'

'Yes, *Fashionista* have asked for the photos they want to use for the memorial article, so we need to get to work on them, and when that's done we've got an exhibition to prepare for.'

'Yes, well, I've been working on that while you've been away.'

'Good. I'll take a look at where you're at this afternoon.'

Anna felt a wave of relief wash over her. He hadn't been in touch with her at all since he'd been away and she was beginning to think that he'd forgotten about her exhibition — and her for that matter.

'And,' he continued. 'Charlotte is coming round later to discuss the final arrangements.'

'Oh, good. I hope that means she'll finally tell us where the venue is.'

'Yes.' He frowned. 'I must admit she's being very cagey about that, says it's a surprise.'

'I look forward to being surprised then, as I'd really like to know where it's going to be.'

Daniel nodded. 'I know what you mean. All this secrecy is a bit strange.'

As she worked throughout the rest of the morning, she worried about her debut exhibition. She'd let them both take over and now she had hardly any control over what should be her proudest moment.

* * *

'So.' Charlotte clapped her hands, a huge grin on her face. 'The big reveal is that your exhibition is going to be held at . . .' She paused for dramatic effect. 'The Whigmore art gallery.'

Anna eventually found her voice. 'The Whigmore?'

'Yes, it's brilliant isn't it? They don't normally exhibit photography, so this is a real coup.'

'I know,' Anna said. 'I used to work there.'

'That's the best bit of all. You're going to be a huge success and they're going to see how far you've come since leaving them.'

'I'm not so sure about that.' Now Anna realised the reason behind Mark's phone call earlier in the week. He'd known all along, and she hadn't, and that made her feel at a complete disadvantage. She looked towards Daniel, hoping for some support. He was obviously as confused as she was.

'Charlotte, can you not see that this might make Anna feel uncomfortable? At the very least you could have run this by her before now. In case it didn't feel right to her.'

For a moment Charlotte looked uncertain, then the smile was back on her face. She looked directly at Anna. 'But that's precisely why I didn't tell you. You don't have the self-confidence and you'd have wanted to back out, but it's too late now. Believe me.'

'If you say so,' Anna said reluctantly. But she had a very bad feeling about this. A very bad feeling indeed.

CHAPTER NINETEEN

'You will come tonight, won't you?' Anna asked on the morning of the exhibition, before her father went to work.

'Of course I will. Harry and I will both be there. I've even had my suit dry-cleaned for the occasion.'

'I'd take you myself, only I have to be there early.'

'Don't worry about that. Harry and I can quite easily get the train, and you'll be busy enough without worrying about the two of us.'

'Just as long as you'll be there,' she said. 'Tonight won't mean anything to me if you're not.'

'I wouldn't miss this for the world.' He pulled her into a hug. 'I know I don't always show it, but I am very proud of you. And your mum would be too.'

And that's what she wanted to do tonight, she thought, as she stood on the threshold of The Whigmore — she wanted to make them both proud. Her mum would have loved to be here and it brought a tear to Anna's eye that she wasn't around to see it. But at least her dad had promised to come. And Harry. And of course she didn't want to fail in front of her former boyfriend, employer and the entire artistic world. She'd bought herself a new dress for the occasion, navy satin that cinched in at the waist, highlighting her figure, before falling to just below the knee in folds, accentuating her long legs. She knew she looked good — she should do, she'd spent a fortune on the dress and ages on her hair and make-up — but did she look like a professional photographer? How many times had she walked through this door without a moment's hesitation? But now this tiny step meant so much.

'You look gorgeous,' Daniel said, his words reassuring as she took a faltering step forward.

'I've never been so nervous in my life.'

'I know what you're thinking,' Daniel said. 'But the only thing that matters tonight is you and your photographs, and I can tell you, without any hesitation, they are absolutely amazing.'

'You think so?' Anna asked, seeking further assurance.

'I know so,' he replied.

* * *

Charlotte had been busy setting up the exhibition, not letting Anna even see what she was doing, never mind giving her any say in how the photographs were displayed. Initially Anna had been furious with her — they were her photographs after all. But Charlotte had reassured her that she knew what she was doing and that she was determined to make the exhibition a success, so she'd felt she had no choice but to let Charlotte get on with it, no matter how alienated it made her feel. But now, as Charlotte led her around the gallery, she had to admit the woman had exquisite taste. The photos were hung to show their greatest dramatic effect. Even though she'd spent the last few weeks staring at them while she edited, here in the gallery they looked completely different. Anna allowed a small smile to play on her lips. Daniel was right — they were good. And even if tonight wasn't a success, she knew she'd done her best work, and for that she could be proud of herself.

'Happy?' Charlotte asked.

'Very,' Anna replied. 'You've done an excellent job.'

Charlotte smiled. 'And I've enjoyed every minute of it.'

'I still think I should be paying you commission for anything that sells. That's if anything does sell,' she added, feeling a small crisis of confidence.

'And I've told you before, I don't want, or need, your commission. You've given me something to get my teeth into and I haven't felt this motivated in a long time. If my name is linked with launching your career, that will be payment enough. I'm thinking of setting up my own agency to launch young talent and to organise their events.'

'Daniel did mention that, but all the same, you've put a lot of effort into this.'

'It has been an absolute pleasure, so don't give it another thought.'

'You must be thinking along the same lines as Daniel. He was talking about mentoring young artists.'

'Yes, I know. That's what gave me the idea. He nurtures the talent and then passes them on to me.'

'You have it all worked out,' Anna said. 'I just hope that my photos are a success and I don't let you down.'

'Well, we don't need to worry about that.'

'Don't we?'

'No. I had a bit of a pre-launch earlier this afternoon with some of my contacts and I've already sold half a dozen photos. Have a look for the images with the red stickers.'

Anna gasped as she took another look around the gallery. Some of her favourite pictures had been sold and she felt proud that her work would soon be displayed in other people's homes. At the same time, she was a little sad that she'd have to let go of some of her babies.

'I've got the journos here tonight too, so we should get plenty of publicity, especially after your outing in the press the other week.'

'That's not something to be celebrated,' Anna said abruptly.

'No, of course not. But from what I heard, you and Daniel helped to save lives that night, so you should be proud of yourselves.'

Anna nodded. She didn't want to be reminded of what had happened — she still had nightmares about it.

'But tonight, my darling, is all about you. So let's put our smiles on and go and meet your adoring public.'

And Anna did manage to smile at that, because the thought that little old Anna from Rotherhithe would ever have achieved anything even close to an adoring public was suddenly very funny.

And mingle she did. All night, and as the gallery filled up it became hotter. Her feet began to ache in uncomfortable high-heeled shoes and her head spun from the glasses of champagne that were thrust into her hand.

Daisy was there with Tom, over the moon at her success, enthusing about Anna's talent and how she'd finally got the acknowledgement she'd always wanted. But the best part was when she saw her dad and Harry admiring the photos. She made her way over to them, delighted that they'd arrived. Her father wasn't a man who liked to venture out into unfamiliar surroundings. As the night had drawn on, and there'd still been no sign of them, she'd begun to wonder if he'd decided not to come after all. But they were here now and it felt as though her world was complete.

'I can't get over these pics, Anna, they're bloody brilliant,' her dad said after giving her a hug.

'Do you think so?' she asked, suddenly shy in his praise.

'I certainly do. Look at this one.' He pointed to a picture of St Mary's church. 'I've walked past that church nearly every single day of my life and I've never once wanted to go inside. But the way you've made it look, I want to see more and I'll definitely be paying a visit the next chance I get.'

'I knew you were talented,' Harry said. 'But I didn't know you were this talented. Well done.' He put his arm around her and kissed her on the cheek.

'I'm sorry that I haven't taken you more seriously in the past,' her father added. 'I should have been encouraging you, not hindering you.'

Anna's eyes filled with tears at the words she'd wanted to hear for so long.

* * *

Daniel watched as Anna was hugged by two men, one older and one younger, who he presumed must be her father and brother. He was glad they'd come tonight to support her. He knew she desperately wanted them to be proud of her and so they should be. She had incredible talent. Daniel looked around the gallery lit by her photography. The fact that she was self-taught, yet was able to produce such amazing images, was incredible. He hoped he'd taught her something too over the last few months. He knew that, if tonight was going to be the success he suspected it would be, he would once again be looking for a new assistant. He certainly didn't begrudge her the success, but his life would be poorer without her in it. Although, if he was no longer her employer, would that break down the barrier she had about mixing work with a relationship? He'd thought going away after the explosion would have helped to distance his feelings from her, but he'd spent the whole time thinking about Anna, wondering what she was doing and if she missed him too. And since he'd been back, he'd had to physically keep her at arm's length — the urge to reach out and pull her into an embrace was overwhelming. He'd caught her staring at him with a frown and knew she must have been wondering why he was being so distant, but it was the only thing he could do to stop himself from crossing a boundary.

He'd barely spoken to her all evening, but now he wanted to tell her how proud he was of her and to let her family know what a huge success she was about to be.

* * *

Anna turned from talking to her family to see Daniel walking towards her. She'd barely seen him all night and was keen to know what he thought about the exhibition. He'd been distant with her since he'd come back from Cheshire and she wondered if she'd done something to offend him. Maybe once tonight was over, they'd be able to sit down and have a proper chat, to fix whatever was wrong between them. Now, though, he was all smiles as she introduced him to her father and Harry.

'So you're the man who made all this happen then,' Andrew said once they'd been introduced.

'I wouldn't say that.' Daniel smiled back at him. 'My friend Charlotte did all the organising.'

'Yes, but you're the one who encouraged her. She has nothing but praise for you.'

'Dad!' Anna muttered.

'Well, that's very flattering, but it had very little to do with me and more to do with Anna. She's very talented.'

'It certainly looks that way, but I don't know where she gets it from. Neither me nor her mother were artistic. But I'm very proud of her.'

'We both are,' Harry added.

Anna felt the heat rise in her face, the praise overwhelming her, and once more she wondered what it would have been like if her mum was still here.

Charlotte tapped her on the shoulder.

'I'm sorry to interrupt, but can I borrow Anna? I've got some people I'd like you to meet.'

Anna allowed herself to be led away. It was typical that just as Daniel came over, Charlotte wanted her to go and mingle. But she knew she had to make the most of this opportunity. Although she was usually awkward about talking to new people, this was easier than she'd anticipated. There was no need to make small talk with them — everyone was keen to know all about her and it was simply a case of answering their questions.

As she chatted, she glanced over to where her brother and father were standing. She knew how uncomfortable her dad would be in this kind of environment and hoped he didn't think she was abandoning him. She was surprised to see that Daniel was still talking to them both, and even more so that her dad was laughing and looking completely at ease with him, which was more than he'd ever done with Mark.

Mark. If there was a downside to this evening it was definitely him. Mark was at his best at these events, schmoozing and ingratiating himself with clients, and tonight was no different. But she couldn't help noticing that whenever he glanced across to her, his eyes were as stony as flint. Did he really resent her success that much? His glares made her feel uncomfortable and she wished Charlotte had chosen a different venue. But then, she told herself, she was very lucky to have any venue at all, and she should be grateful. She would just have to avoid Mark and, hopefully, after tonight, she'd never have to see him again.

Eventually she managed to extricate herself from networking and made her way back over to her family.

'Hiya. Are you both okay?'

'We're fine, Anna, love,' her father said. 'We've had a lovely time, but we're going to head home now if that's okay with you?'

'Of course it is. I'm glad that you made it tonight. It means the world to me.'

'Not as much as it means to me. I wouldn't have missed this.'

'Let me get you a taxi. I don't want you two trekking home on the train.'

'Oh, no need to worry about us. Daniel is outside hailing one down for us.'

'He is?' Anna asked, surprised.

'Yes, he's such a lovely fella. I take back what I said about him being a slave driver when you first started working for him, he sounds like a decent boss, much better than that other bloke.' He glared at Mark who was across the room. Mark glared back at them and then turned away. Her dad continued. 'Though I doubt after tonight you'll be working for him much longer. More like you'll be looking for your own assistant.'

Anna looked at him in disbelief. The thought of not working with Daniel filled her with a sense of foreboding.

'Now, Daniel has said you might be going out afterwards, if you wanted to. So, enjoy the rest of the night and I'll see you tomorrow.' He gave her a quick hug and then, before he left, said, 'Enjoy your success. You deserve it.'

Anna watched open-mouthed as her father and brother left the gallery. She couldn't believe that in such a short time Daniel had won them round. And neither could she believe that her father seemed to like him that much. He'd certainly never taken to Mark. As though the thought of him had conjured him up, Mark appeared at her shoulder.

'Well done,' he said. 'Looks like you're an overnight sensation.'

'I'd hardly call it overnight.' Anna tried to defend herself. 'I've worked a long time to get this far.'

'And now you've made it.' The bitterness in his voice brought her up short.

'I'm on my way at least.'

'Good for you.'

'Does that annoy you, Mark? If so, I'm not sure why. You were the one who ended our relationship, remember?'

He ignored her question. 'What I don't understand is why you chose this gallery for your debut exhibition. It very much feels as though you're trying to rub my nose in your newfound success.'

'Of course I'm not. This is the last place I'd willingly choose for my exhibition. It was Charlotte who organised everything — I only found out last week that it was going to be here.'

'Oh, I see, you're not rubbing my nose in it because you're too good for us?'

'You're twisting my words!' she said. 'I just meant that, considering our history, we'd be better staying apart.'

'But unfortunately you did choose here.' His tone had taken a hard note that sent a shiver down her spine. Mark didn't like it when he didn't get his own way and would often lash out. While she had been with him he'd never been physical, but sometimes it had felt as though his cruel words had hurt as much as any blow. 'And Arthur Whigmore agreed to it without even running it past me.'

She looked around for Daniel, or anyone else who might put an end to their conversation, but Mark had cornered her in a place where no one was likely to be passing. 'I can't say I'm happy you've chosen to have your exhibition at the gallery you used to work at, sponsored by your new boyfriend.' He edged even closer to her — she could smell both the cloying fumes of his aftershave and the stench of stale sweat.

'He's not my boyfriend,' she replied, wondering why she needed to protest her innocence to Mark. He should be the last one to criticise someone flaunting a new relationship in front of their ex.

He edged even closer. 'Come off it, Anna. I've seen the way he looks at you, and don't forget about that little publicity stunt. The one after the London Fashion Show, remember?'

'That wasn't a publicity stunt, far from it, Mark.' She tried to keep her voice calm. 'It was a terrifying experience and we were lucky to come out alive.'

'And go on to better things, only weeks later.'

She tried to move away from him, but he grabbed hold of her upper arm and pulled her closer to him.

'What do you want from me, Mark?'

He almost growled at her. 'I'd have thought that was perfectly obvious.'

His grip on her arm tightened when she tried to shake him off. 'Mark, you're hurting me.'

'I don't mean to hurt you.' He loosened his grip on her slightly but didn't let her go. 'But I need you to understand how I feel. Why don't you come into my office so we can talk privately?'

'Because I don't want to. I have nothing left to say to you. So I suggest you let go of my arm and let me get tonight over and done with, then we'll never have to see each other again.'

'Don't be like that. I'm sorry about what happened with Jemima, but I couldn't help it. It felt as though I lost my mind for a little while. It's different now, though.'

'Yes, it is different,' she said, trying to free herself from him once again. 'Because I don't want anything to do with you.'

* * *

Coming back into the gallery after seeing Anna's father and brother into a taxi, Daniel automatically looked around to see where she was. Not finding her at first, he began to search for her. Eventually he spotted her standing in a dark corner, as close as she could possibly be to her ex-boyfriend, Mark. His heart plummeted into his stomach as he watched them. He knew from their conversations that Anna had been in love with Mark and that his betrayal had hurt her deeply. Daniel's first instinct was to get her away from him, so he couldn't hurt her any more, but what if she didn't want to be interrupted? What if she still had feelings for him? Daniel stayed where he was, watching them from a distance, trying to work out what was going on. It didn't take long.

Mark had a grip on her arm and he saw Anna trying to shake him off. Without thinking, Daniel headed straight towards them.

'Anna, this is where you are. I've been looking for you everywhere,' he said as he strode towards them. Mark glared at him, the look of hatred clear in his eyes, and Daniel knew he had been right to act upon his instinct.

'Do you mind? We were having a private conversation.'

'I think our conversation is over.' Anna tried to prise his hand from her arm. 'And if you don't mind, I'd like you to let go of me.'

'I'd do as the lady says,' Daniel said.

Mark laughed derisively. 'Oh, believe me, this one's no lady, but maybe you already know that.'

Daniel took a step closer, his fists balled by his side. Mark dropped his grip on Anna and she moved to stand beside Daniel.

'Don't, Daniel, he's not worth it. Let's go and enjoy the rest of the evening.'

Even though it belied his every instinct — he very much wanted to smash one of his fists into Mark's face — Daniel knew she was right. It would ruin her exhibition if he did anything, so instead he steered her silently away. Despite her upright demeanour, he could feel her trembling as they returned to the centre of the room.

'Are you okay?' he asked as she rubbed her arm. 'Did he hurt you?'

'No.' She shook her head. 'He was just trying to be intimidating.'

'It looks like he succeeded.'

She gave a shaky laugh. 'I suppose you could say he did. Thanks for rescuing me.'

'I didn't really do anything. But I'm glad you're okay.'

She nodded her head. 'I am. Although, I have to admit, it's taken the shine off tonight.'

'Perhaps it was a mistake to have the exhibition here after all,' he said. 'But it's certainly been a success. That's probably what's rattled him.'

She nodded. 'He said it was humiliating.'

'And what he did to you wasn't humiliating?'

She nodded. 'Yes, but I'm not after revenge, I just want to move on with my life.'

And that's what was so special about her, Daniel thought. She was a good and kind person who deserved the best in life, not snakes like Mark.

* * *

There was no doubt that Mark had unnerved her. But while there were still people in the gallery, Anna knew that she had to put a brave face on and pretend she couldn't be happier. In reality, all she wanted to do was to go home and climb into bed. Success was not the delight she had imagined it would be.

An hour later and the rest of the stragglers were getting ready to leave. Charlotte bustled over.

'Well, Anna, I think that's what you'd call an unmitigated success. You're going to be the talk of the town.'

Anna smiled but didn't mention that she didn't want to be the talk of the town. Yes, she wanted her work to be successful, but she'd rather keep everything else private. After tonight, though, she wondered if that would be possible.

'Thank you, Charlotte, for everything you've done.'

'Although next time, maybe choose a different gallery,' Daniel added. He'd stuck by her for the rest of the evening and Anna was grateful. She liked to think of herself as a strong, independent woman, but with Mark still in the room, glowering at her whenever she caught sight of him, it was comforting to have Daniel by her side.

Charlotte frowned. 'Why?'

'Let's just say it ruffled a few feathers and not in a good way.' He glanced towards Mark — Charlotte followed his gaze.

'He's my ex,' Anna added.

Charlotte clapped her hand to her mouth. 'Oh my God! Why didn't you say? I thought it was just your job you were moving on from.'

'Because by the time you told us it was too late,' Daniel answered for her.

Charlotte looked contrite. 'I'm really sorry, I'll make sure you don't have to have anything to do with him for the rest of the exhibition. I'll deal with everything.'

'Thanks, Charlotte. That means a lot,' Anna said.

'Good, well, now that's over and done with, who fancies going somewhere for a little celebration?'

'Not for me,' Anna said. 'I think I'd rather just go home.'

'Oh, but you must celebrate!' Charlotte said.

'Another time maybe.' She knew she was disappointing Charlotte, and that Charlotte was obviously on a high, but she suddenly felt drained, with no energy whatsoever. 'I think I'll just get a taxi home.'

'I'll come with you,' Daniel said. 'You can drop me off on the way.'

Charlotte shook her head. 'You are a pair of killjoys! Never mind, I'll finish up here, deal with his lordship over there. You two get off.'

* * *

Outside, the air hit Anna in a refreshing wave and she gulped it in, glad to be out of the gallery and its confines.

'It's a shame he ruined your big night,' Daniel said, standing close behind her on the pavement.

'What's done is done.' She sighed wearily.

'But whatever he did, everyone else loved you. Hang on to that.'

'I will,' she said, and yawned.

'You're tired. Why don't you stay at mine tonight? It's a much shorter journey and you're welcome to my spare room.'

Her instinct was to go home, sleep in her own bed, but Daniel's was much closer. His spare room was also much more comfortable than her single bed at home. It might be nice to have some company. His company. She knew she was treading on dangerous ground, but tonight she had enjoyed him standing beside her. The thought of leaving him filled her with sadness. 'Okay, I'll just message my dad to let him know I'm with you and I'll be back tomorrow.'

'Have you eaten anything today?'

She shook her head. 'No, I've been far too nervous.'

'How about I cook something for you and we'll relax for a while?'

She smiled. 'That does sound nice.'

* * *

'Oh, that's me stuffed!' Anna said after polishing off an omelette. 'I hadn't realised how hungry I was.'

They moved into the living room so they could sit more comfortably. While Daniel had been preparing the food, Anna had changed out of her dress into the T-shirt and leggings she'd been wearing earlier in the day. She leaned back on the sofa, enjoying the feeling of being able to relax.

'Thank you for tonight,' she said.

'What for?'

'You know, the Mark thing.'

'I didn't really do anything.'

'Yes, you did. Before you intervened I was beginning to get a little scared. And then sticking by me for the rest of the evening when he was glaring daggers at me. It meant a lot.'

'He's a bully, Anna, and I don't like bullies.' He paused. 'Tell me . . . did he ever hurt you?'

'Not physically, no. But he was vicious with his words. And his temper was always a little volatile, especially when he didn't get his own way. I was treading on eggshells a lot of the time.'

'And yet you loved him?' Daniel said quietly.

Anna nodded. 'I did. He wasn't like that at first.'

'No, they never are.'

She turned to face him. She needed to explain, because she was worried he thought she was foolish for having loved Mark.

'He can be very charming when he wants to be and that's what he was when we first met. I was vulnerable back then and didn't have much faith in myself. I was still struggling without Mum. He believed in me and he made me believe that I could be something too. When I applied for the job as the receptionist at the gallery I didn't even think I would get it, but by the time I left I was practically running the place.'

'Doing his job for him,' Daniel said dryly.

'Yes, I was. But I was good at it and it gave me a sense of accomplishment that I'd never had before.'

Daniel laughed. 'Why ever not? By all accounts you've practically held your family together since your mum died, as well as dealing with your own grief. You were only a teenager, don't forget. Most people would have gone off the rails, but you didn't. You should give yourself credit.'

'Maybe,' she said thoughtfully. She'd never looked at it like that before. She'd just done what she needed to do. What was expected of her. 'By the way, thanks as well for charming my dad.'

'I didn't charm him.'

'Well, he was full of praise for you, so you must have done something. Dad's not good with new people or environments.'

'I really liked him and we just got on. I could see he was uncomfortable but he came anyway, because he wanted to support you. He knows how much you do for him, for all of them, but he doesn't have the words to express that.'

Anna nodded. 'You're right. He doesn't show his emotions, so it's not easy to see what he's feeling.'

'Still waters run deep and all that.'

'Well, you've certainly got the measure of him. Which is more than Mark did. He didn't like my family and they didn't like him.'

'Can't say I'm surprised.'

'Whereas, you've got them eating out of your hand.'

'What can I say?' He grinned. 'I'm just a very special person.'

'Yes,' she said. 'I think you are.' She smiled at him and their eyes locked. The look of longing in his eyes took her breath away. She gazed back at him, time seeming to stand still. Then slowly, very slowly, they both leaned towards each other until their lips touched. The kiss was gentle at first, sending waves of heat tingling through her body. He pulled her closer — she pressed herself into him, wanting to feel the strength and warmth of his body against hers. Wanting to be as close to him as she could possibly be, wishing that they could morph into one being. The kiss deepened and so did her longing for him. Feeling bolder than she ever had done, she tugged at his shirt, wanting to touch his skin. Between kisses they undressed each other until they were both naked on the sofa.

He broke away and looked her in the eyes. 'Are you sure you want to do this?'

She nodded. 'I've never been more sure of anything in my life.'

He nodded and moved away from her, and she felt suddenly cold at his absence. She was relieved that he was only leaving her to make sure they were protected.

He began to kiss her again, their passion mounting once more, and then he was inside her, making her feel complete. Her longing built into a crescendo, followed by a glorious relief.

Afterwards he pulled a throw from the back of the sofa over them.

'Are you okay?' he asked softly.

'No,' she said, and watched him frown. 'I'm very much more than okay.'

The frown transformed into a smile and he nipped her neck gently with his teeth. 'That's not playing fair. Men can be vulnerable too. Especially after . . .'

'You've never really struck me as vulnerable.'

'What then? What do I strike you as?'

She hitched herself into more of a sitting position, making sure that the throw was covering her, suddenly feeling modest.

'Well, when I first met you, I thought you were the rudest man I've ever met.'

He laughed. 'No surprise there. I was pretty rude that day. But then I was in a bad mood and you were late.'

'Because I got lost!'

'And after the day I'd had, I was beginning to think that no one could be relied upon.'

'Well, then, I'm glad you gave me the chance to prove you wrong.'

He kissed her gently. 'Oh, so am I.'

She laid her head on his shoulder. 'You know, after Mark, I swore that I'd never get involved with someone I work with again, and here I am.'

'Well, I can understand why you'd think that. I've wanted to do this for so long, but I held off because of our working relationship. But we're more equal now.'

'Are we?'

'Of course we are. After tonight, your own career is really going to take off. If you want it to, that is?'

'It's what I've always dreamed of. But does that mean I'm out of a job?'

He grinned. 'I'll still need someone to help me, if you want to, but things are changing for both of us, especially if I develop my idea of setting up a school in Manchester.'

She frowned at his words. Being in Manchester would take him away from her. 'I guess you won't be around that much then?'

'I'll be spending more time up there, yes, but I'm not moving away, and it means that potentially our work won't need to interfere with our relationship.'

Despite her doubts about him working away, she decided to focus on the word 'relationship'.

'Our relationship?'

'If you want one?' he asked hesitantly.

She nodded. 'Yes, I think I do.'

'You're not the only one with doubts you know. I've got Ben to think about as well. And if I'm going to bring someone into my life then they have to be right for Ben too.'

'Yes, I completely agree.' She smiled, knowing how easy it would be to grow fond of Ben. Another hurdle crossed.

* * *

She was disorientated when she woke up the next morning, being in neither her own bed nor the spare bedroom in Daniel's house. The large bed seemed to engulf her, the pillows soft, the sheets made from crisp Egyptian cotton. She could have lain there all day given the chance. As she looked around the luxurious bedroom, she smiled at the memory of last night.

They'd woken in the early hours of the morning and made love again, that time being even more glorious than the first time. There was something about Daniel that made her feel protected and cared for. She feared she may need to guard herself — that was how she'd felt about Mark when they had first got together. She knew it wouldn't be easy negotiating both their careers, but at least now she had one, and that was down to Daniel encouraging her to believe in her abilities, which was more than Mark had ever done. It was different with Daniel, though. Unlike Mark, Daniel supported her and pushed her to achieve her own ambitions. Mark had been happy for her to achieve at work, as it reflected well on him, and had made it easier for him to do as little work as possible. But he'd never encouraged her photography. He could have easily hosted an exhibition for her ages ago, but all he'd done was put her down. Admittedly, then her work would have shown little of the quality it had now, but he hadn't even given her a chance.

CHAPTER TWENTY

'Someone looks happy,' Daisy said as she joined Anna at their regular table in the Angel.

'Do I?' Anna could barely keep the smile off her face. She felt like she'd been grinning like a fool since the night of the exhibition.

'I've seen that look before,' Daisy said darkly. 'And this time you can't deny it.'

'Deny what?' Anna took a sip of her wine.

'You know what. You and Daniel.'

'Maybe.' Anna's smile widened even further.

Daisy groaned. 'What is it with you and your bosses? Haven't you learned anything from last time?'

'This time it's different.'

'How is it different? He's still your boss.'

'Technically, yes, but things are changing.'

'How so?'

Judging by the frown on Daisy's face, Anna knew that she'd take some convincing. 'I'm still working for Daniel, but he's setting up a new project in Cheshire, so he's going to be spending more time up there. Which will give me time to concentrate on my own photography.'

'So it's going to be a long-distance relationship? How's that going to work?'

'It doesn't have to be long-distance, not initially anyway.'

'How come?'

'I'm thinking that when Daniel goes up to Cheshire, I can go with him, at least some of the time.'

Daisy had been about to take a sip of her wine but she banged her glass back on the table, causing some of the wine to spill over the top. 'And how exactly does that further your own career? This is just typical of you, going in all guns blazing.'

'I'm not,' Anna protested. 'And I have thought this through, I'm just not explaining it very well.'

'Go on then,' Daisy said, her face still sceptical.

'Okay, well, the exhibition was a huge success, and Charlotte has done a brilliant job on my PR. So I've got to work hard on getting my next exhibition together while people still remember my name.'

'And?'

'And, when I first went to Cheshire with Daniel I took some pictures in Chester. It's a fascinating city, so I'm going to contrast the buildings in that landscape to those here.'

'And conveniently your work will take you to where he is when he's there.'

'Yes.' Anna beamed. 'It's brilliant, isn't it?'

'Just be careful.'

Anna frowned. 'What do you mean?' She'd hoped her best friend would be happy for her, not critical of her.

'Just that you're pinning all your hopes on one person, and he does have a bit of a reputation, you said so yourself.'

'He was very lonely for a long time after his wife left, but he's not been like that recently.'

'Since he met you, you mean?'

Anna could clearly hear the sarcasm in Daisy's voice. She chose to ignore it, smiling instead. 'Maybe. And he absolutely adores his son. Surely that's a good reflection on his character?'

'Maybe, but doesn't that mean his son will always come first?'

'That's as it should be.'

'What about his ex-wife? Will she always come first?'

'No, of course she won't. There's a reason why she's his ex, you know?'

'Okay, have it your way.' Daisy sighed.

'Honestly, Daise, I thought you'd be pleased for me.'

'I am. I just don't want you to get hurt, that's all.'

'I won't.' Anna smiled at her. 'I know what I'm doing.'

Daisy's returning smile was rather more hesitant. 'I hope so Anna, I really do.'

* * *

The following weekend saw Anna heading back up to Cheshire with Daniel. She was looking forward to spending the weekend with both Daniel and Ben, as well as getting on with her project. They'd set off late, so instead of picking Ben up from school, Daniel drove straight to Lucinda's. Anna sat in the car while Daniel rang the doorbell to Lucinda's impressive home.

Anna thought about the wealth this family must have amassed between them, and she remembered the conversation she'd had with Daisy. She knew Daisy thought she was getting in too deep too soon, and she had to admit, albeit only to herself, sometimes she was afraid Daisy was right. Not that she doubted Daniel's feelings for her. Ever since the night of the exhibition they'd spent almost all their spare time together. They still had a good working relationship, but now that had been extended. She enjoyed cooking for him and enjoyed it even more when he cooked for her. After their meal they'd curl up on the sofa together to watch television, but they rarely managed to watch anything to the end because they soon became engrossed in each other. She couldn't get enough of their lovemaking — Daniel seemed to know exactly which buttons to press to send her to heights of passion she'd never known before.

And while they were in their little cocoon, she was content and at peace, confident in his love for her. It was only when they ventured out into the world that the doubts crept in. Watching Lucinda, her head bent close to Daniel's as they spoke on the doorstep, Anna's anxiety edged up a notch. Ex-model Lucinda was completely at ease in Daniel's world, as she was in this massive house in the country. She, Anna, was an East End girl, brought up in a small terraced house, who'd never experienced the wealth or lifestyle that came so naturally for these two. It made her wonder if she and Daniel had a long-term future or whether this was a happy dalliance that wouldn't last. Lucinda looked up and stared at her, frowning, and then turned back to Daniel, gesticulating as she spoke. She noted that Daniel's hands clenched and his shoulders looked tense. He shook his head and she wondered what they were arguing about. Was it her? Then Ben appeared in the doorway and suddenly they were all smiles again. He was carrying a small weekend bag and kissed his mother goodbye, before heading confidently over to the car. He flung his bag onto the back seat.

'Hi, Anna,' he called out cheerily as he clambered in and did his seatbelt.

'Hi, Ben, how are you?'

'Good, thanks. Are you and Dad working this weekend?'

She knew that Daniel hadn't told Ben about them yet, so she was careful in her answer. 'Not your dad, no. But I've got some work to do in Chester, so your dad offered to put me up.'

'That's great. Will you be working all weekend?'

'No, just Saturday, I think,' she replied, keeping a careful eye on Daniel and Lucinda who had returned to their arguing stances. 'It depends on how it goes really.'

'Oh, that's good. Do you think we might be able to go out together on Sunday, like we did before? I really enjoyed that.'

Anna smiled. Lucinda might not like her, but her son was a different matter. 'I enjoyed it too. Maybe we can ask your dad. I don't know what his plans are.'

'Maybe we can ask him together? He won't be able to say no if we both ask him.'

Anna laughed. 'I think that's a great idea.'

* * *

Anna spent a lovely day on Saturday wandering around Chester city centre. Whereas last time she'd taken in the sights that were iconic to the city, today she wandered round the back streets, focussing on the lesser-known architecture. She was fascinated by the city and thought it had been a day well spent. She was exhausted by the time she returned to Daniel's house and was more than happy to play board games with Ben while Daniel cooked dinner. She found it hard not to touch Daniel while she was here, used to the familiarity of each other when they were in London, but she knew he wasn't ready to reveal their relationship to Ben. Not being able to touch him during the day was a price she was willing to pay just to be here.

'So, the weather forecast looks good for tomorrow,' Daniel said as he served up dinner. 'Who fancies going to the zoo?'

'Yeah!' Ben shouted. 'I love going there!'

'I haven't been to a zoo for ages,' Anna said. 'So that's good for me too. Might get some photo opportunities as well.'

'I'm going to take my camera!' Ben said enthusiastically.

'So you're a photographer too?' Anna asked, surprised.

'Yes, I love it. Dad bought me a camera and showed me how to use it properly.'

Daniel grinned. 'And he's pretty good.'

'Must be in the genes.' Anna smiled at them both.

'Must be,' Daniel replied.

'Why don't you take some photos as well, Dad? Then we can have a competition to see who takes the best.'

Anna nodded. 'That sounds like a really good idea.'

Daniel groaned. 'Sounds more like a busman's holiday to me, but yes, count me in.'

* * *

As predicted, the weather was sunny the next morning. Daniel and Anna were up bright and early to pack a picnic before they left. She was so happy that she felt like singing as she worked. She liked spending time with Daniel on her own, but she realised that time with him and Ben was just as special. Although she didn't feel she had any right to it, she thought they made a proper family unit.

* * *

Daniel watched with pride as Anna and Ben oohed and ahhed at the animals in competition with each other. He hung back, letting them get the best shots, happy to watch how well they got on together. Anna's enthusiasm was incredible — the fact that they both seemed at ease in each other's company was extremely important to him. The only real fly in the ointment was Lucinda. She'd been pretty scathing about Anna when he'd gone to pick up Ben, had instantly guessed their relationship was a lot deeper than he'd been letting on. And judging by the catty remarks she'd made about Anna, he wouldn't be surprised if she was the tiniest bit jealous. Not that she had any right to be, as she had Axel. But he suspected that, while she didn't want him for herself, she didn't want anyone else to have him either. She'd just have to get used to the idea. Anna was in his life and that was the way it was going to stay.

Later that afternoon, as a roast chicken cooked in the oven, they judged the photographs they'd all taken that day. Ben won of course, as he'd taken some amazing photographs, which made Daniel incredibly proud. Ben had many hobbies, but it gave Daniel a special buzz to think that he was following in his own footsteps. He would never dictate what Ben should do with his future — Daniel would always encourage his son to follow his heart — but he was glad they had a shared interest. They spent so little time together.

* * *

Back in London, having returned from their time in Cheshire, Anna's phone rang with an unknown number.

'Hi, is that Anna?'

'Yes,' she answered cautiously.

'I'm Eva, I don't know if you remember me?'

'Eva, from the fashion show?'

'That's right.'

'Of course I remember you. How are you?'

Eva gave a small laugh. 'Well, let's just say I've been better.'

'Are you still in hospital?'

'Yes, I'm going to be here for a while.' Her voice cracked. 'They had to amputate my leg.'

'Oh!' Anna cried out. 'I'm so sorry. I could see that it was in a bad way. I put a tourniquet around the top of your leg — you were losing a lot of blood.'

'You did that?' Eva's voice was quiet.

'Yes, I'm sorry it didn't work.'

'But it did. I may have lost my leg but I'm still here, and that's thanks to you.'

'Oh, I see.' Anna was humbled. 'I'm glad I could help.' Once more she was thankful that she'd gone on that first aid course for The Whigmore. Some kind of instinct or retained learning must have kicked in, and it meant Eva was still alive.

'You did more than help.'

'I did come to see you at the hospital.'

'I know, that's where I got your number from. You left a note.'

'Yes, of course I did. Sorry, I'm not thinking straight.'

'It's probably a shock to hear from me.'

'Yes, it is a bit.'

'Well, the thing is, I wonder if you can come and see me? I've got a favour to ask.'

'Of course, whenever you like.'

'How about tomorrow?'

'Tomorrow?' Tomorrow Daniel was heading back up to Cheshire to do some research on his photography school project, and she'd been planning to go with him . . . but this seemed more important. She could always get the train up afterwards. 'Tomorrow's fine. What time?'

* * *

Anna sat next to Eva's bed, feeling humbled by the young woman. She was obviously in a lot of pain, had lost her leg and probably her livelihood, all from being in the wrong place at the wrong time. And yet here she was, looking positively upbeat.

'I can't believe that after everything that's happened to you, you've still got a smile on your face.'

'Oh, don't get me wrong, I have my bad days. I've lost so much, and life will never be the same again. But then I think about the people who didn't survive and I give myself a stern talking to. Which is why I asked you to come and see me today.'

'You wanted to ask me a favour?'

'Yes, that's right. I've been reading a lot about you recently. Since your exhibition. I'd have loved to have come and seen it, but obviously . . .' She looked towards her leg.

'I'm working on another one — maybe next time?'

'I'll definitely be there if I can. I've seen some of the photos online and they look incredible.'

'Thank you.' Anna felt the heat rise in her face. She didn't know if she'd ever get used to hearing praise about her work.

'And you work for Daniel Redfern, is that right?'

'Yes. That's why we were at the fashion show. I'm his assistant.'

'And he took the photos that have been in *Fashionista*.'

Eva handed her the magazine and Anna saw the model's face staring out at her. She couldn't believe the difference between the woman in the glossy pages to the diminutive person in the hospital bed, with no make-up and her blonde hair scraped back into a ponytail. Not that she wasn't still beautiful, she just looked very different.

'We weren't sure what to do with the photos at first. We sent the unedited versions over to the magazine so the police could see them, but then they asked us to edit the ones of people who either died or who were injured, as they wanted to do a tribute to them. They did ask for your permission, didn't they?'

'Oh yes, of course they did.'

'I wasn't sure whether people would think it distasteful. But it wasn't my decision to make.'

Eva took the magazine back from her and focused on the pictures in front of her. 'I think they handled it really well. It's not distasteful at all. At least I don't think so, and it's wonderful to have a record of what life was like the moment before it all changed.'

'Oh!' Anna said. 'I'm not sure whether to be happy or sad about that.'

'It is what it is.' Eva forced a smile. 'I didn't mean to make you maudlin. I like the pictures. In fact, I think they're brilliant, which is why I asked you here.'

'Go on.'

'I want to document my recovery on Instagram. I want people to know that, as devastating as losing a limb is, it's not the end. I will recover from this and I will go on to do bigger and better things.'

Anna was speechless. She was astounded by Eva's bravery and determination. Eventually she found the words. 'I have absolutely no doubt that you will.'

'And the favour I'm asking, is will you photograph it for me? I'll pay you of course.'

'No!' Anna said, and then realising Eva could take her response the wrong way, hastily added, 'I mean, yes, of course I'll photograph you, but I wouldn't dream of taking any payment.'

'But you must.'

'No. I want to do this for you and I'll be offended if you even mention money again.'

Eva nodded. 'Fair enough.'

'So, when do we start?'

'How about tomorrow? I've got a physio session to help me develop strength in my upper body. That should be a laugh.'

Anna smiled at Eva's self-deprecating humour. It would mean putting her Cheshire plans on hold, but she really wanted to do this. More so, she *needed* to do it.

'Tell me when and where, and I'll be there.'

CHAPTER TWENTY-ONE

'So, does that mean you won't be coming up this weekend?'
Daniel asked when Anna phoned him later that afternoon.

'I'm sorry. I wanted to, but I couldn't say no to Eva.'

'Of course you couldn't. I understand that.' And he did,
but that didn't mean he wasn't disappointed. 'I'll miss you.'

'Me too.'

After they said their goodbyes he switched off the phone,
aware of two pairs of eager eyes watching him.

'Anna's not coming?' Ben asked, his voice full of
disappointment.

'No, I'm afraid not.'

Lucinda, who'd brought Ben round to stay for the weekend, snorted. 'Letting you down already, is she?'

Anger rose at his ex-wife's comment. 'No, she's not.
There's something important she needs to do. It's a work thing.'

'That's what you get when you give your assistant ideas
above their station.'

'Lucinda! Please!' He glanced at Ben to warn her not to
behave like this in front of him. She'd been tetchy since he'd
arrived back in Cheshire. He wondered if she was annoyed
with him wanting to see more of Ben — perhaps it was

upsetting her routine. But on a more cynical level he thought she might be jealous. He'd come clean to both of them the previous night about Anna and him being together. He'd thought it best to tell them when Anna wasn't around, give them time to get used to the idea before they saw her next. Ben had been delighted at the news. Lucinda not so much.

'Right, well, I'll leave you to it,' Lucinda said.

'Can you come and see my room first, Mum? You've never seen it before,' Ben asked. Lucinda looked to Daniel for approval and he nodded. While they were gone, Daniel put the kettle on to make some coffee. It didn't bother him if Lucinda was jealous of him and Anna. In fact, he understood it — he'd felt the same way when she'd first got together with Axel. But her snide comments were something he wasn't going to put up with. Despite their differences, they'd always worked hard to put Ben first, and he didn't want that undermined just because the dynamics had changed.

'Mum loves my room,' Ben said when the pair of them came back downstairs.

'Yes, it's very nice. You're a lucky boy to have two such wonderful bedrooms.'

'I am, aren't I?' Ben said, smiling. 'Can I go and watch some telly now?'

'Yes, of course you can.' Daniel was glad of the chance to speak to Lucinda alone. 'Do you want some coffee?'

She looked surprised for a moment. 'If you want me to stay?'

'Yes, I think we need to talk.'

She groaned as she pulled out a chair. 'I knew it! I'm about to get a lecture.'

'I'm not going to lecture you. Have I ever done that?' He brought over two mugs of coffee and sat down next to her.

'No, I suppose not, but I sense your disapproval.'

'I appreciate that things are changing and that can be difficult to deal with. But we've always promised that, whatever happened, we'd do right by Ben. I realise I've upset the apple cart by wanting to see more of him, and I do appreciate you letting me do that. You'd be quite within your rights to make me stick to our agreed routine.'

'I've never wanted to stop you from seeing him,' Lucinda replied. 'It's always the location that's got in the way, what with your work being in London. This is my home and I never want to move from here again. But now that you're planning on spending more time here, perhaps we could . . .'

'Perhaps we could what?'

Lucinda shifted uncomfortably in her chair. 'You're right, we've always tried to be amicable for Ben's sake, but a lot has happened since we split and maybe now we can start being better friends.' She placed her hand over his. 'We used to be really good friends, didn't we?'

He pulled his hand away. 'I think being amicable is enough for now.'

She scowled. 'Why, wouldn't Anna like it?' Her voice was bitter.

'I don't think Axel would like it much either.'

'No, I suppose not,' she said swiftly. 'Well, I'd better go. I'll just say goodbye to Ben and then see myself out.'

Daniel stared after her as she left, convinced she'd implied they could be a lot more than friends. He wondered if her sudden change in attitude was a knee-jerk reaction to him no longer being available. There had been a time when he would have jumped at the chance of getting back together, but meeting Anna had made him realise how wrong he and Lucinda were for each other. And while, from Ben's point of view, being a family again would be ideal, he knew it would never work. Not with Lucinda.

* * *

It had been five days since Anna had seen Daniel. While she'd been incredibly busy, she'd missed him desperately and couldn't wait to see him again.

She'd decided to cook a meal to welcome him home. She'd dressed up in a little black dress, set the table with candles and queued up some music to play softly in the background while they ate.

As he walked through the door he dropped his bag, pulled her into his arms and kissed her thoroughly.

'Wow, you look amazing. And something smells amazing too.'

'Welcome home,' she said simply and kissed him again.

'Whatever it is you have cooking, would it spoil if it waited a while?'

'I think it will be okay.' She made sure that everything was turned off before she allowed herself to be led upstairs.

Afterwards, they sat at the dining table in their dressing gowns, eating the beef bourguignon she'd cooked for him.

'This is delicious,' he said between mouthfuls. 'And it's so good to be here with you. I've missed you.'

She smiled at the thought of him being here with her. It was his home, not hers, but she'd been spending so much time there recently, she could almost imagine it was her home too.

'I've missed you too. Did you make good progress?' she asked him.

'I did. I met a woman who had her own school and she was happy to show me round.'

'Wasn't she worried that you'd be in competition with each other?'

'No, it's a completely different market. She's catering for the hobbyist who can afford it. It was interesting to see what courses she runs, although I think mine will have to be more structured, maybe even leading to a qualification.'

'That could mean a lot of red tape.'

'Yes, it would. So I went around a couple of colleges to see what they're offering. I'm still not sure I know which way I want to go with this, but the research is good. I don't want to commit to anything before I'm good and ready.'

'So it looks like we're going to be spending more time apart then?'

'Unless you come with me?' He reached for her hand.

'Well, I still need to do some more work on my Chester exhibition, but after that I don't know what I'll be doing.'

He squeezed her hand. 'I don't like being away from you any more than you do, but whatever happens we'll make it work.'

'We'll just have to, won't we?' She'd realised that being apart from him for a while was better than not having him at all.

'You know why I'm doing this, don't you?'

'Of course. I know how much you miss seeing Ben, and I'd never begrudge you spending more time with him. How is he?'

'Great.' The way Daniel's face lit up when he spoke about his son made her realise the joy he'd miss out on if he didn't see more of him. She could never stand in the way of that. 'In fact, he breaks up for the summer on Wednesday, and Lucinda was talking about bringing him down here for a week during the holidays.'

Anna nearly choked on a mouthful of food. 'Really? I thought she hated London.'

'She hated living here. But Axel's going to be down here recording, so she's coming with him. She thought it might be nice for me to see more of Ben without me doing the travelling.'

'That's nice of her.' Anna could barely keep the scepticism out of her voice. From what Daniel had said, however much they tried to make it work for Ben, it had largely been on her terms.

'She was a bit frosty when I first told her about us, but maybe she's coming round to the idea.'

'Maybe.' Anna didn't believe that for a second.

Daniel leaned back in his chair. 'Enough about my ex-wife. Tell me all about your meeting with Eva.'

'Oh, she's so amazing. I can't believe how upbeat she is.'

'It's good that you're helping her.'

'How could I not? And I'm enjoying it. She's great to be around and I think it's important people realise the long-term effects these things have.'

'Yes. Once the headlines disappear, it's easy to forget about it, but not for those who were there or lost someone.'

'No, it's not.'

'Still having nightmares?'

She nodded. 'Although I think I'll sleep better tonight with you by my side.'

'I think I will too.' He smiled.

* * *

It was great to have Daniel back — they soon fell into a routine of working together and separately on their individual projects. Eva's Instagram posts were getting great engagement and she'd even been asked to do some magazine articles, for which she had insisted that Anna provide the photographs. It felt strange going out on shoots where she was the lead photographer rather than the assistant. But Daniel was on hand to give her all the advice she needed, and plenty of moral support. Sometimes she wanted to pinch herself — she could barely believe she'd been catapulted into the career she'd always dreamed of, with a handsome and loving partner who supported her all the way. When she compared it to the life she had had only a few months ago, which had consisted of drudgery, conflict and heartache, she was amazed to realise how far she'd come in such a short time. She just hoped that nothing would come along to burst the bubble.

* * *

Anna was just packing up in the studio late the following Wednesday when her phone rang. She picked it up from the desk, startled to see Jack's name flash up on the screen. No one had heard from him since he'd left, though she'd tried to contact him several times.

'Jack.'

Daniel looked up as she mentioned her estranged brother's name, a frown creasing his forehead.

'Anna, hi.'

'Long time no hear. How are you?'

'Not so great to be honest. I'm at the City of London police station. I've been arrested.'

Anna gasped, dropping onto a chair. 'What for?'

'Robbery.'

'Robbery? Jack, what on earth's going on?'

'It's a long story. And I don't have time. I need a solicitor. They've given me a duty solicitor but he's useless. I know I shouldn't expect any help from you after all I've done, but can you? Can you help me, Anna? Please?'

'Jack, I don't know any solicitors.' She looked across to Daniel in a panic. Jack sounded desperate, not the self-assured cocky young man he'd been at home.

'I'll sort it,' Daniel said.

With a wave of relief Anna told Jack, 'Don't worry, we'll find someone and we'll be with you soon.'

She heard Jack exhale. 'Thank you, Anna. You don't know how much this means to me.'

'You're my brother,' she replied. That's all that mattered.

'I won't forget this,' he said. 'Anna, please don't tell Dad.'

'I won't. Not now at least. But when this is sorted you'll need to tell him yourself.'

'I can't.'

'You can and you will,' she said sternly. 'That's my condition for helping you. I want you to sort things with Dad. A family needs to stick together.'

'Okay, I'll try.' She heard someone in the background. 'My time's up. I've got to go. But thank you, Anna. I really mean that.'

She ended the call and sank down in her chair, suddenly deflated. Immediately Daniel was by her side, holding her close to him as she tried to regain her equilibrium. Eventually he pulled away from her.

'I'll try to get hold of my solicitor before he leaves the office. He works for a big firm so I'm sure he'll know a decent criminal lawyer.'

'Thank you, Daniel, I really appreciate it.'

'That's okay, family is family.'

'I doubt Jack can afford it, but I'll pay whatever it costs.'

'Don't worry about that. We'll sort out the finances later. The most important thing for now is helping Jack.'

* * *

Anna and Daniel had been sitting in the waiting room of the police station for what seemed like hours. True to his word, Daniel had found a lawyer, who was with Jack while he was being questioned. Anna was sick with worry, wondering how bad things really were. Eventually the solicitor appeared.

'How bad is it?'

He shook his head. 'Let's go somewhere away from here.'

Anna's stomach lurched. If he didn't want to talk about it at the police station, it must be worse than she'd thought.

They went to a wine bar near to the station. Daniel went to the bar while Anna sat down with the solicitor.

'Please, Mr Braithwaite, how much trouble is Jack in?'

'Call me Simon,' he replied. 'And I'm afraid it's not good. It seems that Jack and two other men attempted to rob an off-licence.'

'Oh, God! I can't believe it. My dad kicked him out and no one knew how he'd been living since then. But I never thought it would lead to this.'

'That's not all. Two of the men were carrying guns. When the owner refused to hand over the money, he was shot.'

Daniel put the drinks down on the table with a thump. 'Was he badly hurt?'

Simon shook his head. 'Fortunately the man was a pretty poor shot, or only intended to wound, and shot him in the arm.'

Finally able to speak, Anna asked, 'Was Jack carrying a gun?'

'No, he was the look out. The shopkeeper must have had a panic button, because soon after the shooting the police arrived. The other two fled but Jack stayed behind to administer first aid, and that's when he was arrested.'

'But if he tried to help and he wasn't carrying a gun, will that be better for him?'

Simon paused before answering. 'Well, you'd hope so, wouldn't you? But have you heard of joint enterprise?'

She shook her head. 'No.'

'It's where someone can be convicted for the crime of another, if the court decides that they either encouraged the crime or foresaw it could happen.'

Anna felt sick. 'So he could be convicted of the shooting, even though he wasn't carrying a gun and he stayed to help?'

'I'm afraid so.'

Daniel put his hand over hers and she was grateful for its warmth. She felt icy cold.

'There are many people who don't believe that joint enterprise is just, so that could work in Jack's favour. He told me that he was coerced into being there because he owed one of the men money, and that they told him the guns were firing blanks. So we'll have to work the evidence to try to prove he was there unwillingly and that he couldn't have envisaged the outcome.'

'Will that work?'

'We can try. But your brother will be spending time in prison, whatever the outcome. Tomorrow he'll go to court and it's likely he won't get bail.'

'So he'll go to prison straight away?'

'I'm afraid so.'

'And the other men? Have they been arrested?'

'Yes. But because they were both armed they'll be sent to higher security prisons, so hopefully that will keep your brother safe.'

'Because he's testifying against them?'

'Yes. I've made him aware of the consequences, but he's insistent that he wants to tell the truth.'

'Well, at least there's some good in him.' Anna sighed.

CHAPTER TWENTY-TWO

Anna heaved the bags of food into the hallway, put them down and closed the door behind her. It was Ben's last night before he went back to Cheshire and Anna wanted to make it special. It had been a joy having him around this week and she'd seen firsthand how much Daniel had enjoyed spending more time with his son. He'd miss him all the more after today, but she'd do her best to distract him next week. Part of her wished Lucinda could settle in London so that the separation wasn't so great, but then she didn't think she'd enjoy having her any closer. She'd been a constant irritation this week. Anna had noticed her linger far longer than was necessary to either drop Ben off or to pick him up. She also hadn't missed the way Lucinda's eyes constantly strayed to Daniel, or the way she had to touch him, resting her hand on his arm whenever she had the opportunity. It was definitely odd behaviour for an ex-wife.

She heard voices in the kitchen and wondered if Charlotte had called round as she often did, but as she went down the hallway she realised it was Lucinda speaking. She froze for a moment, wondering what to do. She needed to go into the kitchen to put the food away, but she couldn't face seeing Lucinda.

'Daniel, we were good together once. We could be again.'

Anna's mouth dropped open in shock at Lucinda's words — she found that she couldn't move.

'Lucinda, I—'

'Please just hear me out. I know we couldn't make it work before, but a lot of water has gone under the bridge since then. I'm much happier now. Going back home has given me the stability I never had when I was here. It was the location that got in our way before. But now that you're not so focused on living here, we could make it work together in Cheshire, with you coming back to London when you need to.'

'Lucinda—'

'Think about it. It would be so much better for Ben to have us under one roof rather than being shipped from pillar to post every other weekend.'

Lucinda paused when Daniel remained silent, and Anna could only assume he was considering her proposal. When he didn't reply, Lucinda continued.

'We had such a good time together the other week, just the three of us. Imagine that happening every day.'

Anna felt sick. He hadn't mentioned anything about the three of them spending time together when she wasn't there. But then of course he wouldn't, would he? Unable to face hearing his reply, Anna left her shopping bags in the hallway and fled.

* * *

At first, all he could think about was living back with Ben again. Not having to spend only every other weekend with him, but be involved in his life on a daily basis. But that, of course, came with a price. He'd loved Lucinda once, a long time ago. Over the years he'd taken off the rose-tinted glasses and begun to see her for what she was. Needy, for one. Highly strung for another. And her mood swings were phenomenal. When he'd lived with her, he'd never known what he'd be coming home to. A lot of that had been due to hormones, both pregnancy and postnatal, but he could still see it in her now, the need to always have her own way. There was no such thing as compromise in Lucinda's book. Did he really want to go back to that?

And then he thought of Anna and the relationship he had with her. Theirs was a truly equal partnership. They understood each other, could talk to each other, were interested in the same things. And she went out of her way to make him happy, as he did her. Anna was easy-going and she was beautiful on the inside and out. Did he want to swap that for living with Lucinda? The honest answer was a definite 'no', even if it meant not living with his son.

'Lucinda, I . . .' Daniel hesitated, knowing that the words he used now could change everything. She would expect him to jump at this opportunity and wouldn't like being turned down. If he got it wrong, it could jeopardise his flexible access to Ben. 'I'm very flattered by you asking me. And it would be great to spend more time with Ben. But . . .' He paused. 'But I don't think getting back together would work. You know we drive each other crazy, and if we tried and it didn't work out, that would really hurt Ben.'

'You're turning me down?' Her voice was full of steel.

'I am. But only because I think it's the right thing to do. We nearly destroyed each other before. It took me so long to get over you and I suspect it was the same for you. I couldn't bear to hurt you or be hurt like that again.'

'I see. And here's me thinking that's what you wanted. You've certainly made it seem like that recently.'

'I'm sorry if you think I've misled you. That was never my intention.'

'You'd prefer to keep your little photographer girl, would you?'

'It's not about Anna. It's about us.'

'Well, have it your way. I'll bring Ben over later and he can spend his last night with you. But we're leaving first thing in the morning, so he'd better be ready.'

She turned on her heel and stalked off down the hallway towards the front door. On one hand, that had gone better than he'd been expecting, but still, he thought as the door slammed behind her, he didn't think this was the last he'd hear of it.

* * *

Anna wandered aimlessly until she found herself beside Hyde Park. She walked in, found the nearest bench and sat down. She could scarcely believe what she'd just heard. Was there a chance that Daniel and Lucinda would get back together? She wondered if she should have stayed to hear his answer, then she would've known for certain. But that moment's hesitation had told her he was at least thinking about it. Or perhaps he was just in shock. She wanted to believe that. But she kept remembering how Lucinda had said they'd spent time together when she wasn't there. And Daniel hadn't told her. Surely if there was nothing in it, he would have mentioned it to her? From now on, whenever he was in Cheshire without her, would she be wondering whether he was with Lucinda? The mother of his child. They'd be a family again. The three of them. Daniel could be the parent he wanted to be. If Daniel and Lucinda could make it work a second time around, it would be the perfect solution.

Of course it would crucify her. The thought of not having him in her life produced a stabbing pain in her chest. But she loved him so much she couldn't bear for him not to be happy. And so she decided that, if that's what he chose, she wouldn't stand in his way. Her life was here in London. Her career was taking off. She had her next exhibition coming up and Eva's Instagram was such a success. Eva was thinking of writing a book, using Anna's photographs to illustrate it. Anna could certainly keep herself busy. And then there was her family — especially Jack.

Anna had managed to convince Jack that their father needed to know what had happened before the court hearing. She'd wanted Jack to be the one to tell him, but it had been impossible from his police cell, so she had been the one to break the news. Of course, her father had been devastated, and he'd blamed himself for throwing Jack out of the house.

'You couldn't have known it would come to this,' she'd said in an effort to reassure him.

'I knew the way he was going, I should have tried harder to help him, not turn my back on him.'

'I doubt he would have listened to you then.' She paused. 'I know it might not seem like it now, but this could be a good thing for him in the long run.'

'How on earth do you make that out?'

'I only spoke to him briefly on the phone, but he was a different Jack. I think this has been a real wake-up call for him. He's hit rock bottom and now the only way is back up.'

'I hope you're right.' Her father didn't sound convinced.

'I do too. I think we need to look to the future, not the past. Right now, Jack needs our support, not recriminations or guilt.'

He nodded slowly. 'Yes, I think you're probably right.'

And so they had both attended the court hearing where, as the solicitor had predicted, Jack had been remanded in custody until sentencing.

Anna shifted uncomfortably on the bench. At least, as he was pleading guilty, he wouldn't have to wait for a trial before he found out his fate. The one good thing about all this was that Jack had promised to send them both visiting orders. While the prospect of visiting him in prison terrified her, at least now they had a hope of mending the rift in their family. So, right now, her life was here, where she could once more support her family.

Thinking about families reminded her of Ben, and the prospect of never seeing him again brought a sob to her throat. For now, though, until he'd gone back home, she'd just have to put her big-girl pants on, and pretend she hadn't heard the conversation that had shattered her happiness.

* * *

Daniel was still in the kitchen when she arrived back, but there was no trace of anyone else having been there.

'Hey! You've been gone ages. I was beginning to think you'd got lost.'

'Sorry, it just took me longer than I'd expected to find everything I needed.'

They were planning a Chinese banquet for tonight, Ben's favourite. Daniel had suggested they order a takeaway, but Anna had wanted to cook things herself, to show Ben the effort she wanted to make for him.

'And you've got everything?'

'Yep. So I want you out of the kitchen. I need to be alone to produce a gastronomic masterpiece.'

'Fair enough. Have you got time for a coffee first?'

'Sure.' She wondered if he was going to talk to her about Lucinda's visit. She began to put the shopping away as a form of distraction. 'What have you been up to this morning?'

'Nothing much. Working mainly. I've just taken a break now.'

He was lying to her. At the very least by omission. She opened the fridge so she had her back to him. He wouldn't see her blinking back tears.

'Productive day?' She hoped her voice didn't sound as strangulated to him as it did to her.

'Not really.' He put the coffee down on the breakfast bar. 'I'd better get back to it, I suppose. Give me a shout if you need help with anything.'

'Sure.' She shut the fridge door, but in the empty kitchen she was still cold.

* * *

Daniel felt like such a coward fleeing from the kitchen like that. When Anna had come back he'd had every intention of telling her about Lucinda's visit but, when it came down to it, he just couldn't find the words. How could he explain to

Anna what had taken place that morning when he couldn't make sense of it himself?

Looking back at the week, Lucinda had certainly been round a lot more than she usually was. Lingering whenever she dropped Ben off or picking him up, and inviting Daniel in whenever he did the same. But he had put it down to the fact that she was in London, out of her comfort zone, and with Axel working he'd assumed she was lonely. And he'd felt sorry for her. He knew how much she hated London, and had even wondered why she'd come to stay in the first place. But he'd been glad of the opportunity to see Ben on his home turf.

Daniel thought about Anna as he tried and failed to work. He should have come clean with her. Told her about Lucinda suggesting they get back together again, but that he'd turned her down. He'd lied by saying the only thing he'd been doing that morning was working — he hated lies. She didn't deserve that, especially as she was in the kitchen preparing a meal for Ben on his last night in London. She was so good with Ben and that made him love her all the more. Love. He'd never told her, but now he had to admit to himself that he was in love with her. And the last thing he wanted to do was to hurt her. He'd noticed how she seemed to go into her shell whenever Lucinda was around. He also couldn't fail to see how Lucinda eyed Anna with daggers, making barbed comments about her whenever Ben was out of earshot. Slowly Anna was growing in confidence, and he knew that if she found out Lucinda had tried to get back with him, even if he'd turned her down, it would knock her. Anna found it difficult to trust and in her mind it would cast doubt on their relationship. On the other hand, he didn't want this to come between them. He would tell her, he decided, but not today. Not when Lucinda would be dropping Ben off later, and they'd be spending his last night with his son. Tomorrow, he decided — he would tell her tomorrow. And he'd try to do it in such a way that she knew she could trust him and had nothing to fear from his ex-wife.

* * *

'Oh, wow, Anna, have you really done all this for me?' Ben's face was a picture when she showed him the food set out on the dining table. That was worth every second of her toiling in the kitchen. As she'd worked, she'd tried to push the thought of Daniel and Lucinda to the back of her mind. It kept popping to the surface, but she told herself to ignore it. Tonight was about Ben and that was all that mattered. Tomorrow she would confront Daniel about what had actually happened this morning, but, for now, she would concentrate on the present.

'Yes, I did do all this for you, because I know how much you enjoy your Chinese. These are just the starters, so let's tuck in before they go cold.'

All through the evening she kept looking at Ben, trying to remember the features of his face, locking in the memory of the three of them together. She feared it could be the last time she'd see him.

After they'd finished eating, the three of them settled onto the enormous sofa in Daniel's living room and watched *Hotel Transylvania*, Ben's favourite film. If this had been a normal night she'd probably have felt utterly content. But tonight it was bittersweet. It was all she could do to blink back the tears and force a smile onto her face.

From time to time she caught Daniel staring at her with a puzzled expression. Was he wondering what was the matter? Or did he know this might be the last time they would spend time like this? It was almost a relief when Daniel announced it was time for Ben to go to bed. She offered to take him up and afterwards went to bed herself. When Daniel came up, she feigned sleep. He didn't attempt to wake her up.

* * *

The next morning she was up early, mixing pancakes for Ben.

'You really do show your love by feeding people, don't you?' Daniel's voice at the kitchen doorway startled her. The whisk jerked upwards, splashing pancake batter over the worktop.

'I just want to give him a good breakfast before his long journey.'

Daniel sighed. 'It's been great having him here, hasn't it? I'm really going to miss him.'

'I know you are. And, yes, it has been great. I'm going to miss him too.' Daniel didn't know how much and Anna decided not to enlighten him.

'You're great with him, you know, and he thinks the world of you.'

'He's a good kid.' She heard the catch in her voice and lowered her head, concentrating once more on the pancake batter. She took a few surreptitious deep breaths to calm herself down. She had to keep it together.

'Are you okay?' Daniel asked. 'You've been a bit down since yesterday.'

'Yes, I'm fine,' she managed to say. 'I'm just going to miss Ben, that's all.'

'Will you be here to see him off?'

'No, I can't. I've got a meeting with Eva.' A meeting that she'd purposely arranged so she could avoid Lucinda.

'Oh, that's a shame.'

'That's why I'm making him breakfast,' she said brightly.

Ben came stretching and yawning into the kitchen.

'Morning,' she said. 'Did you sleep well?'

'Great, thanks. Are you making pancakes?'

'I am.'

'My favourite.'

'I know.' She smiled back at him and he walked over to her, put his arms around her waist and hugged her to him. She put her hand on his head, feeling the silkiness of his hair beneath her fingers. God, she was going to miss him. 'Come on, then,' she said, affecting cheerfulness. 'Let's get this pancake show on the road, otherwise you won't have time to eat them before your mum picks you up.'

When breakfast was over and the washing-up done, Anna made her escape, not wanting to say a long goodbye to Ben.

CHAPTER TWENTY-THREE

Eva was sitting up in bed with her make-up done, her hair tied back and a cheery smile on her face. Anna didn't know how she managed it. She quickly took some snaps of her sitting up in bed. Later they would get to some grittier photos as Eva worked on her physio, which usually saw sweat pouring off her with the effort, but today she also wanted some happy snaps to put on Eva's Instagram. The world needed to know how well she was adapting to her new circumstances.

'If you don't mind me saying,' Eva began, 'you look a little downcast today. It's not something to do with Daniel is it?'

Anna sighed. 'It's nothing really. Not compared to . . .' She trailed off.

'Everyone has their problems, it's all relative, and if it's troubling you then it's important.'

'It's just Daniel,' Anna said. 'I think I've fallen in love with him.'

Eva nodded. 'And he isn't in love with you?'

'No, I think he does love me actually.'

'So, what's the problem?'

'It's his son, he lives in Cheshire, and Daniel only gets to see him every other weekend. He misses him and wants to spend more time with him, so he's set up a project there.'

'And you're worried that will take him away from you?'

'A little bit. But it's more about his ex-wife. I overheard a conversation between them yesterday. She wants him back.'

'And does he want to be with her too?'

Anna shook her head. 'I don't know. I was too scared to hear his answer, so I legged it before he had a chance to reply.'

Eva snorted. 'You idiot!'

'What?'

'What if he said no? You're probably worrying about nothing.'

'Am I? I also overheard that they'd spent time together recently, as a family, something he hasn't mentioned to me. And he didn't tell me Lucinda had come to see him either — he told me he'd been working. He lied to me.'

'What if he hasn't said anything to you because there's nothing to tell? You could be getting your knickers in a twist over nothing.'

'I know, but I also know how desperate he is to spend time with Ben. It would be the perfect solution.'

'Not if he doesn't love her.'

'But she's the mother of his child.'

'Maybe so, but there's a reason they split up. And if he says he loves you, why would he want to lose that? He can still be with you and spend time with Ben. He doesn't have to be with his wife.'

'But what if he wants to be?'

Eva frowned. 'That's a lot of "buts". I heard a lot about Lucinda Redfern back in the day and, if what I heard is true, there's no contest. You're far nicer than she ever could be.'

Anna felt her face flush. 'Thanks, but she's beautiful.'

'And so are you. But what's even more important is that you're beautiful on the inside too.'

Anna stared at her friend open-mouthed, unsure how to take her compliments, but Eva rushed on. 'My advice to you is to come right out and ask him. Whatever he says can't be worse than what you're already imagining.'

'Maybe,' Anna replied hesitantly. She'd decided yesterday that she was going to confront Daniel about it. But now the time was nearly here, she wasn't sure she could do it. What if he told her something she didn't want to hear? She wasn't sure she could bear losing him.

'Ah, here comes my torturer.' Eva said as her physiotherapist arrived with a wheelchair. 'Come on, you. We've got work to do.'

* * *

Anna opened the front door to Daniel's house, her hands trembling as she took the key out of the lock. As she'd photographed her friend during her arduous physiotherapy session, she marvelled at how resilient she was. Eva never complained, no matter how many times the physio asked her to repeat the movements. Whenever she failed, she just dusted herself off and tried again. If Eva could be that brave in the face of adversity, then Anna could force herself to ask the questions about her relationship that she needed to. But that didn't make it any less scary.

'Anna, is that you?' Daniel called from the top of the stairs.

'Yes, I'm back.' She made her way up to the studio.

'How's Eva?' he asked when she walked through the door.

'Good. She's working hard on her physio and doing really well.'

'That's great.'

'Has Lucinda been to pick up Ben?'

'Yes, they'll be halfway home by now.'

Home. Did he think of Cheshire as home now?

'You're going to miss him.'

'I am. But I'm taking a leaf out of Eva's book and looking on the bright side. I'm going up next weekend so I'll see him then.'

It was now or never, she decided. 'And you'll see Lucinda too?'

He frowned. 'Of course, when I'm picking up Ben and dropping him back off again.'

'And not at any other time?'

'I doubt it. Anna, why all the questions about Lucinda?'

Anna took a deep breath and plunged in. 'Yesterday. I came back from the shops earlier than you thought I did. Lucinda was here.'

The confusion cleared from his face. 'And you heard her asking if we could try again?'

Anna nodded.

'And did you hear my reply?'

She shook her head. 'No, I couldn't face it.'

'So you didn't hear me turn her down?'

'You turned her down?'

'Of course I did.' In two strides he was across the room and had pulled her into his arms. She rested her head on his chest, listening to the reassuring thud of his heartbeat, and allowed her breathing to return to normal. He bent his head to the top of hers and kissed her hairline, sending shivers down her spine. 'Why would I go back to Lucinda when I have you?'

'So you can be a family again. With Ben.'

'That would be the only thing that would draw me back to Cheshire, but not to Lucinda. It didn't work before and it wouldn't work again.'

'Really?' She tipped her head back, searching his eyes for the truth.

'Yes, really.' He kissed her tenderly on the lips. Their kiss deepened and he began to kiss her more urgently. She wrapped her arms around his neck, wanting to feel his body as close to hers as possible. Her own body was on fire with need — need that was more emotional than physical. After he led her to his bedroom, she allowed him to undress her, kissing every part of her skin tenderly with butterfly kisses until she could stand it no more and the only thing she wanted was to feel him inside her.

Afterwards, she felt as though a huge tension had been released, until he turned on his side and gently entwined his fingers in hers.

'You do believe me when I say that I don't want to get back with Lucinda, don't you?'

'Yes, but . . .' She trailed off, not wanting to voice her fears.

'Yes, but what?'

'You didn't tell me.'

'No, I didn't want to worry you. Lucinda asked me to go back to her and I said no. And I thought that if you knew, every time I was alone in Cheshire you'd be worrying about me and her together. Afterwards I felt awful for not telling you, and I made my mind up that I'd come clean today, after Ben had gone home.'

'Really?'

'Yes. Lucinda and I are in the past. It's you I want to be with.'

'But what about the other things you haven't told me?'

'What other things?'

'About the three of you spending time together.'

'What? When?'

'I heard her say it, Daniel. I heard her say how much she'd enjoyed the three of you being together the other week.'

'Oh, that!' His frown disappeared. 'That was nothing. Ben wanted to show her his bedroom and afterwards I offered her a coffee. I don't think she was very happy about us being together and I wanted the chance to talk to her about it. She was in the house no more than half an hour, tops.'

'I see. She made it sound like so much more.'

'Well, that's Lucinda for you, making something out of nothing.'

'And you didn't tell me because it was nothing?'

'It was important in the sense that she needs to accept that you're in my life, but there wasn't anything untoward about it. You can trust me, you know.'

Anna sighed. 'It's Lucinda I don't trust. How did she take you turning her down?'

'Not great, to be honest. And she was decidedly frosty with me today as well. But she'll get over it. And even if she does try to play games, I'm not going to play back. And neither should you. Tell you what, why don't you come with me next weekend? We'll show her a united front and then things can get back to normal.'

She nodded. 'Okay.' It would be good for Lucinda to see them still together and she wanted to go into Chester to redo some of the shots she wasn't quite happy with. But deep down she suspected it was only a short-term solution. Despite what Daniel had told her, she wasn't convinced Lucinda would give up the fight that easily.

CHAPTER TWENTY-FOUR

It felt good to be travelling back up to Cheshire side by side in Daniel's Range Rover. She wondered if it was because, only a week ago, she'd convinced herself she'd never be making this trip again. She risked a sideways glance at Daniel and her heart thumped heavily in her chest at the sight of his profile — high cheekbones, sturdy chin, lips that she knew were soft when she kissed them, the way his dark-blond hair curled at the nape of his neck.

As though sensing her scrutiny, he glanced at her and smiled. 'What?'

'Nothing. Just happy to be here.'

'I'm happy you're here too.'

It had been a busy week, both at work and on the home front. She and her father had gone to see Jack where he was being held on remand. And while it wasn't the kind of prison he would be staying in once he had been sentenced, it was still a terrifying and depressing place.

When they'd walked into the visitors' room, it had taken her a while to spot Jack. He had lost a lot of weight and his hair had been greasy and his skin sallow. But when he'd looked up and smiled at them, she'd caught a glimpse of

Jack the boy. The boy she had helped bring up and who she loved dearly.

Hesitantly they had made their way across the room. He'd stood up briefly. Anna had gone to hug him but he'd hung back.

'We're not supposed to have contact,' he'd said. She moved backwards, embarrassed that she didn't know the protocol.

They sat down.

'How are you?' Andrew asked.

Jack shrugged. 'Okay, I suppose. I'm just trying to keep my head down. I never thought I'd end up in a place like this, but it's my own fault.' He looked away, but when he turned back towards them his eyes were shining with tears. 'I'm sorry, Dad. I know I've let you down. I've let you all down. You've only ever tried to do your best for me and I've thrown it back at you all.'

Their father made a noise as though he was trying to clear his throat. 'I'm sorry too. I should never have kicked you out.'

'Yes, you should,' Jack said. 'It's what I deserved. If you hadn't done that, I would never have known how good I had it then. When I think about what I did, I'm so ashamed. Dad, I never should have stolen from you, and Anna, my behaviour and violence towards you was unforgivable. To Harry too.'

Anna couldn't speak she was so moved by his words, but their dad said, 'We all make mistakes, son. Some bigger than others.'

'I can't change the past, but I can learn from it. And if you can find it in your hearts to forgive me, I promise I'll never do anything like that again.'

Andrew nodded. 'I can see that you regret it. And I won't turn my back on you now.'

'You'll always be my brother, Jack,' Anna finally managed to say.

It was an emotional visit, but Anna was glad that they were reconciled. Whatever the future held, they would face it together as a family. That evening, her dad went out to meet someone, though he wouldn't say who, and Anna had a chance to catch up with her youngest brother.

'Harry,' she said she saw him. 'It feels like ages since I've seen you. How are you doing?'

'I'm doing good. I've got myself a job to earn some money before uni, working in a restaurant, and I'm spending time with friends.'

'That's good.'

'How was Jack?' he asked.

'Oh, Harry, it was horrible. He looked broken.'

'Only what he deserves,' Harry said gruffly.

'I know what you mean. But he really regrets what he's done. He's not the Jack he used to be before.'

'Well, something good has come of it then.'

'Yes,' she said. 'I actually think it has. I don't know how long he'll have to spend in prison and I hate the thought of him in there, but I think when it's all over he'll be a different person.'

'Can't be worse than what he used to be.'

'No.' She paused. 'I suppose, being the closest in age, you've borne the brunt of his behaviour more than any of us. But I'd like to think that eventually we can put the past behind us.'

'And that's why I love you so much,' Harry said gently. 'You really are a good person.'

Anna blushed. 'Don't be daft.'

'I mean it,' Harry replied. 'But you're right. We do need to look to the future. And I can't wait to get to uni.'

'I'm glad for you. I feel sorry for Dad, though. He's going to be all on his own.'

'Um, I don't think so.' Harry grinned. 'You know he did that cookery course?'

'Yes, I was amazed by how much he seemed to like it.'

'That wasn't the only thing he liked.'

'I don't get you.'

'I don't know how you're going to take this, but he's met someone.'

'He has?' Anna was amazed. She couldn't imagine her dad being with someone other than her mum. But he deserved some happiness after all these years. 'That's great news. What's she like?'

'I don't know, I haven't met her yet, but he's always smiling these days.'

'Just wait till I see him,' Anna said. 'He's going to get a grilling.'

And she did just that when he returned later that evening. It felt strange talking to him about another woman, but it also felt good. With her and Harry moving on, and Jack where he was, it gave her some comfort that her dad wouldn't be lonely any more.

* * *

'I thought we'd go straight to Lucinda's to pick Ben up.' Daniel interrupted her thoughts. 'That way we can get it over and done with, like ripping off the plaster.'

'Good idea,' Anna said. Although they'd agreed they were here this weekend to show a united front, Anna was dreading seeing Lucinda again. At least this way she could stay in the car.

'And as it's such a nice afternoon,' Daniel continued, 'I thought we could take Ben to the park for a while and then go for a pizza.'

Anna smiled. 'I think that's Ben's idea of perfection.'

'But is it perfect for you, too?' Daniel looked concerned.

'I couldn't wish for anything better,' she replied, wanting to reassure him.

When they arrived, Lucinda opened the door but didn't come out. After a quick exchange with Daniel, Ben scurried out of the house and straight into the back of the car with an exuberant hello. Anna smiled. It was all going to be okay and she was overjoyed at seeing him again.

After that they spent a happy few hours at the park, kicking a ball about, pushing him on the swings and watching him trying to master the monkey bars.

As they ate pizza later, Anna felt a bubble of happiness explode in her chest as she watched father and son laughing together. This was what it was all about, spending time with loved ones. And with tears in her eyes, she realised that she loved Ben almost as much as she loved his dad. She would remember this moment for the rest of her life.

* * *

Anna was packing her bag to take more photographs in Chester when the doorbell rang. Puzzled, she went to answer it. Daniel had taken Ben out and, as far as she knew, he wasn't expecting anyone. She hoped whoever it was wouldn't keep her too long, or she'd miss the bus into town. She almost gasped in surprise when she opened the door to see Lucinda standing on the doorstep, looking as immaculate as ever in cropped trousers, a white linen shirt and pristine white trainers.

'Oh, hello.' Anna was hardly able to mask her surprise. 'If you're looking for Daniel, he's taken Ben out.'

'That's okay. It's you I've come to see.'

'Oh?'

Lucinda raised her eyebrows. 'May I come in?'

'Yes, of course.' Anna's face flushed as she opened the door wider to allow Lucinda inside. When she'd closed the door behind them she led the way into the kitchen, her mind furiously trying to work out what Lucinda wanted. She hoped she wasn't here to cause trouble. Lucinda hopped herself on a bar stool, as though she was perfectly at home.

'Can I offer you a drink? Tea? Coffee?'

'Thanks, I'd love a latte.'

Silently Anna reached into the cupboard for a tall latte glass and pushed a pod into the Nespresso machine. She handed the coffee to Lucinda, who raised her eyebrows in what was becoming a familiar gesture.

'You not having one?' Lucinda asked.

'No, I was just about to go out actually.'

'Oh, I'm sorry, I should have phoned you first, but I thought you'd probably refuse to see me.'

'I . . .' Anna wasn't sure what to say. Her instinct was to agree.

'I think we got off on the wrong foot,' Lucinda said.

'Did we?'

'Yes. I'm afraid I'm very protective of Ben and wary of anyone who comes into his life.'

'That's perfectly natural,' Anna replied. 'I'm sure I'd be the same.'

'And Daniel was very quick to introduce you to our son.'

'As a work colleague, yes,' Anna said defensively. She sighed as she said it. She was getting sick of defending her and Daniel's relationship. They were two consenting adults, neither of whom had been involved with anyone else when they'd got together.

'But you're together now and that does affect my son.'

'As does you being with Axel,' Anna said, still on the defensive. 'It's not just Ben you're protective over, though, is it?'

Lucinda shrugged and held her hands up. 'Yes, you've got me there.'

'I don't mean to be rude, but I do have work to do, so could we get to the point of why you're here?'

'Yes, of course. I seem to be rubbing you up the wrong way.'

Anna was silent, refusing to deny something she knew was obvious.

'I don't mean to,' Lucinda continued. 'In fact, I come in peace.'

'Really?' Anna found that very difficult to believe. Only a week ago she'd been trying to get back with Daniel.

'I suppose Daniel has told you about the fool I made of myself last week.'

'He did, yes.'

'It was a mistake. I just got carried away for a moment with the idea of us being a family again. It wasn't even about Daniel really.'

Anna was glad to hear it, even if she wasn't convinced Lucinda was telling the truth.

'But I've been doing a lot of thinking this last week and I've realised that, although we can successfully co-parent, we will never be a family again. And Daniel made quite clear the depth of his feelings for you.'

'He did?' She felt a surge of relief at Lucinda's words, and also a little foolish that she'd doubted him in the first place.

Lucinda smiled wistfully. 'Yes, he did. And I can accept that.'

'Well, that's all right then.' Anna still couldn't see why Lucinda was here, and she wasn't sure she even wanted to know.

'I can see why you might be prickly towards me, but I really would like to get to know you better, now that you're going to be a much more permanent fixture in our lives.'

'You would?'

Lucinda smiled. 'Yes. Maybe even one day we could be friends?'

Anna would rather pally up with a cobra, but she kept her thoughts to herself.

When she didn't say anything, Lucinda continued, her tone a little harder. 'If nothing else, we can try to get on for Ben's sake.'

'Yes, of course we can.' She could do that for Ben. In fact, she'd always been civil to Lucinda, even when the other woman was giving her daggers and throwing barbs at her.

Lucinda got up elegantly from the table. 'Good, I'm glad to hear that's settled. And if you're going to be spending more time up here, maybe I could introduce you to some of my friends.'

'That would be nice.' Anna was already thinking how she'd get out of that one. Hopefully, eventually, Lucinda would get the message.

'Well, then, I'll leave you to whatever you were planning to do before I barged in.'

Anna shut the door behind Lucinda, breathing against it with a sigh of relief. She wasn't sure she was comfortable with this newfound desire for friendship. Friendship required trust. Anna didn't trust Lucinda, and she couldn't envisage a time when she ever would.

CHAPTER TWENTY-FIVE

That afternoon, Anna lost herself in her work. She was always happiest with a camera in her hands and Chester offered a wealth of interesting photo opportunities. As she had last time, she investigated some of the lesser-known architecture. Daniel had told her about Albion Street, a row of Victorian terraced houses, which was used as a location in the World War Two drama *Foyle's War*. She was fascinated by how it fitted into life today while still retaining its original charm. It made her wonder how many other hidden gems were around, what opportunities there were for her camera lens, if only she looked for them.

She returned to Daniel's house tired but full of inspiration. And after Ben had gone to bed they sat happily entwined on the sofa together, chatting about their ideas.

This was something she loved about being with Daniel — that they could talk to each other about their ambitions. Daniel was a willing sounding board for her ideas, as she was for his, and she liked that they pushed each other to be the best that they could be.

After much research Daniel had found a venue on the outskirts of Manchester where he was going to launch his photography school. He was going to stay here while she got the train back to London on Monday morning.

When the time came for her to go, Daniel gave her a long final hug goodbye. 'I'm going to miss you.'

'Me too,' she said quietly, wishing that they didn't have to be apart. She pondered their situation as she sat on the train. She could see how much Daniel enjoyed his time in Cheshire and how he was beginning to think of it as home more than he did London. Whereas her roots were firmly embedded in London. She liked going to Cheshire, but it wasn't where she needed to be, either for work or for her family. So, for the moment, she hoped that she and Daniel would cope with this hybrid living, although she feared that in the long term one of them would have to compromise on where they wanted to live. With Ben being a big part of the equation, she was all too aware that she would be the one making the sacrifice.

* * *

As Anna got off the train at Canada Water, she spotted Daisy, whom she hadn't seen since her exhibition. Immediately she called out, 'Daisy, hi!'

Daisy turned and Anna was shocked at how drawn she was looking. What on earth had happened to her happy-go-lucky friend?

'Oh,' she couldn't stop herself from saying, 'you don't look great, are you okay?'

'Thanks a lot.' Daisy managed a smile. 'But to answer your question, no, I'm not feeling particularly good.'

'Are you ill?'

'Not ill, no.'

Anna suddenly felt guilty that she'd been so wrapped up in her own life recently. 'I don't suppose you've got time for a drink and a chat, have you?'

Daisy sighed as though letting go of pent-up stress. 'Actually, I'd love to. If you've got time, that is?'

'Of course I have.'

* * *

Finally they were seated at a table in the Angel, a bottle of wine and two glasses in front of them.

'I'm really sorry, Daisy,' Anna said. 'I know I haven't been a very good friend. I've been so busy, but I'm here for you if you want to talk to me.'

Daisy poured the wine and took a large gulp. 'Thanks, Anna, I do appreciate it. A lot has happened and I haven't wanted to be a burden, not when everything is going so well for you.'

'Daise, that's madness. I know what it might look like, but I'm always at the end of the phone. Don't ever feel you can't talk to me.'

Daisy smiled. 'Thanks. Truth is, Tom and I are over.'

'What!' Anna gawped at her. She knew it wasn't a good look, but she couldn't help herself. 'I thought you two were solid.'

'So did I.'

'What happened?'

Daisy laughed bitterly. 'Same old story. He went out with his mates, got drunk and ended up in bed with some girl.'

'And how did you find out? Did he tell you himself?'

'Nope. Tried to pretend nothing had happened, until someone tagged me on my socials with a picture of them together.'

'Ouch.'

'Exactly. So, I confronted him and he admitted everything. Said it was a drunken mistake that would never happen again, that he was really sorry. It was me he loved, yada, yada, yada.'

'And you don't believe him?'

Daisy shifted uncomfortably in her seat. 'The thing is, Anna, he only confessed when he had to. If someone hadn't tagged me, I'd have been completely oblivious.'

'Maybe he's telling the truth and it was a mistake — but once the trust is gone . . .'

'Exactly. You'd never have trusted Mark again, would you?'

'Never. But Mark wasn't even sorry in the first place. And then he tried to do the same thing to Jemima. Probably even used the same lines. He's completely untrustworthy.'

'I have thought about forgiving Tom. I really wanted this to work, and I thought he was the one, but I just can't. I'd constantly be on tenterhooks, wondering what he was up to whenever we weren't together.'

'Yes, I can see why you'd think that.' She knew how that felt, even though Daniel had repeatedly assured her she had nothing to worry about. She pushed the thought aside. Today wasn't about her. 'And I know it's little consolation, but maybe it was better to have happened now, rather than when you'd moved in with each other.'

'True. But now I'm right back to square one. Still living with my mother.' Daisy shook her head. 'Oh, listen to me, I'm so fed up with thinking about it. I'm even boring myself. Changing the subject, there's something I've been meaning to ask you. Why did you have your exhibition at The Whigmore? Was it to stick one up at Mark?'

'Not really, no,' Anna said. 'I didn't want it there. I didn't even find out until just before the event. Charlotte who does my PR organised it all.'

'Fancy that! You have come up in the world.'

'Hmm, yes. Don't get me wrong, she's really good at what she does, and she's getting me loads of exposure, which I need, and which I certainly wouldn't get without her contacts, but . . .'

'But?'

'But everything feels out of my control. It's my work and I've still got free rein on what I decide to photograph, but sometimes I feel a bit like a puppet on a string. It's really not how I expected it to be.' Anna sighed. 'Oh for goodness' sake! I've got what I've always dreamed of and yet still I'm complaining. How self-centred is that?'

Daisy laughed and gave her a hug. 'We're a right pair, aren't we?'

'We are. But we've been friends for a long time and I hope that won't change.' She reached out and squeezed her friend's hand. 'I know it looks like my life has changed, but I'll always be here for you.'

'Thanks,' Daisy said, but she looked away.

'Daise? Is something wrong?'

Daisy sighed. 'I suppose it's confession time. When Tom and I broke up, I didn't contact you because I was jealous.'

'Jealous?'

'Yes. You seemed to be living the perfect life, with your new boyfriend and job and living a life of luxury.'

'It's not that luxurious,' Anna muttered, although she couldn't deny that living most of the time with Daniel was more luxurious than what she was used to. 'And I do have to work hard. But, yes, I'm finally doing the thing I've always wanted to do.'

'And you have the perfect boyfriend.'

'I wouldn't say that. He is special, yes, but our relationship isn't without its complications.'

'Which are?'

'I'll tell you about them another time. I want to talk about you.'

'Okay, well, there I was in a crappy job, still living at home, and there was no comparison. But I had Tom and I was in love and we were talking about finding somewhere we could rent so that we could live together. As much as I love Mum, I'm thirty and want my own place, my own life and most of all I want to start a family.'

'I know, that's what you've always wanted.'

Daisy shook her head sadly. 'No chance of that happening any time soon now, though.'

'No, I suppose not. But maybe Tom wasn't the right man for you. Maybe you needed to split up so that you can find the right one, the one who does want to commit and have babies. You never know what's around the corner.'

'Yes, that's very true. But for the moment I'm stuck with the single life, a crappy job and living with Mum. Oh, there I go again! Tell me about these complications. Cheer me up by telling me you don't have the perfect life after all.'

Anna laughed. If anyone else had said that, she would've thought they were being nasty, but not Daisy.

'Remember when I told you that Daniel was thinking of setting up a photography school in Manchester?'

'And I said it would be difficult having a long-distance relationship.'

'And I pooh-poohed that.'

Daisy laughed. 'Yes, I do remember your optimism.'

'Well, as ever, my dear and trusted friend, you were right. Oh, I do get to go up there to work on my exhibition, but we're apart much more than we're together, especially at the moment. And Ben's only nine, so it's going to be a long-term thing and I'm really not sure how we can make it work.'

'Can you trust him?'

'I think so.'

'You don't sound so sure.'

'He's nothing like Mark, but his ex-wife lives up there and she's already made a play for him. He turned her down flat, but he didn't tell me until I told him I knew. He says he doesn't want to be with her, that it would never work and it's me he loves, but I don't trust her. I don't think she'll stop until she gets what she wants. Besides, there's Ben and the thought of being a full-time father. That might be too much for him. I guess I'll just have to wait and see how it all works out.'

'Like you said,' Daisy added. '*You never know what's around the corner.*'

CHAPTER TWENTY-SIX

'Daniel, have you got a minute?'

Daniel frowned at the sight, once more, of his ex-wife standing on his doorstep. Despite her assertions that she'd accepted his decision not to get back together, she was becoming adept at finding excuses to talk to him.

He glanced at his watch in an attempt to fob her off. 'I've only got a few minutes.'

'That's fine,' she replied. He felt he had no choice but to invite her in. He led her through to the living room but didn't offer her any refreshment. Unperturbed, she settled herself down on his large sofa. He selected a chair and sat as far away from her as possible.

'I've got a bit of a problem with the charity ball on Saturday,' she said.

'Oh, yes?' Lucinda was a supporter of the Brain Trust — her cousin's husband had died of a brain tumour at the age of twenty-six — and every year she held a charity event to raise funds. With her wealthy Cheshire contacts she usually raised a huge amount of money, and when they'd been married he'd helped her organise it. Since their split, he'd always attended the event in support of the charity, and in memory of Craig, whom he'd grown close to during his marriage to Lucinda.

'The MC for the night is ill and won't be able to attend next Saturday.'

'And?'

'And I need a replacement. I wondered if you would do the honours?'

'Me?' Daniel was astounded. Although he had a certain amount of fame, he much preferred to be behind the camera than standing in front of a crowd. 'Oh, I don't think so — it's not my kind of thing. I doubt I'd make a very good job of it. What about Axel? He's much better suited than me.'

Lucinda pulled a face. 'Axel won't be here. He's doing a gig in London.'

'Oh, I see.'

'I really can't think of anyone better, Daniel. You've been involved with the charity for years and despite your misgivings you'll do a brilliant job.'

Daniel sighed. 'Very well, I'll do it, but don't blame me if I make a hash of it.'

'You won't, I know you won't.' Lucinda leaped up and threw her arms around him. Daniel gently extricated himself from her grasp. He had a feeling he was going to regret this.

* * *

'Dad, when's Anna coming up again?' Ben asked when Daniel dropped him off at Lucinda's on Monday morning.

'I don't know, son,' Daniel replied. 'She's really busy at the moment with her work, but I'm sure she'll be here as soon as she can.'

'I hope so, because I really miss her.'

'Me too,' Daniel replied, wishing he wasn't so bogged down with his own work while she was in London. She never had time to talk when he phoned at the moment, was always just rushing off somewhere and often forgot to phone him back when she'd said she would, and he was beginning to worry that she was avoiding him. He feared that he was losing her. Maybe he should have decided to set the new school up in London, then he would have had more time to spend with her. But the flip side of that would be having less time to spend with Ben. Whatever he did, he was going to lose out. He stayed in the car while Ben got out. Lucinda came out on the doorstep, but he waved to her cheerily and drove off, avoiding yet another conversation.

Charlotte was coming up on the train to see the new venue for the photography school and he couldn't wait to show her what he'd found. The property was in Didsbury, just outside of Manchester, and although it was in the Manchester commuter belt, and a bit of a posh area, he thought that by being based there he might encourage sponsorship. Although he'd be working for free, he hoped he could get others to sponsor the students to help them throughout the course. That way it would spread the costs and give the students a bit of security in the long term. It had been Charlotte's idea and it was one he was really excited about.

'It's a great venue,' Charlotte said as Daniel snapped some publicity shots. It had a number of rooms that could be portioned off for private editing studios, a larger area for portrait work, another area that could be used as a lecture theatre with smaller rooms for offices. Although initially he would be the only teacher, he hoped that over time he would be able to recruit more. That would free him up to concentrate on other things. He wondered if, after her exhibition, Anna might be interested in getting involved too. At least then they would be able to see a bit more of each other.

'So, how's life in London?' he asked when he and Charlotte were seated in an Italian restaurant, enjoying some pasta for a late lunch.

'Great,' Charlotte said between mouthfuls. 'Busy. Things are really beginning to take off. I've rented an office and I've even taken on some staff. Youngsters, mainly, eager to learn the ropes, but their ambition and enthusiasm is amazing, and of course they are so much more tech and social savvy than I will ever be.'

'Sounds good. Have you seen much of Anna?'

He'd tried to frame the question casually, but he realised from the way she was staring at him intently that he had failed spectacularly.

'Some, but she's really busy.'

'So I'd noticed.'

'Something wrong?'

'Not really, no.' He sighed. 'I'm missing her, that's all.'

'I'm sure you are. But don't forget she's covering some of your work while you're up here. She's also working hard on the exhibition, and with Eva. The book's coming along well and I've offered to get in touch with some of my contacts when she's finished so that there's a good chance of getting it published.'

'That's good. I can't wait to see it. It will really raise awareness for what's happened.' The investigation into the cause of the explosion was still ongoing, but while no one knew how it had happened, the effects of it were more than evident.

'And she's been spending time with her family of course,' Charlotte continued. 'I think she's feeling guilty because she's not been spending so much time with them recently.'

'Yes, she did mention that. It's just so hard trying to fit everything in.'

'I think she's worried about the exhibition too, because it's up here and not on her home turf.'

'She's no need to worry about that. I've seen the photos and they're brilliant.'

'I know, I've said the same. And the good thing is, at least being up here, she doesn't need to worry about her ex trying to sabotage it.'

'The slimy git.'

Charlotte nodded in agreement. 'But I think he'll be getting his comeuppance soon.'

Daniel looked up from his pasta. 'How so?'

'Well, you know Daddy's a golfing buddy of Arthur Whigmore?'

'Yes.'

'They met up recently and Arthur's noticed that his gallery isn't being run as successfully as he thought it was. Not like it was running when Anna was there.'

'That's because she was doing Mark's work for him.'

'Precisely. Arthur's getting more involved in the gallery and Mark's job is on the line. So I think he's got enough to worry about at the moment.'

'And would Arthur sack his future son-in-law?'

Charlotte laughed. 'That's the other thing. Mark's been a bit of a naughty boy there, too. Jemima's got wind of it, so there might not even be a wedding.'

'Karma.' Daniel smiled, glad that Anna's ex might be getting what was coming to him.

'And as for Anna,' she said. 'There's a very good chance that you'll be seeing her at the weekend.'

'I will?'

'Yes, she's talking about coming up to do some last-minute photography. Some of the shots she took aren't quite what she wanted. Didn't she tell you?'

'Not yet, no,' he replied, wondering why she hadn't. And then, in a panic, he remembered the charity event. If Anna was coming up at the weekend, she'd need to know about that.

As soon as Charlotte was on the train back to London, he phoned Anna from the car.

'Hiya.' She answered the phone cheerily enough. He let out a breath he hadn't realised he'd been holding. He'd been half-expecting that she wouldn't even answer his call.

'Hi, how are you doing?'

'I'm good, thanks,' she replied. 'Although I'm having difficulty with some of the images I took in Chester for the exhibition. Daniel, I could really do with your help.'

He felt a rush of elation that she still wanted his opinion. 'Of course, I'm happy to help, whenever, you know that.'

'I'm glad you said that.' He thought he heard a note of relief in her voice. 'I wasn't sure. I know you're busy and I didn't want to disturb you.'

'I'm never too busy for you. Charlotte said you were thinking of coming up for the weekend.'

'I was thinking of it, yes, but I didn't want to make a decision until I'd spoken to you first. Would that be all right?'

'Of course it is.'

'Great, I'll get the train up on Friday afternoon then?'

'Perfect. I'll meet the train. There is one thing, though. I've been asked to MC at a charity event on Saturday night.'

'Oh, that's posh. I wouldn't have thought it would be your kind of thing.'

'It's not really. I've been kind of press-ganged into it. It's a charity I've been involved with for years. Well, actually, it's more Lucinda. She hosts an annual event and the MC has let her down, so she's pushed me into doing it.'

'Oh, I see. Well, that's not a problem. I don't mind staying in on Saturday.'

'I'd rather you came with me.'

'You would?'

'Yes, of course I would.'

'But won't you be otherwise engaged?'

'Only for some of the time. There'll be plenty of time for us to be together, and it will be a much better evening if you're with me.'

'Then of course I'll come.' He couldn't help noticing the hesitation in her voice.

'Let me know what time your train is on Friday and I'll pick you up.'

As he ended the call, the world seemed a much brighter place. He'd missed Anna so much and he couldn't wait to see her in a few days' time. When they were apart the doubts began to creep in, but at least while she was here they could talk about the future face to face. Beyond everything, he knew with certainty that he wanted to make it work between them. Whatever it took.

CHAPTER TWENTY-SEVEN

Anna laid the phone down on the desk with a shaking hand. She was relieved that Daniel had made it clear he wanted to be with her. She'd been worrying that Lucinda might be trying to manipulate herself back into his life, so she'd been making herself extra busy to stop herself from dwelling on it. Sometimes that meant she had missed his calls. But she realised if they were going to spend so much time apart, she was going to have to get over these silly insecurities. Though the thought of going to a posh charity do hosted by Lucinda filled her with dread. She wouldn't know anyone and she'd be completely out of her depth. But he wanted to go to the ball with her, which was a plus. The only problem now was: what on earth was she going to wear?

She poured out her problem to Eva the following day. Eva was doing well with her physio and was due to go home shortly. First, though, her home had to be adapted and Anna had come to pick up her keys so that she could let the workmen in. Then she was going to take some photos for both the book, and Instagram, as the adaptations were put in place. For a good while yet Eva would need a wheelchair, so the doors needed to be widened and bars fitted for her to pull herself up when she was strong enough to stand.

Eva smiled when Anna talked about her dilemma.

'What? It's not funny. I haven't got a clue what the dress code is, Daniel didn't say and, even if I did, I'd have to go and buy something because I don't own anything remotely suitable.'

'Oh, don't worry about that. What did you say the charity was?'

When Anna told her, Eva typed rapidly into her phone and turned the screen towards her. 'Here are some pictures from last year's event.'

Anna gasped. All the women were impossibly glamorous and their outfits were definitely designer.

'I haven't got the kind of money to spend on something like that. At least not for a one-off event.'

Once again Eva smiled. 'Never fear, Eva is here.'

'What?'

'You might not have a dress, but I've got a wardrobe full of them. You're going to be at mine tomorrow. Have a shufty through them. I'm sure you'll find something that fits — we're a similar size. In fact, I've got a Stella McCartney little black number. It's in a dark-green suit bag in my far-left wardrobe. I think it would be perfect.'

Anna breathed a sigh of relief and thanked her lucky stars that she had a friend who was used to this sort of glamour.

* * *

Anna was nervous on the train journey up to Cheshire, but as soon as she saw Daniel and he gathered her into his arms, all her fears melted away. Feeling his solid arms around her, breathing in his familiar citrus aftershave, made her feel like she'd come home.

'It's so good to see you,' she murmured into his chest.

'You too.' He kissed the top of her head. She looked up and his lips moved to hers. Their kiss deepened until they both realised they were making a spectacle of themselves.

'I'd better get you home and then I can kiss you properly,' he said as he led her to his car.

Ben was staying at Lucinda's for the weekend, so they had the house to themselves. They enjoyed getting to know each other again over the next few hours. As Anna lay contentedly in Daniel's arms, he said, 'I'm so glad you're here. You've been a bit distant recently and I thought you were going off me.'

'I've been busy and I wanted to give you some space.'

He leaned over, a puzzled expression on his face. 'Why would I need space?'

'To be with Ben. Without being conflicted, because you're not with me.'

He sighed. 'I know I wanted to set the photography school here, to enable me to spend more time with Ben, but I didn't realise just how much commitment it would take to get it running smoothly. I think I've bitten off a bit more than I can chew. But when I think about how much good it can do, well, it's something I don't want to give up on.'

'It makes you feel more fulfilled than photographing models with diva-like tendencies?'

He laughed. 'Something like that. I've been doing that for years, so I think I've earned the break.'

'And yet you're so good at it.' She laughed. 'You should see the look of disappointment on their faces when I turn up instead of you.'

'Bet they're happy with the end result though.'

'So far.' Anna sighed. 'Your commitment here is obvious, and the only way I can see an end to that is if I moved up here.'

'Is that something you'd think about?' he asked, hope rising.

'I don't know,' she paused. 'I need to be in London at the moment to support Jack, and with Harry moving away Dad will be on his own, and I know he has a new girlfriend, but . . .'

He nodded. 'Your life's in London, and that's how it should be. You have your family, a new career and your work with Eva. It would be too much of a sacrifice for you to give up all that because of my whims.'

'But if it meant we could be together more . . .' She paused. 'I promise I'll think about it, but I really don't know if it's feasible at the moment.'

'I think you're probably right. Just remember, I really do want this relationship to work, so at least let's promise to speak to each other more on the phone when we're apart, and I'll see if I can spend more time in London. At the moment it feels like you're doing most of the legwork.'

He kissed her gently, then pulled away. 'Now, I'm starving, and if we carry on like this, we'll never get to eat. So come on, get yourself up, you brazen hussy, while I get dinner on the way.'

He was just serving up pasta in tomato sauce with garlic bread when the doorbell rang. He groaned as he put a dish down in front of her.

'Go on, you eat, I'll get rid of whoever it is, then we can spend the rest of the evening in peace.'

She listened as she heard voices on the doorstep, then the sound of feet rushing towards the kitchen. Ben burst through the doorway and hurled himself into her arms.

'Anna! I didn't know you were going to be here until just now, it's so good to see you.'

'It's good to see you too, Ben,' she replied. She looked up as Daniel came into the kitchen, then her heart sank as he was followed by Lucinda. That woman really was becoming something of a bad penny.

'Anna, Daniel said you were here.'

Anna smiled but didn't reply. She didn't like the way Lucinda looked as though she owned the place. She didn't trust herself to say anything, but she did wonder just how often Lucinda took it on herself to pop round.

'I've invited Anna to the ball tomorrow,' Daniel said.

'Oh, really? Actually I don't think there are any spare tickets. It's a sell-out, you see.' She smiled at Anna.

'Oh that's all right,' Daniel replied. 'I've already got one.'

'Great,' Lucinda said, and Anna was sure she must be clenching her teeth.

'So, Lucinda, to what do we owe the honour?' Daniel asked.

'Well, actually, I've got some things I want to go over about tomorrow night.'

'Anna and I were just about to eat.'

'It's a bit late, isn't it? We ate hours ago.'

'We've been busy,' Daniel said meaningfully, and Anna noticed that Lucinda had the grace to blush.

Daniel sighed, picked up his bowl of pasta and put it in the microwave.

'Ten minutes,' he said. Lucinda smiled as he led her into the living room.

'Sorry for interrupting your tea,' Ben said.

'Not your fault, love,' she said, smiling at him.

'I've already had mine, so I don't mind if you carry on eating.'

She pushed her bowl to one side. 'No, I think I'll wait for your dad. Now tell me about your week.'

They chatted happily for much longer than ten minutes. Occasionally Anna's eyes strayed towards the living room, wondering how much longer Daniel and Lucinda would be and feeling more resentful by the minute. Why did Lucinda feel she had the right to commandeer Daniel's time, when they had so little time together? And why on earth was Daniel letting her?

'We had to make a model for school today,' Ben said. 'Mine's in the car. Do you want to see it?'

'I'd love to,' she said brightly.

Ben strode into the living room, interrupting Daniel and Lucinda. 'I want to show Anna my model,' he said. 'Can I have the car keys?'

'Of course,' Lucinda replied, reaching for her handbag.

Anna stood in the doorway, gratified at least that the pair of them were sitting at either end of the sofa. With Lucinda concentrating on finding her keys, Daniel shrugged apologetically, which caused a further burst of irritation. Why didn't he just tell her to get off home?

Anna complimented Ben's model. It really was very good, but she wasn't entirely convinced it was the work of a nine-year-old. She'd bet Ben's school was one where the mums were in competition with each other, even over a simple piece of homework.

Ben was putting the model back in the car when, thankfully, Lucinda came out of the house. Daniel remained at the doorway as she walked over to the car.

'Come on, Ben, we'd better get off home now, leave your dad and Anna to their evening.'

'What's left of it,' Anna muttered.

'Well, I hope you enjoy the ball tomorrow night.'

'I'm very much looking forward to it.'

'It should be a good night. Exclusive.'

'And hopefully it will raise a lot of money for your charity.' Anna ignored the way Lucinda had looked her up and down when she'd said the word "exclusive". So much for the fake show of wanting to be friends. The gloves were definitely off.

'Oh, there's no doubt about that. I hope you've brought your best frock with you.'

'I have.' Anna returned the fake smile. 'A little black Stella McCartney number.'

'Sounds perfect.' Lucinda got into her car.

Anna watched as she moved away, the tyres spitting up gravel on the drive. Her stomach was wound into tight coils of anger. She hated the way Lucinda acted so superior around her. But most of all she hated the way she reacted to it. Just as Lucinda wanted, it made her feel as though she didn't belong here. With Daniel.

'Well, thank God she's gone,' Daniel said when Anna reached him.

'Finally,' Anna added.

'I know, I'm sorry she interrupted our evening. She's just nervous about tomorrow.' He put his arm around her as they went inside.

'She didn't seem very nervous to me.'

'Ah, well, she puts on a front to people she doesn't know.'

'I just wish she wouldn't turn up unannounced, like you haven't got anything better to do.' She knew she sounded like a petulant child, but she couldn't help herself.

'I know, but I couldn't really turn her away, not with Ben standing there.'

'No, I don't suppose you could.'

'Come on, let's go and finish our dinner. I'm starving.' He led Anna back into the kitchen.

While Anna sat in front of the reheated food, she could only pick at it. Her stomach was still twisted into knots, her appetite vanished.

'Does she do that a lot?' she asked eventually.

'What?' Daniel said between mouthfuls.

'Turn up on your doorstep.'

'A couple of times. Not really,' he said evasively. 'Come on, let's forget about Lucinda and enjoy our evening.'

But that was the problem — she couldn't forget about Lucinda, even though she desperately wanted to.

* * *

Anna got up early the next morning and headed into Chester. Normally she liked to amble around, taking her time to find the perfect shot, but today she was on a mission. She had a list of places to go for her reshoots and she was determined to get through them as quickly as possible. She knew she would need all her confidence to face tonight, so that morning she'd booked herself into the hairdresser's and was going to have her make-up done too. A quick blow-dry and a flick of mascara, her usual routine, was not going to cut it tonight.

Daniel was dressed and downstairs by the time Anna had finished getting ready. She barely recognised herself as she looked in the mirror. Her make-up was much heavier than she was used to and she wasn't sure if it was really her, but it would certainly help her blend in with the other women. She liked the way the hairdresser had piled her hair on top of her head, though, with a few tendrils coming down the sides. And Eva's dress was stunning. Skimming her curves and accentuating her slim waist, it made her legs look incredibly long. The dress was perfect and she couldn't wait for Daniel to see her in it. She picked her way downstairs, hesitant in the unfamiliar high heels.

As she descended the stairs, Daniel came into the hallway, wearing a white tuxedo. She hadn't envisaged that — she'd imagined him wearing black.

As he saw her, a look of anguish crossed his face. 'Oh, shit!'

'What? What's the matter?' she asked anxiously. 'Is it the dress? Do I look all right?'

'No, no, you look wonderful, it's just that . . .'

'What is it, Daniel? You're really starting to worry me.'

'You look amazing.'

'And that's bad?'

'No, it's just that . . .' He paused. 'It's just that it's white tie.'

'White tie?'

'Yes, it means that everyone wears—'

'White. I know what it means. But why didn't you tell me?'

'It slipped my mind.'

'It slipped your mind? Surely you knew you were wearing white.'

He hung his head. 'I'm really, really sorry. I don't suppose you've got—'

She interrupted him again. 'A white dress? No, Daniel, I'm not like the other women you know. I don't have a whole

214

wardrobe full of dressy clothes. In fact, this dress isn't even mine — I had to borrow it from Eva. But if I'd known about the dress code, if you'd even stopped to mention it, I might have borrowed something in *white*!'

'Maybe you could borrow something from L—'

'Don't even finish that sentence!' she almost shouted, remembering she'd told Lucinda last night that her dress was black. Lucinda hadn't mentioned the dress code. If she had, then Anna might have been able to salvage things by buying a dress in Chester today. But Lucinda wouldn't have wanted her to do that, would she? Lucinda would prefer the humiliation of Anna turning up in something that was completely unsuitable.

'She's got loads of dresses. I'm sure she wouldn't mind.'

Her anger stuck in her throat and for a moment she was speechless. What she wanted to do was scream at him. Why didn't he understand that she wouldn't want to go cap in hand to borrow something from his ex-wife? Why did he not see that? She'd thought he was more emotionally switched on than this.

'For a start, we are a completely different shape and size, which you, as a photographer, might have noticed. And for another, why would I ask a favour from her when she set me up?'

Daniel frowned. 'What do you mean, set you up?'

'I told her last night my dress was black. She knew I didn't know the dress code.'

'Oh, shit,' he said again.

All of a sudden she felt the anger dissipate and, feeling as though she couldn't hold herself up, sank down into a sitting position on the stairs, uncaring of how she might crease the dress.

'Well,' she said sadly. 'I hope you enjoy your evening.'

'You're not coming?'

'How can I? Dressed like this.'

'You look amazing.' He walked up the stairs, sitting down on the step in front of her. 'You really do. Who gives a stuff about some shitty dress code?'

'It's not about the dress code. It's about fitting in. And I don't. This is Lucinda's turf and I'd say she's gone out of her way to make sure I know it. And that I'm not welcome.'

'Not by her maybe.' He ran his hand up her black-stockinged leg and, despite the fact that she'd just been so furious with him, the action sent shivers down her spine. 'Who cares what Lucinda thinks? I want you here, and I'd be so proud to have you by my side tonight. Black dress or not.'

'I'm not sure I'm brave enough for that.'

'You're the bravest person I know. Think about what we went through together only a few weeks ago. That would have most people breaking down, but you, you took it in your stride, you tried to help as many of the victims as you could, and you're still supporting one of them now. What's a bunch of bored rich people compared to that?'

She laughed shakily. 'That's scarier than anything else.'

'You're worth a hundred of them.'

'Glad you think so.'

He reached up and kissed her. She closed her eyes as she revelled in the tender feel of his lips on hers. Outside a car beeped its horn.

He pulled away from her. 'That's the taxi.'

'We'd better go then, hadn't we?' She pulled herself up into a standing position.

Daniel stood up, grinning, and put his arm round her. 'Really? You'll come with me?'

She nodded, even though it was against her better instincts. 'Like you said, who cares about a stupid dress code.'

'Not me. Can you tell the taxi to hang on for five minutes?'

'Why? We're both ready aren't we?'

'No. I need to go and change. If you're going to be in black, then so am I.'

'You can't do that. You're the MC.'

'Just you watch me,' he said as he raced up the stairs.

CHAPTER TWENTY-EIGHT

The ball was being held at a posh Cheshire golf resort and spa. As their taxi made its way through the sandstone archway and up the driveway to the main building, Anna felt as though a whole barrage of butterflies were fluttering about in her stomach. She gaped in awe as the taxi stopped in front of another, larger, sandstone building. A number of expensive cars were parking up, out of which stepped amazingly glamorous men and women, all dressed in a concoction of white.

'I'm going to stick out like a sore thumb.' Anna's throat was suddenly dry.

'Because you're going to be the most beautiful woman here and I'm proud to have you on my arm,' Daniel replied.

'Cringe.' She laughed shakily at him. 'But you're going to have to stick by my side all night and defend me. Tonight you're going to have to be my knight in black armour.'

'I won't let you down.' He kissed her on the cheek.

'You'd better not.' She gritted her teeth, getting out of the car as gracefully as she could.

* * *

Daniel took her arm, leading her up the stone steps and into the foyer, which was decorated with so many pedestals of white roses that it looked like the inside of a florist's. Anna felt growing fear, aware of the curious glances being cast their way as they walked into the large reception room.

'This is a disaster,' she muttered to Daniel. 'Look at the way they're staring at us. I feel like a freak.'

'Take a deep breath and hold your head up high. Most of all, remember you look stunning.'

And then Lucinda was coming forward to greet them.

'Daniel, darling, so good to see you, but why are you in black?' She glanced swiftly at Anna. 'Did you not get the dress code?'

'Well I didn't, although you could have let me know last night, when I told you I was wearing a black dress.' Anna swore she saw a slight smile on Lucinda's lips, but only for a brief second.

Instantly Lucinda sounded contrite. 'Oh, no, I'm so sorry. I thought Daniel would have told you.'

'He forgot, which is why he's wearing black too, in solidarity.'

'Really?' She looked back to Daniel. 'But you're the MC. I really think—'

He interrupted her. 'If Anna's wearing black then so will I. And if that doesn't suit, then maybe you'd like to find a replacement for me?'

'No, no of course not. Don't be like that Danny.' She glared at Anna and put a hand proprietorially on Daniel's arm. 'Could I borrow you for a minute?'

Danny? Anna had never heard anyone call him that before. Inwardly she groaned. So this was what it was going to be like. Lucinda grabbing what she wanted and Anna left high and dry. She wished she'd stayed at Daniel's house after all. But Daniel's response surprised her.

'I thought we went through everything last night. That's why you came round to the house, wasn't it?'

'Yes, but I didn't remember everything. And now we're in situ so to speak.'

'All I need is for you to let me know when you want me to start and to provide me with a microphone. But, right now, I'd like to get a drink and introduce Anna to a few people. That's okay with you, isn't it?'

'Of course,' Lucinda replied, her lips tight. 'As you wish. Now, I must mingle.'

As she stalked off, Anna turned round to Daniel and whispered, 'Thank you.'

'Not a problem,' Daniel replied. 'I agreed to MC as a favour and against my better judgement. To be honest, I'm terrified. But Lucinda is taking the role a bit too far. I'm not about to become her puppet.'

'Glad to hear it,' Anna replied.

'Now, how about a drink?'

'Definitely, yes,' Anna said. She felt as though she would need one if she was going to get through tonight, but she was determined to take it steady. She needed to keep her wits about her.

Daniel took two champagne flutes off a passing waiter and handed one to her. She took a sip, relishing the tartness and the bubbles in her mouth. She had a feeling this was going to be a very long night.

* * *

Half an hour later, Daniel had introduced her to so many people her head was swimming.

'Daniel, darling, how nice to see you.' A woman dressed in a tight sheath dress, demonstrating she didn't have a spare ounce of flesh, enveloped Daniel in a hug, her elbows almost poking Anna in the face. She had no choice but to move a step further away. When the woman eventually released him, she said, 'So good of you to fill in as MC. Lucinda's beyond grateful — she can't stop talking about what a saviour you are.'

As Daniel extracted himself from her grasp he said, 'Nice to see you, Verity. This is Anna, my partner. Anna, this is Verity, Lucinda's best friend.'

Verity looked Anna up and down with a barely concealed smirk. 'Oh dear,' she said. 'Didn't anyone tell you the dress code?'

Anna felt her cheeks flush at the question and wished the floor would swallow her up.

'I . . .' She tried to answer, but Verity turned away to screech at a woman dressed in a full-length white silk gown festooned with roses around the neckline.

'Felicity, how lovely to see you.' Verity air-kissed the woman around both cheeks. Briefly she turned to Daniel. 'Lovely to see you, Daniel, but we must mingle.' She linked her arm through Felicity's and moved away.

'Rude,' Anna muttered.

'Pay no attention,' Daniel replied. 'Those two are a right pair.'

But it was the same for the rest of the cocktail hour as Anna tried to ignore the numerous barbed comments about dress code, even though her face flushed whenever it was mentioned.

'Just ignore them,' Daniel murmured. 'They get off on feeling superior.'

'Funny how it's me they're targeting. Your lack of dress code barely gets a mention.'

'They're just jealous,' he replied. She was grateful for his reassurance, but that didn't make her feel any less like she didn't belong.

Lucinda grabbed him as they were sitting down to dinner, so he could formally make the introductions for the evening. Anna was left with an empty space beside her at the dinner table. She looked around for someone else to talk to, but the woman on her other side was deep in conversation with the man next to her. The table was so large it made conversation difficult with anyone other than the person sitting next to you. Everywhere people were deep in conversation with their neighbours and no one made any effort to talk to her, despite the fact that she was sitting on her own. They certainly were a cliquey bunch.

Introductions over, Daniel came back to the table. As he sat down, he took her hand.

'I'm sorry, it looks as though I'm going to have to keep abandoning you.'

'It can't be helped.' Anna noticed the guilty look on his face.

'I wish I'd just given a hefty donation to the charity and was curled up next to you on the sofa with a takeaway and a good film.'

'Oh, me too. Shame we can't just slip away, but I think people might notice if you weren't here.'

He squeezed her hand. 'I know and I'm sorry to put you through this.'

'It's okay,' she said. 'Once the dinner and auction is over, will there be dancing?'

'Yes, till the early hours if I know this lot, but we don't have to stay that long.'

'Might be nice to have a dance together though.' She was looking on the bright side. 'We've never done that before, have we?'

'No, we haven't,' he said thoughtfully. 'There's a lot of things we haven't done together. Like go on holiday for one.'

'There hasn't been time.'

'No, we've both been so busy, but once the school holidays are over, I've got the school more organised and you've done your next exhibition, maybe we could get away together, just the two of us, even if it's only for a long weekend.'

'Yes, I'd like that,' Anna said, thinking how wonderful their relationship was when it was just the two of them. It was only when the rest of the world stepped in that the problems started.

After dinner, Daniel was dragged away to compere the charity auction and Anna was left on her own again. She was

surprised by how rude these people were. After a few perfunc-
tory sentences, they quickly returned to their conversations.
She wondered if it was because she was with Daniel and their
loyalty was to Lucinda, or whether it was because they were
so shallow they didn't want to take the time to get to know
anyone new.

She watched, mesmerised, as the auction continued. If
they weren't interested in conversation, they certainly enjoyed
flashing the cash, or, she thought cynically, making themselves look good in the process. She couldn't imagine they
were doing it for the sake of the charity.

When the auction drew to its close, Anna thought Daniel
would come back to the table, but Lucinda clearly had other
ideas and took him off to mingle with her guests. At first
Anna waited patiently, but after a while her resentment began
to rise. Fuelled by champagne, she decided to make a stand.
Getting up, she made her way towards them, determined to
be included, even if she wasn't accepted.

Walking up behind Daniel, she put her arm around his
waist. He jumped, but when he looked down a smile spread
over his face. He extricated himself from Lucinda and drew
her to him. Then, turning to the man he was speaking to, said,
'You haven't met Anna, my girlfriend, have you?'

For a moment a flash of doubt crossed the man's face
as he looked from Anna to Lucinda. Then he recovered.
'Delighted to meet you. How did you two meet?'

'Anna's a photographer too,' Daniel said on her behalf.
'She's just had her first exhibition, which, if I say so myself,
was a bit of a hit. Anna Wright? You may have heard of her.'

'Anna Wright? Urban landscapes?' the man asked. 'Yes,
I've seen your photographs and I love them.'

Amazed that he had even heard of her, she replied shyly,
'I've got another exhibition coming up soon. And the landscapes this time are much closer to home. Well, closer to your
home anyway. I'm focussing the exhibition on Chester.'

'Really? How wonderful. I can't wait to see that.'

And they began Anna's first genuine conversation, with the exception of Daniel, that she'd had all night.

After a few moments, Lucinda cleared her throat. 'Well, I think I'd better mingle with the other guests. Daniel, will you—'

'Yes, thank you, I will enjoy the rest of my evening, now that I've completed my duties as MC.'

'Yes, well, um, thank you for doing that. You really helped me out.'

'My pleasure,' Daniel said. 'Anything to help raise money for such a worthy charity.'

'Enjoy the rest of your evening then.' She turned to Anna and said coldly, 'You too, Anna.'

'Oh, I intend to,' Anna said, suddenly realising there was only one way to deal with the Lucindas of this world, and that was to show no fear.

* * *

Anna kicked off her shoes as soon as she was through the door, groaning.

'I don't know how women wear these all the time, they're so painful.'

'But you do look sensational in them. Mind you, I think you look gorgeous in anything.'

Daniel nuzzled the back of her neck and she leaned into him. 'And I do like it when you have your hair up,' he said between kisses. 'You have such a beautiful neck.' She wriggled in enjoyment at the tingles he was sending up and down her spine. 'And although you look amazing in this dress, I can't wait to get it off you.'

She turned to face him and wrapped her arms around his neck, pushing herself closer to him. 'I'm not sure I've quite forgiven you about the dress,' she said. 'The way some of those women looked at me.'

'Forget about them,' he said. 'They're not important.'

He kissed her and then took her hand to lead her up the stairs. She was glad that the evening had ended so well after such an unpromising start. For the rest of the evening Lucinda had kept her distance — Anna and Daniel had danced and laughed and even had some nice conversations with people. She realised it was always going to be difficult when she was on Lucinda's turf, but she hoped that tonight Daniel had seen how manipulative Lucinda could be when it came to him.

* * *

On Sunday they took a drive out to Lyme Park with Ben, and spent a happy day in the August sunshine followed by lunch in a country pub. Afterwards, when Ben was playing on a slide, Daniel said, 'I meant it last night when I said we should go on holiday together.'

'Good, I'm glad. That would be really nice.'

'We do need to spend some more time alone with each other. I'm aware that even today Ben is with us.'

'I don't mind Ben being with us. I enjoy his company and he's part of you. It's just his mother I don't like hanging around.'

'I know what you mean. I'm sorry, I have tried to put her off, but she's not getting the message. I'll have to try harder. Lucinda has a habit of not giving up until she gets what she wants, but it's not going to work this time. I'm with you and she's just going to have to get used to the idea.'

'Good.'

'I've got some work I need to do here in the early part of the week, but then I'm coming back to London to spend some time with you before your exhibition.'

'Oh, I'd like that,' Anna said, hoping that things would be all right after all.

* * *

Anna leaned back in her seat on the train and closed her eyes. For once the train wasn't busy — she was the only one sitting at a set of four seats with a table. While it had been a difficult weekend, she was happy that she and Daniel had had a great day yesterday spending time with Ben, but part of her was glad to be going home, where she could concentrate on her own life and career without having to be part of the drama.

Her phone pinged and she picked it up. It was a text from Daniel saying how much he was going to miss her over the next few days. She smiled sadly at that. She was going to miss him too.

Idly she started to scroll through Instagram, looking at Eva's account to see if she was up to anything. She hadn't seen Eva since she'd offered to lend her the dress and she was determined to go and see her as soon as possible. She wondered what she'd make of the situation. She hoped Eva didn't blame herself for the choice of dress, because the only people who could be blamed for it were Daniel and Lucinda. And while she was still annoyed at Daniel for not telling her in the first place, his was an oversight, whereas Lucinda had been acting out of spite.

She typed Lucinda's name into the search engine of Instagram and opened up her page. As she had expected, many of the pictures were of the ball, with lots of comments of congratulations. She couldn't help noticing so many of the pictures were of Daniel and Lucinda together, which made it look as though they were still a couple. She scrolled through the photographs until she saw one of herself, sitting alone on the table looking forlorn. She looked across to the comments. Lucinda hadn't posted any, but plenty of others had.

Who would be stupid enough to wear a black dress when the dress code was white?

Doesn't she know anything about dress code?

No wonder no one wanted to speak to her.

Definitely not our sort.

Two of the comments, unsurprisingly, were by the lovely Verity and Felicity. *No*, Anna thought as she flicked her phone off, tears welling in her eyes. *I wouldn't want to be one of your sort either.* It would be nice if she never had to go to Cheshire again, but she had the exhibition to get through. Right now, she wished she'd stuck to taking photographs of London, but it was what it was. She'd just have to make sure the exhibition was as good as it could be. She'd show them she was not someone to be ridiculed.

* * *

Daniel had had a busy morning, meeting the building contractor first thing to go through the renovations to the photography school. He was satisfied that the team knew what they were doing, and hopeful that the work would be completed on time. When he got home he'd work on the text for the pages of the website so that it could go live as soon as possible. And then they would start marketing. He was looking forward to getting his first students through the door. The first course would start at the beginning of January. Initially he would run three-month introductory courses, with a certificate at the end of them. If that went well, he would apply to teach more formal qualifications from September next year. He was also looking forward to actually getting back to his camera, rather than having to deal with estate agents, solicitors and builders. He'd enjoyed project-managing the venture but he'd missed the photography, and being with Anna.

It wouldn't hurt to spend more time with her and much less time around Lucinda. He'd been nice to his ex-wife to keep the status quo for Ben, but after the way she'd tried to manipulate him recently the gloves were definitely off.

He pulled into his driveway, opened the front door and headed to the kitchen for a much-needed cup of coffee. His phone pinged with an Instagram notification and he opened it up. Social media was an important part of his job and that was what he used it for, but he wasn't interested in gossip and the tittle-tattling that went on there. He opened up Lucinda's post, horrified to see there were a lot of pictures of him and her together. Why did that not surprise him? And then he saw the photograph of Anna, sitting alone, looking forlorn, and his heart clenched. He should never have asked her to go with him. He should have known it would be like throwing her to the lions. When he saw the comments he was even more enraged and immediately dialled Lucinda's number. It took a while for her to pick up, but eventually she did, sounding a little out of breath.

'Daniel, hello! How nice to hear from you.'

'I've just seen your Instagram post.'

'Oh, have you? Didn't the photos come out really well? Not to your standard, of course, but good all the same.'

'Could you take down the photo of Anna, please?' He refused to engage in conversation.

'Oh, don't you like it? I must admit she looks a bit sad but—'

'No, I don't like it. Neither do I like your friends' comments. You know full well that the dress wasn't Anna's fault and you should be ashamed of yourself for trying to make a fool of her.'

'Daniel, I never meant—'

'I don't care what you meant. Please just take it down.'

'Of course, Daniel, yes, I didn't think. I haven't actually seen the comments yet, so I don't know what you're talking about, but if my friends have been unkind, then I'm sorry.'

'So am I, Lucinda. I expect to see that removed immediately.'

'Yes, of course.'

'And, just for the record, next time you find yourself short of an MC, find someone else.'

He ended the call with an angry jerk of his thumb. Her protestations of innocence angered him even more. Who was she trying to fool? Not him, that was for sure. At least not any more. He just hoped Lucinda took that picture down before it could do much damage. Certainly before Anna saw it anyway.

* * *

227

Anna's phone rang as she made herself a cup of tea in the kitchen. It was Daniel. She paused for a moment, wondering whether or not to answer it, and then accepted the call.

'Hi,' she said.

'Are you home yet? I waited until I thought you would be.'

'Yes, all arrived safely.' She tried to make her voice sound breezy, but the memory of those catty comments weighed heavily on her.

'Yours or mine?'

'Mine.' She needed to be around her own family for a few days, with the familiarity of her own life, not a reminder of Daniel's.

'Oh. I thought you were going to stay at mine, make it easier for editing.'

'I was. I might. I'll probably go there during the daytime, but I wanted to spend some time here.'

'Of course. I'm sorry. We're leading a bit of a nomadic lifestyle here, aren't we?'

'Yes. Nowhere really feels like home at the moment,' she said.

'You're talking about the weekend, aren't you?'

'Yes. I thought I could deal with it, but then I saw Lucinda's Instagram post.'

'Ahh,' he said. 'I was hoping you hadn't seen that.'

'Not exactly pleasant, is it?'

'I'm furious about it. I spoke to Lucinda earlier and told her to take it down. It's gone now.'

'That's something, I suppose.'

'I also reiterated that you were here to stay, so she'd better get used to it and rein her friends in.'

'Daniel?'

'Yes?'

She paused, not quite knowing how to frame her words. 'What if it's not a question of Lucinda reining her friends in?'

'What do you mean?'

'It's just a feeling. She didn't make any nasty comments on the post, or at the ball, but I get the feeling that she's behind it all.' When he didn't say anything, she continued. 'I mean, what if she's loading the gun and getting her friends to fire the bullets?'

'I don't think she'd do that.'

'Don't you?'

'No.' He paused. Then, sounding irritated, he carried on. 'Look, the main thing is that we don't let them get to us. I've made it quite clear to Lucinda that I'm not happy and I'm definitely not going to be doing her any favours in the future. From now on, our only contact is going to be about Ben. She'll get the message. And, in the meantime, we need to concentrate on us and our lives. I'm coming back up on Thursday and we can spend some time alone together.'

'That will be nice,' she said, although she wasn't as confident as Daniel that this would blow over so easily.

* * *

'It was white tie?' Eva was aghast after Anna filled her in during their visit the next day.

'I'm afraid so. I stuck out like a bloody sore thumb.'

'Oh, Anna, I'm so sorry.'

'It's not your fault,' Anna put a hand on her friend's arm. 'You weren't to know.'

'No, but you should have. I can understand why Lucinda didn't tell you, but what about Daniel?'

'He forgot.' Anna's tone was heavy with sarcasm.

'Typical bloke.'

'I think he just assumed I would know.' Anna shook her head. 'Sometimes I don't think he sees the difference between us.'

'What do you mean?'

'I'm not from his world. I'm not used to posh restaurants, fancy balls and designer clothes. Even if they weren't all being so vile to me, I think I'd still feel like a fish out of water.'

'I wouldn't worry too much about that. Not being like one of them is a good thing. I thought I was living my best life being a model, but sitting here in this hospital bed, with so much time on my hands, it's given me plenty of time to think about my life. I thought the models I worked with were my friends, but in all the time I've been here, only one of them has come to visit me, and I'm sure that was more out of curiosity than anything else. You've been a better friend to me than any of them and I didn't even know you before.'

'Oh!' Anna felt a lump form in her throat and tears welled in her eyes. Eva was such a lovely person. She deserved to have a close circle of friends.

'I've come to realise that what I had before wasn't friendship. It was more a question of keeping your enemies close. Everyone is competition, you see, and no one trusts anyone. They pretend to, so that they can find out what's going on in everyone's life, but really it's all just fake. I don't want that in my life anymore.'

'I can see why. So have you decided what you do want?'

'Yes. I'm going to get back on my feet.' She laughed. 'Quite literally. And together we are going to create a bestselling book, which is going to make our fortune.'

Anna laughed with her. 'I wish.'

'Well, it will be a start at least. You know, I earned quite a bit of money when I was modelling, and I was working so hard and trying to live a healthy lifestyle so that I could stay in the game, I didn't really have much to spend it on. I'll be comfortable for a while, but, now, I've realised that I want to help other people. I'm not quite sure how, but I'm just going to take one day at a time.'

Anna nodded. 'That's a good philosophy.' She'd been overthinking her and Daniel's relationship. She needed to take a leaf out of Eva's book and concentrate on the now, on what she wanted to achieve.

'It's a shame you won't be able to come to my exhibition, but it's in Chester and will be too far for you to travel.'

'I know. I was hoping to be there too. To be honest, I don't think I'd have been able to make it yet, even if it had been in London. But you won't be able to stop me from being there in the future.'

'That's something to work towards, then. For both of us.'

'One exhibition in particular,' Eva said enigmatically.

'What do you mean?'

'I did have one visitor recently,' Eva said. 'Charlotte.'

'Oh, yes, and what's she been plotting?'

'We were talking about my book. Obviously I can't finish it for a while, because it needs to be about my complete recovery, but we were chatting about the launch. What do you say to it being a joint venture?'

'How so?'

'The launch of my book along with an exhibition of your photos inside it.'

'Genius.' Anna grinned. 'And this was Charlotte's idea, was it?'

'Yes. She's a force of nature, that woman.'

'She certainly is. I hope you're ready for it.'

Eva grinned. 'Can't wait.'

CHAPTER TWENTY-NINE

Anna stood on the pavement of Watergate Street, looking in awe at her name splashed across the window of the gallery, interspersed with some of her images.

'Wow!' For a moment that was all she could say. She could feel the butterflies flitting around her stomach as though they were in overdrive.

'Come on.' Daniel placed his hand gently on the small of her back. 'Let's go in. I'm sure Charlotte has worked her magic.'

'I'm sure she has.' Anna regained her composure. 'I wish she'd let me help with the display beforehand, though. It would stop me feeling so nervous.'

Daniel laughed. 'That's Charlotte for you. Complete control freak.'

The moment she stepped through the door, she was greeted by a tall, immaculate-looking man in a tailored black suit and crisp blue shirt. He held out a perfectly manicured hand.

'Ms Wright, my name's Andrew. I'm so pleased to meet you.' She stalled at his name, thinking of her father, who hadn't felt able to come to Chester. Briefly, once more, she wished she could have held this exhibition on her home turf.

She remembered the glow she'd felt last time with her family's praise embracing her. She shook her gloom off. She was here now and this was her big night.

She shook his hand, noticing how firm his grip was. 'And I you.' She smiled. 'Thank you for allowing me to hold my exhibition here.'

'The pleasure is all ours. Thank you for showcasing our beautiful city in such a stunning way. Let me show you around.'

Once again, even though she'd looked at every detail of every photograph so many times, now that they adorned the walls they were as fresh as though she'd never seen them before. Her heart was hammering so loudly she imagined everyone could hear it quite plainly.

Daniel had his arm around her as they slowly moved through the gallery. When they returned to the open space at the front, he whispered, 'Congratulations, my love, you've done it again.'

She smiled then, relaxing for the first time that evening, and took a calming deep breath in and out. Whether tonight was a success or not, she'd done her best and she was more than pleased with that.

'Thank you.' She looked up at him, so glad that he was by her side, and knew she would never have had the confidence to do this without him. She owed him so much for pushing her forward and reassuring her at the same time.

Charlotte breezed through the door and embraced them, then stepped back. 'Well, what do you think?'

'You've outdone yourself, as usual,' Daniel said.

'Thank you, Charlotte,' Anna added. 'You've done a brilliant job. The photos look stunning.'

'Not difficult, seeing as they're so good to start with.'

'Yes, but the way you've put them together, I never would have thought of it. Next time, please, will you at least show me how you do it?'

'What, and let you in on my trade secrets?' Charlotte laughed. 'I'll think about it.'

A waiter appeared with a tray of champagne glasses and they all reached for one. Anna sipped at hers, the nerves mounting once more as the door opened and people began to trickle in.

At first she stood back, watching in awe as people commented on her work. It was one thing for her to think she'd done a good job, but something entirely different to hear words of praise on other people's lips. Gradually, Charlotte pushed her forward and she began to mingle with the guests, blushing with pride at the compliments she received, relieved that tonight was going to be a success, and that she had nothing to worry about.

As the gallery filled up, the heat rose, and Anna was beginning to feel stifled. She wished she could pop outside for a moment just to get some fresh air, but everyone was clamouring for her attention and it would be rude to ignore them.

A cackle of laughter drew her attention away from the conversation she was having with a rather dull man who was talking to her about the English Civil War, giving her an in-depth breakdown of the siege of Chester, which had lasted for sixteen months. As she turned towards the noise, she saw a gaggle of women enter the gallery, some of them unsteady on their feet, and her body went suddenly cold. Lucinda and her cronies. That was the last thing she needed, especially as they all looked worse for wear.

Daniel was by her side, looking stricken.

'Daniel?' she asked quietly. 'What are they doing here?'

'I might have known they'd show up,' he said. 'But I didn't expect them to be drunk.' He touched her arm. 'I'm going to go over and see if I can get rid of them. I don't want them to spoil tonight.'

Anna nodded, hoping they weren't here to deliberately cause trouble. She excused herself from the dreary conversation and tried to conceal herself in the shadows. It was ridiculous for her to be hiding at her own exhibition, but these women were still pressing all the buttons on her inferiority complex. As Daniel strode towards Lucinda, the group broke up and began to wander around the gallery. Their voices were loud as they commented on the pictures and, in her hiding place, Anna couldn't help but hear them.

'I don't know why she thinks she's so special. I could snap these photos on my phone.' Anna recognised that voice as Verity, the one who'd snubbed her at the charity ball.

'Can't understand what Daniel sees in her. Lucinda's far better-looking,' her partner in crime, Felicity, agreed.

'Probably because she's younger than him. He's only doing this to bolster his ego.'

'He'll soon get bored. Especially now Lucinda's back on the scene. They're hardly ever apart these days.'

Unable to stand listening to the conversation, Anna stepped out of the shadows, startling the women.

Felicity gasped. 'Oh. What are you doing, skulking around in the dark?'

Anna pinned a smile to her face. 'Hello, ladies. Are you enjoying the exhibition?'

'Um, yes,' Verity said. 'It's very good.'

'Oh, I don't know, I'm sure you could take better pictures on your phones.'

They both stared at her, but neither of them seemed embarrassed. 'Yes, well, Chester is a much-photographed city. There's nothing new or special about these,' Verity said.

'Some people seem to think they are special. Judging by the number of red stickers on them. That means they've been sold, if you didn't know.'

'And that's how you judge things, is it? On how much money you can get for them?' Felicity asked.

'I imagine most people around here base their judgements on money,' Anna replied.

'Or style.' Verity sneered. 'Not that you'd know anything about that.'

'Is that style over substance?' Anna asked. She didn't know where this feisty version of herself had come from, but she liked it. She was sick of feeling inferior to these women. Women who were as fake as the Botox in their faces.

A waiter hovered and both the women reached out for further glasses of champagne, while Anna declined politely with a shake of her head.

'Well, even if the photos aren't to your taste, at least you can enjoy the free champagne.' She made to move away from them, but the next comment stopped her in her tracks.

'He'll soon grow bored of you, you know,' Verity said. 'Especially when he has something much better on offer.'

'Really? Well, that's just your opinion.'

Verity smiled. 'We're all entitled to our opinions, but this is a fact. I don't suppose you'd know, being in London for so much of time, but Daniel is spending a lot of time with Lucinda. It won't be long before he has his family back together, which is all he's ever wanted.'

Her words struck a nerve, even though Daniel had reassured her so many times that it was over between him and Lucinda.

'What's up, cat got your tongue? You must know it's true. And where's Daniel now, but talking to Lucinda at your exhibition. Doesn't that tell you something?'

'Not really. She's the mother of his son, and he loves Ben very much. And why would I listen to the likes of you over Daniel himself? You're not the kind of people I would either trust or respect.'

She watched as they registered her words, a look of fury on their faces. Then, as if in slow motion, Verity raised her arm and the contents of her full glass of champagne projected in an arc towards Anna, landing on her face in a cold splash. She gasped loudly in shock and the conversations closest to her died. A hush descended all around. Anna found herself unable to either move or speak she was so stunned. Then the gallery manager moved to her side.

'I think it's time you *ladies* left,' he said, the emphasis on the word "ladies", leaving no doubt what he thought of them.

'With pleasure,' Verity said. 'And that's what I think of your free champagne,' she added before she was ushered off the premises.

Anna watched them leave in a daze as Daniel rushed over.

'What the hell happened?' he asked.

'Your wife's vile friends happened,' Anna said, furious with him for being with Lucinda while she was having to defend their relationship. 'Excuse me, I need to clean up.'

The staring faces parted as she rushed towards the toilets, keen to get away from the unwanted attention. She pushed the door open and breathed a sigh of relief that no one else was inside. What was it about exhibitions and her? First there was Mark, now this. It was almost as if she wasn't allowed to enjoy the fruits of her hard work. And was it any wonder that she felt humiliated being here? She had no doubt that — although the woman was standing away from the action, looking as innocent as could be — this was all Lucinda's work, stirring people up to act on her behalf. Anna splashed her face with cold water, patted it dry with some towels and then attempted to reapply her make-up with the little she carried in her bag. A bit of face powder and some lipstick were all she had. But it would have to do. She needed to get back out there and salvage what she could from what was left of the evening. The door opened and Charlotte walked in.

'Are you okay?'

'I'll live,' Anna said through gritted teeth. 'Not as though there is any physical harm.'

'It's still classed as assault. You could call the police.'

'And waste their time? I don't think so. But do me a favour, Charlotte, and remind me to stick to subjects, in future, which have nothing to do with this city.'

'Oh, Anna.' Charlotte sighed. 'Don't let them win. They're not worth it.'

'No they're not.' But Anna felt drained. There was no fight left in her. And why should she have to fight for her relationship anyway? Why was Daniel letting Lucinda get away with this?

When she stepped back out into the gallery, there were only a few stragglers left, and thankfully Lucinda wasn't among them.

'Why don't you get off home and I'll finish things up here?' Charlotte said.

Anna laughed but without any mirth in her voice. 'Ever had the feeling of déjà vu?'

Charlotte smiled back. 'Yes, this is becoming a bit of a habit. I wonder what the next exhibition has in store for us?'

Anna couldn't think that far ahead. All she knew was that it wouldn't be here.

'But, despite that little hiccup,' Charlotte continued, 'tonight was a success. Most of your pictures have already been sold. Just remember that and don't dwell on the rest.'

Daniel came towards them. 'Are you okay?'

'I'm fine, just a little sticky. Nothing that a shower won't fix.'

'I can't believe she did that,' he said.

Anna nodded. 'It surprised me too. But I'm having to learn to put nothing past these women.'

'What I don't understand is why Verity did it.' Daniel frowned.

'I think that's easy enough to work out. Someone put her up to it.'

'What? You mean Lucinda?'

'Of course I mean Lucinda.'

'But she was with me.'

'Of course she was. Playing little Miss Innocent, while commandeering your attention as usual.'

'No, I really don't think—'

'No, Daniel, you don't. That's the problem.' She paused. 'Look, it's been a long night and I'm tired. Can we just get a taxi home?'

'Yes, of course.'

They sat in the taxi in an uncomfortable silence. She was furious that Daniel couldn't see the game Lucinda was playing, but she was tired of it going round in her head.

'I'm sorry tonight ended this way,' Daniel said eventually. 'The exhibition was a success, though. Everyone was blown away by the photos.'

'Not everyone.' Anna remembered Verity's words.

'Everyone who counts,' he said.

'They're just photographs of a much-photographed city, that's all,' she said, quoting Verity. What good was taking them even doing? She'd wanted this kind of success all her life but, now she had it, it felt hollow. Perhaps it was the effect of the explosion, perhaps it was Eva, but she suddenly realised she wanted her photographs to do more, to make a change in some way, to make people see things differently. What use were pictures of buildings to the world?

'I think you're doing yourself down,' Daniel said.

Anna sighed. She was too tired to make any sense of it tonight.

When they got home, Daniel tried to embrace her in the hallway, but she gently pushed him away.

'I need a shower and then I'm going to bed.'

'Anna, don't leave things like this. We need to talk.'

'Fine. But let me have a shower first.'

The pounding of the hot water over her body was comforting, but fear gnawed at her. She didn't want this conversation with Daniel as she was afraid it would only go one way.

After her shower, she wrapped herself in a bathrobe and towelled her hair before heading back downstairs, her legs feeling like lead.

In the kitchen, Daniel handed her a cup of tea. 'Here, drink this.'

'Thanks.'

She wandered into the living room and slumped onto the sofa. Daniel sat next to her and took hold of her hand. She resisted the urge to snatch it back from him.

'I'm really sorry about tonight,' he said.

'So am I. But we all know who's behind this. Why would Verity want to have a go at me like that? I don't even know her.'

'She's always been a pot stirrer and likes to be the centre of the drama. But Charlotte was right, you know. You could report it as an assault.'

'And what good would that do? It would only stir up more trouble.'

'I'll have a word with Lucinda if you really think she's behind this.'

'No, I don't want you to have a word with Lucinda.'

'So what do you want me to do?'

'I want you to stop running back to Lucinda all the time. You tell me it's over between you, but your actions are telling me something completely different. And they're telling everyone the same thing.'

'But I'm not running back to her. I'm just trying to get through to her that we are together and she can't keep behaving this way.'

'But don't you see that's exactly what she wants? She's finding ways to keep that connection between you, giving you reasons to speak to her. And you fall for it every time.'

'We'll always have a connection. We have Ben.'

'Yes, I know that, and I'd never get in the way of that. But this isn't about Ben. It's about you and her, and the fact that I'm in the way now and she doesn't like it. Don't feed the flames, Daniel.'

He sighed. 'I can see what you're saying. But I just think she needs to get used to the idea. Give it—'

'Don't tell me to give it time. How can I, Daniel? What do you want me to do? Accept that, every time I go out here, I risk the chance of being publicly humiliated? Is that what you want for me?'

'No, of course it isn't. I just think that if we stick together they'll get bored.'

'Do you know what? Until tonight I thought that too.' She turned to face him — all she could feel was sorrow. 'After the exhibition I'd planned to tell you that I was going to help you with the school. I was going to put my own ambitions on hold, and spend more of my time up here with you and Ben. I'm sick of us being apart so much, and I thought that was the answer.'

His eyes lit up. 'But it still can be. We can make it work, here together. It's being apart from each other that's killing this relationship.'

'It's part of it, yes. But me moving up here wouldn't work.'

He frowned. 'Why not?'

'How can I make this place my home when all I'm met with is hostility? And why should I give up my life in London, my own career, my family and my friends, when you're happy for me to be treated this way?'

'I'm not happy about it. Not by any means, but it would be different if you were here.'

'No, it wouldn't,' Anna said. 'She'd just up the ante to drive me away.'

'But we'd be together. I wouldn't have to be on my own with her.'

'You mean I'd be your guard dog, your protection. That you wouldn't be able to do anything without me by your side?' She shook her head. 'No, Daniel, that would never work, and I'm not going to come here to be treated the way I was tonight.'

She got up from the sofa and kissed him lightly on the cheek. 'It's been a long day and I'm tired. I'm going to bed.'

When she was in bed, she listened for him coming up but was glad when she didn't hear his footsteps. She longed for the oblivion of sleep, but she lay in bed, watching shadows through her tears as she cried silently. In the past she'd felt lost and alone, but she'd never felt as lonely as she did tonight. In the silence, she admitted to herself that this was the end. No matter what Daniel said about loving her, no matter how much she loved him, their relationship couldn't survive while he was still a puppet at the end of Lucinda's string. Daniel wasn't about to make the break. It would have to be down to her.

She slept fitfully during the night, later finding that Daniel was sleeping next to her. She edged herself away from him when she realised he was there. She didn't want to risk touching him or waking him, because if she did she knew she would want to make love to him and that would be her undoing.

She woke for the last time just as the light of dawn was streaking through the curtains. She got up as quietly as she could, tiptoeing around the bedroom as she collected her things before getting dressed in the bathroom. Downstairs she called for a taxi and took out the notepad she carried around in her bag. She paused before writing. How could she tell him that she was leaving and she wasn't coming back? In the end she wrote it the simplest way she could.

> *I'm sorry, Daniel, although I love you, I can't do this any-more. Thank you so much for everything you've done for me. I will always appreciate the chance you've given me. Give Ben a kiss goodbye. I'll miss you both. Xx*

She was waiting outside when the taxi arrived at the gates, glad that it didn't have to draw up outside the house. Although Daniel was a heavy sleeper in the morning, she didn't want to risk waking him. She didn't think she'd have the willpower to walk away if he was there.

She said a breezy hello to the driver, but then was silent as he drove her to the station. Her throat was thick with unshed tears and she was glad he was the silent type. She didn't think she'd be able to speak. Tears gathered behind her eyes but she refused to let them spill over. She would only allow herself to cry when she was behind the closed door of her childhood bedroom. Back to safety, back to where she belonged. As she boarded the train, she tried to ignore the ache in her stomach, the hollow feeling — the space that Daniel had left inside her.

She dozed on and off throughout the journey, relieved to be getting off the train at Euston. Back on familiar ground, she headed home. She put the key in the lock and listened as she opened the door. Thankfully all she could hear was silence — she was grateful that no one seemed to be there. She couldn't face anyone right now. She tiptoed up to her bedroom, undressed and climbed into bed. She was so exhausted that she fell into a deep sleep, but even on the verge between wakefulness and sleep, she knew that the tears would come. They were just lying in wait.

CHAPTER THIRTY

When Daniel woke, the sun was already streaming through the curtains. He lay on his back, allowing the events of last night to return to him. With a groan he remembered his conversation with Anna when they'd arrived home. He rolled over to reach out to her, but her side of the bed was flat and empty. She was always an early riser — he hoped her absence just meant she was downstairs.

* * *

Daniel drove towards Lucinda's house, his hands gripping the wheel with fury. Anna hadn't been downstairs in the kitchen as he'd hoped. Instead, a lone piece of paper had greeted him with her final words of goodbye. At first he'd been dismayed that she'd left, then angry that she'd slunk away without even facing him. As he re-ran the conversation in his head from the previous night, though, he realised she'd been saying her goodbyes then. If only he'd seen it, maybe he could have talked her round. His emotions had swung back from anger to dismay. He'd thought he'd found real love with Anna, his soulmate, someone with whom he could share everything, his hopes, his dreams, his thoughts, his body. But there had always been Lucinda. And Anna had been right when she'd asked why she should have to risk humiliation at the hands of his ex-wife and her friends, just because Lucinda didn't want him to find happiness with her.

After reading the note he'd grabbed his phone and rang Anna, but his call went to voicemail. He texted her but there was no reply. She obviously didn't want to speak to him. And that was when the fury began to grow. Fury at Lucinda that, although it had hurt him when she'd moved on with Axel, and he hated the thought of another man playing father to his son, he'd stepped aside and treated her relationship with respect. Why couldn't she give him the same?

Anna's words rang in his head — that Lucinda wanted him to react — and she was right. But what Anna didn't know, what he'd never been able to share with her, was that there were reasons he'd always treated Lucinda with kid gloves. Reasons why he needed to keep the status quo to preserve the relationship between her and him and Ben. And Lucinda had known that, and now she had pushed things too far. She had pushed him too far, because his life was empty without Anna in it.

Gravel sprayed from the sides of his tyres as he pulled to an abrupt stop in front of Lucinda's house. He stormed down the driveway, before banging on her front door and simultaneously ringing on the doorbell.

'Hold your horses! Where's the fire?'

'Well, I hope you're happy now.' He hurled the words at her the moment she opened the door.

'Daniel, what—'

'You've got what you wanted. So I hope you're pleased with yourself.'

'Daniel, what on earth are you talking about?'

'Last night!'

'Oh.' Her eyes widened. 'Yes, I'm sorry about last night. Verity had too much to drink and got carried away. She should never have thrown a drink over Anna.'

'And why would she do that?' Daniel asked. 'She doesn't even know her. So why would she have a go unless she'd been egged on? By you!'

'Daniel! I don't know how you can say that. I was with you at the time, if you remember.'

'But you weren't with me before, were you? When you were all getting sloshed together. Were you feeding them vitriol? Just like you did before the ball, so that no one would speak to Anna, and then afterwards, when they wrote those snide comments on Instagram.'

Lucinda gripped the door as though she was about to slam it in his face. 'Maybe that's because Anna clearly doesn't fit in. Nothing to do with me!'

'She doesn't fit in because you and your friends haven't given her a chance. I don't care if you don't like her. You don't have to. But I do, and now, because of you, because of how you've treated her, Anna doesn't feel comfortable being here anymore. So if your aim was to drive her away, then congratulations! You've done it. She's gone!'

'Mummy, Daddy, please don't argue.' A voice behind them stopped Daniel in his tracks. They turned to face Ben, who had tears streaming down his face. 'I hate it when you argue.'

Lucinda threw Daniel a look that clearly said *Now see what you've done?* Daniel knelt down and held his arms out, and Ben ran past his mother to throw himself against his father's chest.

'I'm sorry, Ben,' Lucinda said. 'We don't mean to argue. It's just that sometimes grown-ups get frustrated with each other. We'll try not to argue in front of you again.'

Ben looked up at Daniel. 'Has Anna really gone?'

Daniel nodded. 'Yes, I'm afraid so.'

'Is she coming back?'

Daniel shook his head. 'No, I don't think so.'

'Can't you go and get her?'

Again Daniel shook his head. 'It's a bit more complicated than that.'

'But I really liked her!'

'Me too,' Daniel said softly.

'That's just not fair!' Ben pulled himself away from Daniel, looked at the two of them and then, with tears still spilling down his face, ran upstairs.

Daniel pulled himself back to his feet, glaring at Lucinda.

'Daniel, I—'

'I don't want to hear it. And I think Ben needs you now.'

He began to walk towards his car, his anger spent, but then turned back to Lucinda. 'From now on I don't want anything to do with you apart from access to Ben. Whatever we had has been destroyed and there's no going back. So please, don't call me or come round on some pretext because I'm really not interested. Do you understand?'

Lucinda nodded sadly. 'Yes, I understand.'

'Good. I'm glad you've finally got the message.'

* * *

Anna woke to the sound of her phone ringing. Confused, she looked at the screen, saw it was Eva and answered it.

''Lo.'

'You weren't asleep, were you?' Eva's bright and breezy voice came down the phone. 'Good God, woman! It's the middle of the afternoon.'

'Oh.' Anna sighed. 'I didn't get much sleep last night.'

'Too much partying, I hope. Did the exhibition go well?'

'Um, sort of. A bit mixed really.'

'Oh!' Eva paused. 'Want to talk about it?'

'Not really. Not yet anyway.'

'Okay. Well, when you're ready, you know where I am.'

'Thanks.'

'But that wasn't the only reason I was calling you. I'm getting my new leg tomorrow.'

'That's brilliant news!' Anna sat up in bed, genuinely happy for her friend. Eva had been waiting for news on her prosthetic limb for a while — Anna knew she was desperate

247

to get going with it so she could be up and walking again. 'Do you want me to come and photograph it?'

'If you're up to it?'

'Of course I'm up to it. I wouldn't miss this for the world. What time?'

* * *

Feeling thirsty, Anna made her way downstairs to make a cup of tea. She couldn't remember the last time she'd eaten, but couldn't face the thought of food. She was grateful that the house was empty to give her time to process the situation. She was on her own now. Her dreams of a life with Daniel gone. She shook herself. There was no point dwelling on it. She would just have to get on with things. She was glad she had tomorrow to concentrate on. She would focus on that for now, then take a leaf out of Eva's book and take it one day at a time. She sat down at the kitchen table and braced herself to pick up her phone. There were several missed calls from Daniel and a ream of text messages. Anna deleted them without reading them. She knew she had to speak to Daniel — he deserved that at least. She should try to make up for the way she'd slunk out in the early hours of the morning. But not now. She couldn't face it now.

She took a deep breath and steeled herself for the next thing she needed to do. She clicked into Instagram, looking for the post she hoped she wouldn't find. But there it was. The very moment Verity had launched her glass of champagne into her face. Almost as though the photographer had known it would happen and when. *What a coincidence*. The phrase "today's news is tomorrow's chip wrapping" ran through her head. Only these days it wasn't like that. These days, once something was online, it was there for life, for all to view for ever. Whenever there was anything new to say about a person those photographs could be dragged up in an instant for all the world to see.

'Well, thank you, Lucinda,' she muttered. 'Now my humiliation is complete.' She sipped at her tea, grimacing because it had gone cold. Lucinda may have won in terms of splitting her and Daniel up, but Anna wouldn't let her win completely. *The best revenge is success*, she told herself. She was determined that whatever she decided to do she would be successful, just to spite Lucinda and her friends.

* * *

'So, here she is, your new leg,' the physiotherapist said.

'She's beautiful.' Eva stroked the metal lovingly.

'Most people give them names. But that's up to you.'

'I will give her a name. Something that's going to give me my independence deserves one. I'll have to think about the right one though.'

'I know this is a cliché, but you need to understand it's going to take time. It's going to be metal against flesh for a while, so it will rub at first and you'll have to take it in small bursts, while you become acclimatised.'

'Okay, I understand.'

Standing in the background, filming the first time Eva would put on her prosthetic limb, Anna marvelled again at how upbeat and positive Eva always seemed to be. She was sure that she had her moments, where despair would hit her, but she never showed it in these sessions. Here she was always prepared to go the extra mile, to make the best of her situation. Eva was definitely the kind of person Anna wanted to emulate.

The time passed quickly as Anna concentrated on getting the best shots and videos of her friend, and she was glad that she had something positive to focus on.

* * *

Daniel groaned as his phone rang and Lucinda's number flashed up. Hadn't she got the message? He stared at his phone as it rang, contemplating whether or not to answer it. But what if she was phoning about Ben? And there it was. The reason they'd always have to stay connected.

He accepted the call. 'Lucinda,' he said curtly.

'Daniel! He's gone!'

'What do you mean? Who's gone?' He wondered what drama Lucinda was trying to create. Had she split up with Axel? Was she using that to try to pull him back in?

'Ben! Ben's gone.'

A shiver of fear ran down Daniel's spine. Not just at her words, but at her voice, which he now realised was genuinely hysterical.

'Ben's gone? Where's Ben gone?'

'I don't know! He didn't come down for breakfast so I went to wake him up. His bed was empty and his backpack is gone.'

'Shit!' Daniel was suddenly very afraid. 'Have you phoned round all his friends?'

'Not yet, no. I thought he might have come to yours.'

'Start phoning. I'll be round as soon as I can.' Daniel picked up his keys and ran to his car.

The journey to Lucinda's house was a blur. All he thought about was Ben. Where had he gone? Was he safe? And he thought of all the dangerous people who were out in the world, who could harm his precious, innocent nine-year-old son.

* * *

Lucinda had rung everyone she knew. 'No one's seen him or heard from him. No one.' A tear slid down her cheek. In the past Daniel would have comforted her, but today he had no time for emotion. If he gave in to any emotion, either hers or his own, he would break down, and then he wouldn't be able to find his son.

'So now it's time to phone the police,' he said, in his most matter-of-fact tone.

CHAPTER THIRTY-ONE

'I think we'll call it a day now. You've done enough,' the physiotherapist told Eva.

'But I want to carry on. I'm fine.'

'No.' The physio was firm. 'If you overdo it on day one,
you'll chafe the skin too much, then you won't be able to do
anything for a while. A little bit each day will get you where
you want to be.'

'Okay,' Eva said reluctantly. 'If you say so.'

'I do.'

Anna chipped in. 'The footage is great and, besides, you
want to give your readers something to look forward to. Little
and often works for me.'

'All right!' Eva held her hands up in mock surrender. 'I
get the message.'

The sound of Anna's phone ringing cut into their conversation. Anna looked at the screen, it was an unknown number. She still hadn't returned any of Daniel's calls — briefly
she wondered if it was him ringing on someone else's phone.
She hesitated, wondering whether to answer, but decided to be
brave. She'd have to face him sometime.

'Hello, is that Miss Anna Wright?' an unknown voice asked her.

'Yes, that's me,' Anna said, frowning. 'Who is this, please?'

'I'm phoning from British Transport Police.'

'British Transport Police?' she repeated, even more confused. 'I'm sorry, I don't understand.'

Eva looked over, a surprised expression on her face.

'I'm here with a Master Benjamin Redfern.'

'Ben?'

'Yes. He's run away from home and he was coming to see you.'

'What? Is he okay?' she asked, horrified.

'Yes, he's fine. One of our train conductors spotted him on the London train alone, and flagged it up with us. We were there to meet him from the train.'

'Oh, thank God! Does his dad know he's safe?'

'No. That's the problem. He only wants to speak to you. Can you come to meet him?'

'Of course. If you give me an address I'll be there as soon as I can. And I'll let his dad know.'

'Thank you.'

'What's the matter?' Eva asked when Anna ended the call.

'It's Ben, Daniel's son. He's run away from home and he's at Euston with the transport police.'

'Why would he do that?'

'Daniel and I have split up.'

'What?'

Anna sighed. 'It's a long story. I'll tell you all about it, but right now I need to phone Daniel, then I need to get to Euston and speak to Ben.'

'Of course. You get on.'

* * *

Daniel snatched up his phone as it started to ring, hoping it was Ben. His heart flipped a little when he saw it was Anna. He'd been longing for her to phone, but now he needed to concentrate on finding his son.

'Anna, hi, I'm glad you called. But I'm sorry, now's not a good time.'

'I know. It's Ben.'

'Yes, we can't find him. How did you know? Did he call you?' He felt as though he was holding his breath. All he wanted was to be able to reach out and hug his son, to know that he was okay.

'Not as such, no. But, first of all, he's safe. He somehow managed to get on a train to London, but he was spotted by himself and the transport police picked him up at Euston. He's refusing to speak to anyone but me.'

'Oh, thank God!' He smiled at Lucinda, who was frowning at him from across the kitchen table. He moved the phone away from his ear and told her, 'Ben's in London. He's safe.'

For a moment her face lit up, then she frowned again. 'What's he doing in London?'

Daniel waved her question away and turned his attention back to Anna. 'So have you spoken to him?'

'Not yet. I'm on my way over now, but I thought I'd better let you know straight away that he's safe.'

'Thank you, Anna. Thank you so much.' Daniel didn't know how he felt about Ben not wanting to contact him, but the main thing was that he was safe, and soon he'd be with someone who loved him. 'I'm on my way.' He ended the call.

'What's Ben doing in London?' Lucinda repeated.

'I don't know, but the only person he wants to speak to is Anna.'

'Anna! That bloody woman!'

'No!' Daniel almost shouted at her. 'I won't have you bad-mouthing her. She knew nothing about this. And I think we've both underestimated how much Anna means to Ben.'

'Because of you!' Her voice rose. 'Because you let her into your life.'

'Yes, I did,' Daniel said. 'Because she is a good and kind woman, who I love very much. And because I was misguided enough to let you drive her away. If we want to apportion blame here, Lucinda, then we need to look at ourselves before we start blaming anyone else.'

'I don't think—'

'I don't care what you think. All I care about right now is Ben. So I'm driving down to London. You can either come with me and keep your opinions to yourself, or you can find your own way there, or even wait here until we come back.'

'No, I'm coming. I'll just get my coat.'

* * *

The train journey seemed to take ages, lumbering slowly towards each station. Sitting in an almost empty carriage, Anna willed it to go faster. All she wanted to do was get to Ben. To make sure he really was all right. She'd thought she was doing okay, that she'd be able to cut both Daniel and Ben out of her life. That she'd be able to take one day at a time and gradually become stronger. But at the news that Ben might have been in danger, and wondering what kind of hell Daniel was going through, had brought that house of cards crashing down. She desperately wanted to be with them, with both of them, and that would never change. The fact that Ben had run to her filled her with both horror — that she might be the cause of him running away — and a huge rush of love — that he'd turned to her for help. But most of all, she realised, this should never have happened in the first place. She should never have allowed Lucinda and her nasty friends to drive her away. What she felt for Daniel, and his son, was too strong. She had been a fool not to fight for it. Daniel hadn't helped by the way he dealt with Lucinda, but she understood he had to tread carefully because of Ben. She still thought he should have backed her up more, but she did at least understand his motives. She wondered if now things could be different. Could a nine-year-old boy show them all the error of their ways? She certainly hoped so.

* * *

After what seemed like an interminable journey, Anna finally reached Euston Square and headed out towards the police station. She hurried as fast as she could, out of breath by the time she entered the station and headed for the desk.

'Hi, I'm Anna Wright. I'm here for Ben Redfern — he's nine years old and was on a train to Euston on his own.'

'Yes, of course, just take a seat and I'll phone through for someone to take you to him.'

She sat nervously, her legs shaking as she waited for what seemed like for ever. Eventually a middle-aged woman came through.

'Anna Wright?'

'Yes, that's me.' She stood up quickly. 'How's Ben?'

The woman smiled. 'He's fine. But, before I take you to him, I need to go through a few things first.'

'Okay.' Anna followed her to the desk, wishing they could get this bit over and done with as quickly as possible.

Anna showed her identification as requested, giving her personal details as the woman filled in a form.

'So you're Ben's stepmother, are you?' the woman asked, putting the form to one side.

'Ah, no, I'm afraid Ben's been a bit stretchy with the truth there. I was in a relationship with his father, but we're not married.'

'Was?'

'Yes, we split up yesterday.' The words stuck in her throat as she said them. It was still hard to believe that they weren't together anymore. 'Ben lives with his mother in Cheshire. Daniel, his dad, splits his time between London and Cheshire, and I live mainly here.'

'Sounds complicated.'

Anna sighed. 'Yes, it is.'

'Well, unfortunately, that changes things. If you're not his next of kin, or even his guardian, then I'm afraid I can't release him to your care.'

'No, I don't expect you to. His dad's on his way, but it's going to take him several hours before he gets here. I just want to sit with Ben until he gets here. Ben did ask for me. By name.'

'Yes, he did. But he said you were his stepmother and that's clearly not the case.'

'That is correct, but he's a nine-year old boy, he must be very distressed to have tried to make this journey in the first place.'

The woman's face softened slightly. 'Why don't you take a seat? I'll have a word with my superiors and see what we can do.'

Anna sat down, her body feeling as though it was jittering with tension. All she wanted to was to be with Ben. To hold him in her arms and tell him everything would be alright.

Finally the woman returned. 'Well, I've spoken to my superiors, and although this is not normal protocol, in the absence of his next of kin, because of the time it will take for his father to get here, and because Benjamin asked for you specifically, we will allow you to sit with him until his father gets here. However, one of our officers will be present with you in the room at all times. Do you agree to that?'

'Yes, of course I do,' Anna said, relieved that she was finally going to be allowed to be with Ben.

* * *

'Anna!' Before she was even through the door, Ben jumped up from the chair he was sitting on and hurtled into her arms.

'Oh, Ben!' She clutched him to her. 'Thank goodness you're safe.'

'I'm glad you're here.'

'I'm glad I am too. But, Ben, what were you thinking?'

He shook his head and she could see tears welling in his eyes. She realised she was being too heavy-handed.

'I'm sorry. Please don't cry. Take your time.'

'Can I get any of you a drink?' the woman from the desk asked as Ben pulled away from Anna.

'I'd love a coffee,' Anna said gratefully.

'And perhaps some squash and biscuits for Ben?' The woman looked to the officer who was already sitting with Ben. 'Coffee? it might be a long wait.'

'That would be good thanks.' The officer took out his phone — an attempt to give some privacy while still being in the room.

'I'm sorry,' Ben said, hugging Anna once more, his words muffled by her jumper. 'I've caused a lot of trouble.'

'Come and sit down,' she said, guiding him back to the sofa. 'I'm sure you had your reasons.'

'I did, but they seem a bit silly now.'

'Never mind about that. The main thing is that you're safe. I spoke to your dad and he was worried sick. I bet your mum was too.'

He nodded. 'I know, but they were arguing. I hate it when they argue.'

'That must be hard for you. But what made you get on a train here? It can't just be because of an argument?'

'They were arguing over you. Dad said it was all Mum's fault, that she'd pushed you away. I heard them so I came downstairs. I asked Dad if you were coming back and he said no. I didn't want to never see you again and I was cross with them for you not being there, so I thought I'd come and see you myself.'

'Oh, Ben!'

'I'm sorry.'

'No, I'm sorry. I should have realised. I shouldn't have gone without speaking to you myself. That was bad of me. I was upset and I didn't think things through. See, we all make mistakes when we're not thinking properly. You could have phoned me, though. You've got my number in your phone, haven't you?'

He nodded. 'Yes, but I didn't know if you'd speak to me. I thought that if you were angry with Dad then you might be angry with me too.'

'Oh, Ben!' She reached out and hugged him. 'It wasn't about you, although I should have been more careful with your feelings.'

'Did Mum really push you away? Did she hurt you?'

'No, she didn't push me like that! I . . .' Anna paused, knowing she needed to phrase her words very carefully. 'This might sound like a grown-up trying to brush things under the carpet, but sometimes relationships can get very complicated. Sometimes people do strange things because they're afraid.'

'Was Mum afraid I'd love you more than her?'

'I don't know about that,' Anna said, shocked at how perceptive he was. 'And that would never happen, because you'll always love your mum the most.'

'I do, but sometimes she can be a bit . . . I don't know, I can't talk to her like I can to you.'

'That's because I'm not your mum, so it might be easier to talk to me about some things. But I know that your mum loves you very much. And she does things because she wants it to be right for you and to keep you safe.'

'Okay.' He nodded. 'I understand. I think.'

'Good. Well, when I spoke to your dad, he was relieved to know that you were safe and sound. He said he was coming straight down here.'

Ben nodded. 'Was he really mad at me?'

'Not mad, no. I think he was just relieved. He might have a few words to say to you when he's got over the shock, though. Because what you did was very dangerous. You should never do something like that without speaking to your parents.'

'I know. I'm sorry about that. It's just that things are very complicated with Mum and Dad and you.'

'Oh, tell me about it. And if we find it complicated, you must find it even harder. It doesn't help with us all living in separate places.'

'Do you think you and Dad will get back together?'

'I don't know,' Anna said, wishing she could wave a magic wand and make it all right for all of them. But in the absence of a magic wand, she added, 'Whatever happens between me and your dad, I'll always be there for you and you can ring me if ever you need someone to talk to.'

'Okay.'

'Now, you tell me something. How did you manage to get all the way to London with no one knowing?'

Ben smiled. 'Well, I knew where the train station was, so I packed my bag and snuck out of the house before anyone else was up. And I walked to the station. It was a long way, but I was determined to get there.'

'Wow, you certainly were determined. And what did you do for a train ticket?'

He blushed. 'Mum has a train app on her phone. I know the code to her phone — she told me what it was before I had my own and I used to play games on it. And I . . .' He faltered. 'I booked a ticket on her app.'

'Oh, Ben! You shouldn't have done that.'

'I know, and I know she'll be angry. She'll probably take my PlayStation off me for at least a month.'

'And the rest!' Anna laughed. 'But honestly, that was not a good thing.'

'I know and I'll never do it again.'

'Well, that's something you need to talk to your mum and dad about. But I'm still curious — a young boy on a train alone is going to look odd. How did you even get on the train in the first place?'

'I waited until there were people around and I tagged along with them, so it didn't look like I was on my own.'

'Mmm, very clever. But will you promise me one thing?'

'What?'

'In future, will you only use your cleverness for good things, not for bad?'

Ben grinned. 'I promise.'

* * *

Daniel drove as fast as he could, his need to be with his son paramount. He couldn't believe Ben had actually taken it on himself to travel to London. Alone. Without telling either of them. He was nine years old. Nine years. Anything could have happened to him! Daniel silently thanked the person who'd spotted him and delivered him safely to the transport police, rather than leaving him exposed to the dangers of the capital city. Daniel shuddered at the horror of the alternative. He had to stop thinking like this — Ben was safe and that was all that mattered. And he was with Anna. He almost gasped at that thought. Not only would he be seeing Ben soon, he would be seeing Anna too.

'Are you okay?' Lucinda asked. It was the first time she'd spoken since they'd got into the car.

'I'm fine.' He didn't want to speak to her. She was just a passenger as far as he was concerned, and not a particularly welcome one. How would Anna feel when they arrived together? he wondered. Would she think that nothing had changed? He hoped he'd have a chance to speak to her alone, to explain to her how he felt, how he was desperate to make things work between them. He was even prepared to spend more time in London, maybe employ someone else to oversee the opening and running of the photography school. It would mean seeing less of Ben, of course, but somehow he'd just have to make it work. One thing the last few days had taught him was that he definitely didn't want to live without her.

'I'm sorry,' Lucinda said into the silence.

'What are you sorry for exactly?' He wished he'd insisted she find her own way to London, or better yet stayed at home until he returned with Ben. But they'd only been focused on Ben when they'd left and he'd understood she would be as desperate to see their son as he was.

'For everything really.' Her voice was so quiet he almost didn't catch her words.

'What do you mean?' He hoped this wasn't another one of her games. Pretending to be contrite so that she could get back into his good books.

'I'm sorry for being so nasty to Anna. I'm sorry for causing you two to break up. I didn't realise how much she meant to you, or to Ben.'

She sounded genuine enough, as though she meant her words, but he didn't know how to answer her. What could he say? That's okay? Because it wasn't okay. Her saying she was sorry wouldn't bring Anna back. The damage had been done.

'I was jealous,' she said.

'Of me?'

'Of your relationship.'

'You've got Axel. Why couldn't you let me move on too?'

She sighed. 'It's different. Axel and I, well . . . it's not really working. He's like you, married to his job. He's either on tour or recording, he's not cut out for a ready-made family. Not yet anyway.'

'Is that why you said you wanted us to try again?'

'Yes. I was scared. I'm no good on my own.'

'It would never work between us, you know?'

'I do know. I suppose I always knew it. I was just clutching at straws really. I was jealous of what you and Anna had together. You seem so perfect, so much in love, and I wanted that too.'

'And if you couldn't have it, you decided that I couldn't have it either.' He clenched the steering wheel, trying to contain his anger towards her. Why couldn't she have been happy for him?

'Yes, but it wasn't just that.' She paused. 'I was also jealous of her and Ben. I thought she might take him away from me.'

'That would never happen! You're Ben's mum.'

'But they got on so well together. And who was it he ran to?'

'Because we were at loggerheads with each other. He ran to the only other person he felt he could trust. It's not a competition. You've got to get over this, Lucinda. Start to have a bit of faith in yourself. So it didn't work out between us, but you're a brilliant mum and you need to trust in that.'

'I haven't always been a great mum, though, have I? Not at the start anyway.'

Daniel sighed. He'd lost count of the number of times they'd been through this before. 'That wasn't your fault. You were ill. You've got to stop beating yourself up about it.'

'It's not that easy.'

'Then do something about it. Get some therapy.'

'See a shrink, you mean?'

'See a counsellor. If you'd broken your leg you'd go and see a doctor, wouldn't you?'

'Yes, but that's different.'

'It's not different at all. There's nothing wrong in reaching out for professional help. Not if it heals you.'

'I'll think about it.'

'Good.' He knew he was being tough with her, but treating her with kid gloves hadn't done any good before. She needed to face facts. They all did. 'Look, I'm sorry if that seems harsh, but I think it will help. You're a good person — you just need to allow yourself to be that person. And while we're talking about Anna, I can't let you take all the blame. It was my fault too.'

'How do you figure that?'

'Because I didn't stick up for her enough.'

'From what I can see she did a pretty good job at sticking up for herself.'

'But she shouldn't have had to. It wasn't working with us being so far apart, so she offered to move up to Cheshire to help me with the photography school. She was actually prepared to put her own dreams on hold so that I could fulfil mine. But then, after the way she was treated, she felt she couldn't give up her life, her family and her friends to be in a place where she was made to feel so unwelcome. And in hindsight I wouldn't have asked her too. It would have been too much of a sacrifice.'

'Oh, God. Daniel, I am so sorry. Is there anything I can do? Do you want me to speak to her? Tell her I was wrong and I won't behave like that again?'

'Thanks for the offer, but I don't think that will help. It's probably too late now. And I'll forever blame myself for that.'

CHAPTER THIRTY-TWO

The door opened and, suddenly, there standing in front of Anna, were Lucinda and Daniel. Ben looked from one to the other, a worried expression on his face. Then Lucinda started walking towards him, her arms open, and he jumped up and ran to her.

'Oh, my darling.' Lucinda circled her arms around him, kissing the top of his head. 'You've given us all such a fright.'

'I'm sorry.' Ben's voice was muffled in her clothes. 'I never meant—'

'Hush, hush,' she said. 'The important thing is that you're safe. We can talk about the rest later.'

Feeling superfluous, Anna rose from the sofa. 'I'll leave you to it.'

Lucinda looked up from Ben. 'Thank you for looking after him.'

For the first time Lucinda sounded genuine. What a pity it had taken until now — that it had taken this little boy being in danger to make this happen.

'It was the least I could do.'

She dared not look at Daniel as she walked past him, but he caught her arm. 'Anna? Can we talk?'

She dragged her eyes to his and her heart lurched as she saw his desperation. Was it possible that Ben running away had changed things? Lucinda was certainly less frosty towards her. She wasn't sure she dared hope, afraid that would only cause her more heartache. But she'd left without speaking to him, so the least she could do was give him a chance to speak. She nodded.

'Yes, but not now. You need to be with Ben. Call me when you're ready and we'll sort something out.' She could hear the catch in her voice as she spoke and her eyes flooded with tears, but she blinked them back. Then, holding her head high, she walked away.

* * *

She sat in a daze on the train on the way home, unable to sort her scrambled thoughts. She wasn't sure what to do next. Did she and Daniel have a future after all? Could they make this work? Now that the exhibition was over she didn't have much of a demand on her time, apart from documenting Eva's recovery, and she could do that in day trips to London whenever she was needed. In theory she should be planning her next exhibition, but apart from the prospective launch of Eva's book, she couldn't envisage what her next project would be. The last two exhibitions had been a success, both in terms of achieving her dreams and in making a financial profit, but the Chester exhibition had left her feeling rudderless. And it wasn't just Lucinda and her friends and her split with Daniel. It was more about the feeling she'd had when she'd left the venue — of what was the point of it? She wanted to do something useful, something that changed people's opinions and made them think about life in a different way. Pictures of buildings didn't seem to be enough anymore, but for the life of her she didn't know what would be enough.

On a personal level, her dad seemed settled with a new girlfriend, and Jack would be sentenced soon and moved to a new prison that might be outside of London. Wherever he was she would visit him. Harry was going to Durham University. Although her family might be further apart in distance, they were closer than they had been for a long, long time. She should be happy but she wasn't.

Daniel. His name drifted into her mind and she realised she would never be able to settle until she'd spoken to him.

* * *

His call came later that evening. 'Anna?'

'Daniel, hi. Is everything okay?'

'Yes, everything is fine. We both had a good chat with Ben and he knows how dangerous it was to do what he did.'

'I spoke to him too. I hope you don't blame me for him running away.'

'No, I don't! I blame myself and Lucinda.'

'I do feel guilty, though. If I hadn't left so suddenly, had explained to him what was happening, maybe he wouldn't have done what he did.'

'And if Lucinda and I hadn't been arguing over you in front of him . . . I don't know.' He sighed and she felt his deep sadness in that sigh. 'Maybe we're all to blame. But at least no harm has been done.'

'Yes, that's one good thing.'

'But it has made me realise how much you mean to him. And how much you mean to me too.' He paused. 'It's late now, but I could drive over to yours?'

She thought about her dad and Harry downstairs in the living room. She could meet Daniel out somewhere, but she didn't really want to have this conversation in public.

'Maybe tomorrow? I could come over to yours. That's if it's not disturbing Lucinda and Ben.'

'They're not here. They're staying in a hotel and heading back first thing in the morning. Ben starts back at school on Wednesday.'

Her heart started to beat wildly in her chest. She hadn't thought Lucinda would stay in a hotel when he had all those rooms going spare in his house. But as she was, did that mean something had changed after all?

* * *

Anna tried to apply a dash of mascara, but her hand was shaking so much she was in danger of stabbing herself in the eye. She wanted to look good for Daniel but, after another night of barely sleeping, she looked tired and washed out, and no amount of inexpertly applied make-up was going to cover that up. She made one more attempt, then put on some lipstick in the hope that would make the difference.

Her stomach was twisting in anxiety all the way on the Tube journey. She'd bought a takeaway coffee at the station but it just added to the agitation going on in her stomach, and she'd ended up unable to drink it. Her legs were practically shaking as she walked down the road towards Daniel's house. During the long sleepless night, she'd come to the conclusion that, in running away from Cheshire, she'd been a coward. Yes, she had been very unhappy at the way she'd been treated, and she did have a right to defend herself, but when it came down to it, she should never have walked out on Daniel like that. She had let her insecurities and her jealousy get the better of her. If they had any chance of making their relationship work, things would have to change on both sides. And surely the way she felt about him was worth the effort? That was what she was planning on telling him anyway — she just hoped he was prepared to fight for her too.

Although she had a key to his house, she rang the bell instead of letting herself in.

'Anna?' He looked surprised. 'Have you lost your key?'

'No, I just didn't think it was appropriate.'

He nodded and she thought he looked sad. It felt awkward and distant between them, and she wished they could be as free around each other as they used to be.

'Come in. Do you want a coffee?'

She shook her head. 'No, thanks.'

'Come into the living room and sit down. Let's at least be comfortable.'

She perched herself on the sofa, thinking of all the times they'd lain in each other's arms, either just relaxing or revelling in exploring each other's bodies. She shivered and tried to pull herself back into the present. Daniel sat down in the chair opposite.

They stared at each other for a moment and then simultaneously said, 'I'm sorry.'

They laughed. It helped to break the ice.

'I'm sorry for leaving the way I did,' she said. 'It was cowardly. I did it because I was afraid that, if I stayed to say goodbye, you'd talk me out of it. Says it all really, doesn't it?'

'I understand why you left and I'm sorry too. The way Lucinda and her friends treated you was horrible, but I should have done more to put a stop to it or to support you.'

'It's okay, I understand.'

'No, I don't think you do. Let me explain.' He took a deep breath. 'Despite her looks, despite the hard front she puts on, deep down Lucinda is very insecure.'

From the Lucinda she'd seen, Anna didn't think she looked insecure at all, but she kept her thoughts to herself as he continued.

'She had a difficult pregnancy, she was sick as a dog for most of it, not just the first few months like most women, and then when she had Ben she didn't bond. No one realised at the time that she was ill, postnatal depression, and so she wasn't treated. She had a breakdown and refused to look after Ben at all. When we finally got her to a doctor and started on the medication, everything changed, but she's never got over her guilt about not bonding with him at the beginning. And then she became overprotective towards him, pushing everyone away from her, including me. My way of dealing with it was to bury myself in work, so you can see how it would have become a downward spiral. For a long time I've blamed myself for not seeing what was happening and not doing anything to stop them from leaving.'

'I can see that's why you're sensitive around her.'

'We'd been rubbing along fairly well, until you. I'd never really got involved with anyone since she left. Not in any meaningful way, so when she saw you she got scared.'

'But she's in a relationship herself.'

'Yes, but it's not working out.'

'So, she decided she wanted you back?' Despite his empathy with his ex, Anna still couldn't feel it. These were the actions of a spoiled child, not someone she could relate to.

'I can see that's what it looks like. She's not resilient like you. She'd never had to be on her own and she was scared. And then there was the way Ben reacted to you. You're so natural with him and you took to each other instantly. It brought back all her insecurities about being a mother, and she thought he'd end up loving you more than her.'

Anna gasped. 'But that's not possible! And even if it was, I'd never let that happen. She's his mum.'

'I know that, you know that, and even Ben knows that, but it took her a while to see it.'

'And she does now?'

'Yes. She's admitted how horrible she was to you. Ben running away has really opened her eyes.'

'I don't suppose it helped that he ran to me.'

'Initially, no, but Ben explained that it was more about us arguing. You were the only other person he felt he could trust. We had a long chat yesterday and everyone now knows where they stand.'

'Well, that's good.' Anna hoped she'd managed to keep the bitterness out of her voice. She was glad that they were all sorted, but where did that leave her?

'I realise I didn't support you enough. It wasn't because I had any feelings for her, but I was trying not to rock the boat. For Ben's sake.'

'Yes, I think I always understood that,' Anna said quietly. 'But it's really hard to be stuck in the middle. I'm not great at trusting people, especially after Mark, and I needed to protect myself.'

'And so you should. But it's not like that anymore.'

'Isn't it?'

'No. Lucinda is genuinely sorry for the way she behaved towards you, and also grateful that you were here for Ben, despite the circumstances.'

'Whatever happens, I'll always be here if Ben needs me.'

'Thank you. Anyway, she's decided she needs to try some counselling to help her unravel her feelings, and, although I don't think you'll ever be besties, I think things will be a lot easier now. That's if . . .' He paused. 'If you'll agree to give me another chance?'

At those words she was so tempted to rush into his arms, but Lucinda wasn't the only obstacle in their way.

'I don't know,' she said. She could tell by his face that her words had dashed his hopes. 'There's still the question of distance. I have to admit I was jealous and insecure about you spending so much time in Cheshire. In being close to Lucinda. I realise of course, now, that there's nothing between you, but, while you were away, I let those insecurities get the better of me.'

'I can understand that. The photography school is something I really wanted to do, but I think I made a mistake in setting it up in Manchester. I should have done it here instead, then all this would never have happened.'

'But you did it to be closer to Ben. You want to spend more time with him and I totally get that.'

'I did and I do. But I also don't want to lose you. Which is why I've decided that, if you'll give me a second chance, I'll find someone to take over the running of the school and I'll spend more time here. I might even set up another school here. I'll still spend time with Ben, and hopefully you'll join me, but I want to be wherever you are. For the moment that's here, so that's where I want to be.'

His sacrifice pulled at her heart. To give up spending time with his son showed how deeply he loved her.

'I don't want you to do that,' she said slowly.

His face fell and instantly he was by her side, beseeching her. 'But Anna, I—'

'Let me finish.' She held his face between her hands. 'I don't want you to make that sacrifice. I don't want you to give up spending time with your son to be with me. That's not fair on either of you and I would never want to be the cause of that.' She paused. 'So I'll come to you.'

'To Cheshire?'

'To Cheshire.' Her heart lifted at his smile.

'But what about your work, your family, your life? I don't want you to sacrifice that for me either.'

'I'm not. I'm glad I did the exhibitions, and I'm glad they were a success, but being with Eva, surviving that blast, well, it's made me want to give something back. To make a difference. I want to help you run the school. I want to give people the chance that you gave me. Yes, I still do want to pursue the photography but it needs to be more meaningful, and I don't know what that is yet. As for my family, Harry will be off to university next month and Jack, well, who knows where he's going to be for the time being, and Dad has met someone.'

'He has? And how do you feel about that?'

'It's a bit strange, but he's been on his own a long time and, as long as whoever it is makes him happy, then that's fine with me. And besides, I'll still need to come here some of the time so I'll get to see him.'

'And you'll do that for me?'

'I'm not just doing it for you. I'm doing it for me too. But . . .' She paused. 'I'd like us to create our own life in Cheshire. I don't want to be expected to be part of Lucinda's crowd.'

Daniel laughed. 'Neither do I! I promise you, things will be different from now on. We'll build our own life. Together.'

'I'd like that very much.'

She leaned in and he kissed her. Gently at first, but with increasing passion. It was a kiss she hoped would last for ever.

EPILOGUE

Anna paused on the threshold to the London gallery and took a deep breath. Daniel put his arm round her in reassurance. 'There's no need to be nervous — the pair of you are going to blow them away. And you look gorgeous.'

'Thank you.' The deep red dress she'd bought for the occasion clung to her curves and she knew she looked good in it. She'd also had her hair and make-up professionally done. She'd learned over the last twelve months that, if she was going to be photographed, she was going to make sure she looked her best. 'At least this one isn't all down to me.'

In the six months since Anna's move to Cheshire, Eva had made a remarkable recovery. She'd regained her mobility, thanks to her prosthetic limb, and was living life to the full. Whenever Anna had been back in London they'd met up, and Anna had documented everything she needed for Eva's book. As they had discussed many months ago, the book signing would take place along with an exhibition of Anna's photographs, managed by the indomitable Charlotte.

'You've done all the hard work,' Daniel said. 'Now all you have to do is relax and bathe in the glory.'

Instantly her mind slipped back to her last exhibition when she hadn't bathed in the glory but had been left dripping in champagne. She just hoped tonight didn't hold any unexpected surprises, at least not of the unsavoury kind.

'You know I'm not very good at that, and you also know my past history with exhibitions.'

Daniel laughed. 'Yes, but a lot has changed since then, so we'll just have to hope that it's third time lucky tonight.'

He was right. A lot had happened in the last six months. She'd been hesitant at first about the move north, but she could honestly say that she'd never been happier. It had been a relief to settle into family life with Daniel and Ben, and to be out of the limelight. Her camera was still her constant companion whenever she went walkabout. She, Daniel and Ben often took trips so that she could photograph the landscape, usually in competition with Ben, who was developing his love for photography too. But in helping Daniel set up the photography school, she'd realised where her real love lay, and that was in teaching. She loved it when new students came in, with lots of enthusiasm and ambition but little understanding of the complexities of their art. She often felt she learned as much from the students as they did from her, and the best thing was that it was completely out of the limelight.

Her relationship with Lucinda had developed too. They were never going to be friends, but at least they showed each other mutual respect. Daniel had kept his word and made sure that they didn't have to socialise with her crowd. In fact, they lived an almost reclusive life, concentrating on the school, each other and Ben.

But now, she knew that tonight was going to be the exact opposite. Tonight was going to be glamour and glitz, and the only reason she was doing this was for her friend Eva. Their relationship had grown stronger during Eva's recovery, and it was a joy to be there for each other through both the hard and the good times.

The investigation into the explosion had finally reported its conclusions, and Anna vividly remembered the day when they had found out that it could have been easily avoided. For June it had been a cold day, and she remembered how some of the models had complained about the temperature. One kind soul, thinking they were doing them all a favour, had lit the central heating boiler to provide them with some heat. But they had failed to pay any attention to the stickers on the boiler, highlighting that it was faulty and should not be lit. All day the pressure, due to defective safety valves, had been building up, eventually exploding just as the models had been lining up for the final walk down the catwalk.

'To think that people died, and me and others lost limbs, over something so stupid,' Eva had said when she'd read the report.

Anna didn't know how she could lift her friend's spirits. All she could come up with was, 'It all seems so senseless, but there's nothing we can do to change the past.'

And miraculously Eva smiled and said, 'No, but we can change the future, and that's exactly what I intend to do.' And then she told Anna that, as a result of the Instagram posts, she'd been contacted by a charity who helped amputees come to terms with their loss, and to adapt to their new lives.

Eva became an ambassador for the foundation and was busier and more fulfilled than ever before. When she told Anna she needed a personal assistant, Anna immediately introduced her to Daisy. They hit it off and Daisy thrived in her new job. She moved out of her mother's house and was revelling in all the opportunities for travel.

Now, as Anna walked through the door into the gallery, she smiled as she recalled telling Daisy all those months ago, 'You never know what's around the corner.'

'Ah, here you are,' Eva called out. 'Better late than never!'

'I just didn't want to overshadow you,' Anna quipped back. 'I thought I'd give you time to have the limelight to yourself. How are the book sales going?'

Daisy grinned. 'They're going really well. Everyone wants a copy. I wouldn't be surprised if Eva hits the bestseller lists before the week is out.'

'Don't.' Eva groaned. 'It's all very well people buying the book, but what if they think it's rubbish?'

'They won't,' Anna said reassuringly. 'The photographs alone will make it a good buy.'

They laughed.

'Talking of which, Charlotte has done a brilliant job,' Daisy said.

'As ever,' Anna replied. 'It drives me mad that she's such a control freak, but she is brilliant at what she does.'

'Actually, there was something I wanted to talk to you about,' Eva said. 'Not tonight, obviously, but perhaps we could catch up before you go back to Cheshire.'

'Yes, I'd love to have a proper catch up. But you've got me intrigued. Can you give me a hint?'

Eva grinned at her. 'Well, depending on how the book goes, and despite my nerves I'm hoping it goes well, I've got an idea for book two.'

'Go on.'

'Well, now that I've got a platform, there are lots of stories to tell about the bravery and strength of other survivors. And of course, there's no book without photographs.'

'That does sound like something I would be interested in,' Anna replied. She'd been pondering where to go with her photography for some time now, but she had wanted to find something that could make a difference. This sounded like the perfect project. And working with Eva again would be an added bonus. 'Let's catch up tomorrow then.' She glanced to the queue that was forming behind her, waiting for Eva to sign her book. 'But for now, I'll let you get back to your public, while I go and have a look at these snaps that are on display.'

She took Daniel's arm and they moved towards the first prints.

More than any of her previous exhibitions, the photographs blew her away. They began with some that Daniel had taken on the catwalk prior to the explosion, and followed with ones that showed Eva when she was first in hospital.

'God, I love the way you've captured her emotions,' Daniel said as they walked slowly round the exhibition.

'I was lucky,' Anna replied modestly. 'Eva has a very expressive face.'

'No, it's more than that. She knew you were taking the photos, but you seem to have captured her so that it looks as though she is almost unaware. You've documented perfectly the highs and lows of her recovery. Look at the joy on her face here, that she's managed to propel herself right to the end of the bar.'

'That was in the early days,' Anna agreed. 'She said her arms were screaming in pain at the effort of lifting her upper body. She used the gym regularly, but nothing had prepared her for that. It took her weeks to be able to get to the end of that bar, but she persevered, and I'm so glad that I managed to capture the moment she made it. Again, I was lucky she was a very good subject.'

'And I'd say you're too modest.' Daniel kissed her lightly on the lips.

As they reached the foyer of the gallery once more, the door opened to reveal Anna's dad and his new partner, Jane. They'd met at the cookery class Andrew had joined and had developed a friendship, which had led to something more. Her dad looked so much happier than she'd ever seen him, and she was grateful to Jane for bringing that joy into his life.

'Dad! Jane!' Anna went to join them and enveloped both of them in a hug. 'I'm so glad you came.'

'We wouldn't have missed it for the world,' Jane said.

'She's been like a cat on hot bricks all day,' Andrew said.

'Well, why wouldn't I be? It's the first time I've been to an exhibition like this. And to know the artist too — well, that's just the icing on the cake.'

'Oh, you'll have to get used to that, with our Anna,' Andrew said proudly.

'Says the seasoned pro.' Anna laughed. 'Here, take a glass of champers and go and have a look.'

'I've heard so much about these pics,' her father said. 'I can't wait to see them.'

'I'll catch up with you later.' Anna smiled as she watched them walk away arm in arm.

'They seem very happy together,' Daniel said, coming to stand by her side.

'They do, don't they? I'm so pleased for them. I can't believe how much life has changed in such a short time. It seems that everyone I love or care about is in a good place in their lives.'

'I agree. It's a shame Harry couldn't make it, though.'

'I know, he would if he could, but he's got a deadline for a big assessment, and you know how conscientious he is. I'm just glad he's happy.' Despite a disruptive few months in the run-up to his exams, Harry had received top grades and had gone to the university of his choice in Durham. Sometimes, when he had a free weekend, he came to stay with them rather than making the longer journey down to London, and he and Daniel got on well together.

The person who had changed the most, though, was Jack. After being arrested, he'd really turned his life around. A spell in prison, much shorter than any of them had anticipated, had confirmed to him that this wasn't the way he wanted to live his life. Ever since he'd been helping other youngsters turn away from crime.

He was smiling as he approached her now. 'This is amazing, I'm so proud of you.'

'And I'm proud of you too.' She gave Jack a hug. They were closer now than they'd ever been, as he was no longer the angry young man who'd turned on her all those months ago.

When she and Daniel were alone again, Daniel said, 'It's hard to believe that hiring a drowned rat of an assistant could have led to such great things.'

Anna agreed. 'Oh, yes, especially when the person who hired the drowned rat was such a rude man.' She held up her glass. 'I propose a toast.'

'What, to us?' he asked.

'No. To Charlotte, for getting you to hire the drowned rat. She has proved beyond doubt that first impressions don't mean a thing.'

THE END

ACKNOWLEDGEMENTS

I would like to thank the Choc Lit team for their support, encouragement and belief in me as a writer. I am so lucky to have you as my publisher.

Thank you to my editors, Emma Grundy Haigh and Becky Slorach who have worked with me to strengthen this book.

Thank you also to the Choc Lit family who have been an amazing support in my first year as a published novelist.

And a special thank you to my book cover designer — I absolutely love it.

Thank you to The Tasting Panel who said 'yes' to the manuscript and made publication possible.

Thank you to everyone who has supported me this year, it means so much to know that the words I have written have brought others enjoyment.

THANK YOU

I would like to thank you for choosing to read my book. I hope you enjoyed Daniel and Anna's story.

If you enjoyed First Impressions then please do leave a review on the website where you bought the book. Every review really does help a new author like me.

You can find me on Twitter, Facebook and Instagram:

Facebook: www.facebook.com/linda.middleton.735

Instagram: @middletonwrites

X(Twitter): @middletonwrites

Please do get in touch for all the latest news. I look forward to chatting with you.

Much love

Linda x

THE CHOC LIT STORY

Established in 2009, Choc Lit is an independent, award-winning publisher dedicated to creating a delicious selection of quality women's fiction.

We have won 18 awards, including Publisher of the Year and the Romantic Novel of the Year, and have been shortlisted for countless others. In 2023, we were shortlisted for Publisher of the Year by the Romantic Novelists' Association.

All our novels are selected by genuine readers. We are proud to publish talented first-time authors, as well as established writers whose books we love introducing to a new generation of readers.

In 2023, we became a Joffe Books company. Best known for publishing a wide range of commercial fiction, Joffe Books has its roots in women's fiction. Today it is one of the largest independent publishers in the UK.

We love to hear from you, so please email us about absolutely anything bookish at choc-lit@joffebooks.com

If you want to hear about all our bargain new releases, join our mailing list: www.choc-lit.com/contact

Milton Keynes UK
Ingram Content Group UK Ltd.
UKHW020657280824
447448UK00010B/93